Mr & Mrs Smith
Hotel Collection

Australia / New Zealand

FOR TW

It had to happen eventually. Mr & Mrs Smith have finally made it to the sunnier side of the world. And not only have we combed beaches, climbed mountains, trekked deserts and scoured cities in pursuit of the sexiest boutique and luxury hotels down under, but we've also unpacked our cases and decided to stay for good.

Our latest guide comes courtesy of our new Melbourne team, a tight-knit group of native-born Australians and imported Brits, all with the same Smith sensibility and hunger for the good things in life. We've personally visited scores of Australia and New Zealand's most stylish hotels and lodges, then hand-picked the very best to appear on our website and in this book. It's a tough job all right, but someone has to do it. How else are you really going to know if your special weekend away – or long-haul honeymoon – will be everything you're hoping for?

We think you'll like the fruits of our labour. Whether long-standing local favourites, or bold, out-of-the-way newcomers, all our picks have a distinctly southern sense of place. From the lush, wet plains of Australia's Top End, via the iconic beaches and islands of the east coast, right through to the Middle Earth peaks of New Zealand's South Island, we've signposted you to the most seductive stays around. And we don't stop there – we also throw in our top tips on where to eat, drink, party or picnic, wherever you find yourselves.

We also return with a whole new extended family of carefully selected local tastemakers – actress Sigrid Thornton, *Vogue* editor Kirstie Clements, restaurateurs Andrew McConnell and Christine Manfield, and media luminary Deborah Hutton are among our reviewers – and, as ever, we have slipped in a free BlackSmith membership card as a little extra to make your next stay even more unforgettable. Activate it today to get exclusive access to a whole load of great hotel offers when you book through Mr & Mrs Smith. And don't forget to check out our global collection of over 600 gorgeous hotels on **www.mrandmrssmith.com**.

Have fun, best wishes and bon voyage.

Mr & Mrs Smith

(take)

advantage of us

Please help yourseif to your very own BlackSmith card, which entitles you to free membership for one year. From the moment you register it (online, or by ringing our local and freecall numbers in Australia, NZ, the UK or US – see opposite), you can access the members' area of our website to find out about exclusive offers from our hotels and self-catered properties and take advantage of other life-enhancing perks from our many global partners. You get members-only treats every time you check into a hotel; think free champagne, spa specials, transfer and room upgrades, and you're getting the red-carpeted picture. Look for the symbol at the end of each hotel review.

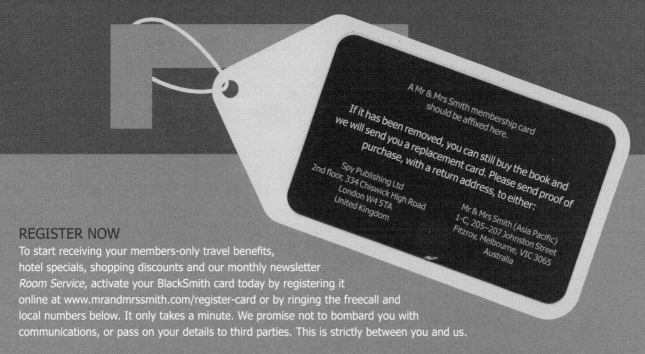

A Mr & Mrs Smith membership card should be affixed here.

If it has been removed, you can still buy the book and we will send you a replacement card. Please send proof of purchase, with a return address, to either:

Spy Publishing Ltd
2nd floor, 334 Chiswick High Road
London W4 5TA
United Kingdom

Mr & Mrs Smith (Asia Pacific)
1-C, 205–207 Johnston Street
Fitzroy, Melbourne, VIC 3065
Australia

REGISTER NOW

To start receiving your members-only travel benefits, hotel specials, shopping discounts and our monthly newsletter *Room Service*, activate your BlackSmith card today by registering it online at www.mrandmrssmith.com/register-card or by ringing the freecall and local numbers below. It only takes a minute. We promise not to bombard you with communications, or pass on your details to third parties. This is strictly between you and us.

AND THERE'S MORE

If all this isn't enough, why not upgrade your membership to our SilverSmith or GoldSmith levels? Get access to VIP airport lounges, automatic hotel upgrades, flight and car-hire offers and your own personal travel concierge.

VAULT VALUE

Depending on your membership level, Mr & Mrs Smith also credits up to five per cent of your booking value to a special member's account, which we call the Vault. Yes – money back to spend on your next stay with us.

ON CALL

Thanks to our new global team, Mr & Mrs Smith now operates a 24-hour travel service five days a week, with round-the-clock weekend coverage to follow. Ring any of the numbers below to activate your membership today, and, better still, start planning your first Smith adventure.

From Australia, local call 1300 896627
From New Zealand, freecall 0800 986671
From elsewhere in Asia, ring +61 3 8648 8871*
From the UK, local call 0845 034 0700
From the US and Canada, freecall 1 866 610 3867
From elsewhere in the world, ring +44 20 8987 6970

*Also check www.mrandmrssmith.com/contact for new free or local call numbers from key territories in Asia.

Small print: all offers are according to availability and subject to change.

(contents)

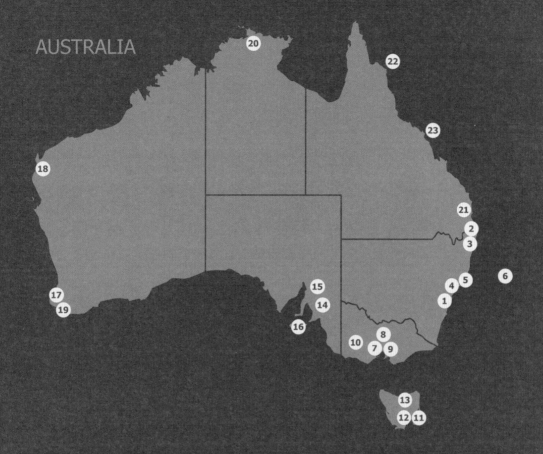

AUSTRALIA

NEW ZEALAND

[at a glance]

NEW SOUTH WALES

SYDNEY
Establishment Hotel
BYRON BAY
Gaia Retreat & Spa
Victoria's at Wategos
CENTRAL COAST
Bells at Killcare
Pretty Beach House
LORD HOWE ISLAND
Capella Lodge

SYDNEY

CITYSCAPE Bridges, beaches, botanical gardens
CITY LIFE Get out and stay out

Sassy Sydney is a supermodel of a city – and she knows it. The eye-popping setting, sprawled around one of the world's best looking harbours, keeps tourists slack-jawed, but locals are more likely to be found ogling fashion-forward labels in Paddington's glam boutiques or downing cocktails in party-hard Darlinghurst. There's a buzzy urban feel here (it's the nation's advertising, media and fashion hub), so visitors may find the pace frenetic, but you can also hone your surf skills at a brace of beautiful beaches. Fancy more nocturnal action? The vibrant gay scene clubs till dawn and even straights aren't backwards in coming forwards.

GETTING THERE

Planes Sydney's Kingsford Smith Airport (www. sydneyairport.com.au), 10 kilometres south of the city, is Australia's busiest. International and domestic terminals are a four-kilometre bus or train ride apart.
Trains Central Station is Sydney's main rail terminus, with a network of inner-city, intercity and country destinations (www.cityrail.info).
Boats Regular ferries depart from Circular Quay (www. sydneyferries.info), with popular routes including Taronga Zoo and Manly on the North Shore, Rose Bay and Watsons Bay in the Eastern Suburbs, and Darling Harbour and Parramatta to the west. There's a ferry information office at Wharf 4.
Automobiles Walking around Sydney is a pleasure, and it's compact enough that you shouldn't need a car. If you're planning a trip out of town though, it's worth having your own wheels. Hire a car at the airport, which has desks for all major companies.

LOCAL KNOWLEDGE

Taxis These are plentiful in Sydney and easily hailed in the street, but if you need to call one try Silver Service Cabs (13 31 00) or Premier Cabs (13 10 17). Drivers don't expect tips but often need directions – so it's best to have some idea of where you are going beforehand.

Packing tips Swimmers, flip-flops and anything flashy – Sydneysiders aren't shy of strutting their stuff.
Recommended reads Richard Flanagan's *The Unknown Terrorist*, set in post-9/11 Sydney, tells the terrifying tale of a pole dancer's fall in seedy, strobe-lit Kings Cross. If you're a fan of the Sydney Opera House, curl up with *A Tribute to Jørn Utzon* by photographer Katarina Stube and the architect's son Jan Utzon.
Local specialities Sydney has blossomed into one of the great restaurant capitals of the world, offering every imaginable cuisine, but it's perhaps best known for pioneering Pacific Rim and Mod Oz dishes. Quality is high and is delivered at reasonable prices.
Do go/don't go Sydney thrives in summer, so any time from December through to March is especially lovely.
Also... With a dangerously thin ozone layer, the sun is Sydney's biggest natural hazard – be sure to cover up.

WORTH GETTING OUT OF BED FOR

Viewpoint Take a walk through Sydney's Botanical Gardens overlooking the Opera House and Harbour Bridge or get up close and personal at the Sydney Harbour Bridge and Pylon Look-out (www.pylonlookout. com.au). The 'Coathanger' was built in 1924 and was at the time the world's largest single-span bridge.

Arts and culture The Art Gallery of New South Wales (www.artgallery.nsw.gov.au) commands a grand classical building in the Domain housing a permanent collection of Australian, European and Asian pieces. In Surry Hills, the Brett Whiteley Studio (www.brett whiteley.org) is a showcase for the late artist's work. There are hot shows at the Museum of Contemporary Art (www.mca.com.au), on the waterside at West Circular Quay (the café is perfect for people watching). The Powerhouse Museum (www.powerhousemuseum. com), located in the inner-city suburb of Ultimo, hosts extravagant and unexpected exhibitions dedicated to design, technology and Australian history. To find out more about arts and culture events, consult Friday's *Sydney Morning Herald*.

Activities For a taste of Sydney street style, head for the Paddington Markets on Oxford Street (Saturdays 10am–4pm; www.paddingtonmarkets.com.au), where you'll find more than 200 stalls selling everything from clothing, jewellery and fragrances to ceramics, artworks and second-hand books. Ditto the Bondi Markets (Sundays 10am–4pm; www.bondimarkets.com.au), and the Rocks Market down by Sydney Harbour (Saturdays and Sundays, 10am–5pm; www.therocks.com), which has recently spawned a spin-off farmers' market on Fridays. All are inspiring places to pick up one-off pieces, and are breeding grounds for tomorrow's design names.

Daytripper The Blue Mountains, just two hours' drive west of Sydney, is a spectacular wilderness with breathtaking walks through bush, hills and river gorges. Don't miss natural rock formation the Three Sisters, at Katoomba. The Hunter Valley, the state's main wine-growing region, is around three hours by car from Sydney. Head for Tyrrell's Winery in Pokolbin (www. tyrrells.com.au), where a one-hour tour is followed by a tasting. While in Pokolbin, stop at the Hunter Valley Cheese Company (www.huntervalleycheese.com.au) to pick up fabulous local vintage cheddar.

Best beach The (in)famous Bondi Beach may not be Sydney's prettiest, but it's definitely the one to be seen on. Bronte Beach, with its child-friendly park and surfeit of barbecues, is ideal for chilling out – have a leisurely lunch at upscale Swell (www.swellrestaurant.com.au), or just grab some fish and chips. Tamarama Beach – 'Glamarama' to locals – is one of the hippest beaches around, with good surf. Palm Beach (where *Home and Away* is filmed) is well worth the hour's drive north.

Children Amuse the kids at Taronga Zoo (www.taronga. org.au) on Sydney's scenic North Shore. If the ferry ride from Circular Quay isn't exciting enough, they'll be met by an array of cool Australian animals, including koalas and kangaroos (adults, AU$41; kids aged 4–15, AU$20; under fours go free; get 10 per cent off with a ZooPass, which includes the return ferry trip). Children over five can even sleep over in safari tents at one of the zoo's popular Roar & Snore slumber parties.

Walks Take in some classic Sydney sites with a leisurely ramble from Jørn Utzon's masterpiece the Sydney Opera House (www.sydneyoperahouse.com), through the Royal Botanical Gardens flanking the CBD to the Domain, home to the Art Gallery of New South Wales. Stroll on past St Mary's Cathedral to pretty Hyde Park and the moving ANZAC Memorial, an art deco edifice where the Pool of Reflection provides pause for thought.

Perfect picnic For wide-open spaces head to Centennial Park (www.centennialparklands.com.au), Sydney's biggest park, beloved of joggers, in-line skaters and horsey types. For a nocturnal picnic in summer check out the Moonlight Cinema (www.moonlight.com.au), where you can munch away to a movie.

Shopping Venture to Paddington where you'll find the best of the fashion boutiques, arthouse cinemas, hip eateries and cool bars. Glenmore Road hosts the biggest designer boutiques such as Ksubi, Alannah Hill, Kirrily Johnston and Scanlan & Theodore. Queen

Street in Woollahra is like an old-fashioned English high street lined with delis and antique shops. Crown Street in Surry Hills is great for vintage finds, while Campbell Parade and Hall Street in Bondi are fun for second-hand, surf and bikini stores. The upscale 19th-century Queen Victoria Building (QVB) in the CBD showcases Australian fashion alongside international designers. Interiors fans should check out Dinosaur Designs on Oxford Street for rainbow-bright tableware and jewellery, and the new Donna Hay General Store in Woollahra for pretty food, books and homewares.

Something for nothing The Bondi to Bronte walk is an easy stroll around the headlands and a beautiful way to see Sydney's Eastern Beaches (if you're feeling energetic, keep going down to Coogee, four kilometres from Bondi). In November the trail comes alive with Sculpture by the Sea (www.sculpturebythesea.com), a free outdoor exhibition.

Don't go home without... posing in a pavement café in boho Darlinghurst, the ideal spot for a skinny latte or fattening cocktail. Accessorise with trainers, a bicycle or a small dog for a sporty but chic look.

SUITABLY SYDNEY

Woolloomooloo Wharf, just a short walk from the CBD, offers the ultimate Sydney experience. Designed to accommodate the fleece-carrying merchant ships that once provided the backbone of Australia's export industry, the dock now welcomes visitors in search of a little luxury and sensational food. With its multitude of alfresco waterfront restaurants and bars, it's a prime haunt for celeb-spotting and people watching.

DIARY

January The splashy Sydney Festival (www.sydneyfestival.org.au) brings three weeks of events to town. **February** Tropfest (www.tropfest.com), the world's largest short film festival, screens in the Domain. The Sydney Gay & Lesbian Mardi Gras hits town with a parade, parties and club action galore (www.mardigras.org.au). **April** ANZAC Day sees two-up gambling pop up in all the pubs. **May** Rosemount Australian Fashion Week (www.rafw.com.au) is a must in a city obsessed with looking good. **June** Vivid Sydney, a music and light festival, illuminates iconic sites including the Opera House. **December** Boxing Day sees the start of the Sydney to Hobart Yacht Race (www.rolexsydneyhobart.com).

'As Mrs Smith attempts to banish all traces of jet-lag with the fragrant Bulgari freebies, we discuss how gracefully this Jane Fonda of a hotel is ageing'

Sydney

Establishment Hotel

STYLE Multi-tasking pleasure palace
SETTING Sydney's glam CBD

It's 6am, Sydney time, and Mrs Smith and I have just arrived in the city's CBD, a little exhausted, despite the generous flat-bed upgrade on our flight from London. We are here on a 'bleisure' trip – business mixed with pleasure – starting with the latter at Establishment Hotel. Approaching the giant metal front door, tucked away in a cul de sac, I notice a few weary revellers leaving Establishment's basement nightclub, Tank. They look about as fresh as we are after our very different all-night session.

A bright-eyed girl from reception shows us to our room. All I can focus on is the bed, which, raised on a platform, hovers before me like a much-craved mirage. Mrs Smith quickly goes to work on making the room as dark as Darth Vader's wardrobe and we slump onto the squishy mattress.

Waking a few hours later, I appraise our surroundings afresh. One of 31 rooms, ours has a New York-loft feel: exposed brickwork, muted greys and creams and a chocolate brown-painted, beamed ceiling. Mrs Smith runs a bath (apparently a decadent use of scarce water that we rainswept Brits wouldn't understand); I opt for the (far more economical) rain shower that, with its oversized head, lives up to its name. A folding door means the bathroom can either feel like an extension of the bedroom (when Mrs Smith needs to call for a cocktail from her tub) or shut off (to contain the downpour sound effects while I shower).

As Mrs Smith attempts to banish all traces of jet-lag with the fragrant Bulgari freebies, we discuss how gracefully this Jane Fonda of a hotel is ageing. Now nine years old, it hasn't become old-fashioned or rough around its minimalist edges. Fuchsia cushions and velvet sofas may come and go, but the heavyweight stone and wood flooring, gleaming marble panels and simple dark-wood furniture stand the test of time and fashion like a Savile Row suit.

We enjoy a late breakfast in the hotel's Gin Garden. Cleverly renovated with a glass ceiling and the original stonework still bearing fire scars (the building almost burned down in 1996), the room is dotted with six-metre potted bamboo plants that tower towards the light. A grand accompaniment to my Vegemite toast, they better suit the room's evening personality as a very cool hangout, adjoining Establishment Bar.

When I say bar, try a 42-metre-long, marble-fronted counter that's studded with grand iron columns, modern light-bulb chandeliers suspended above. This luxe labyrinth also has a bar called Hemmesphere and a sushi bar. Establishment, the building that houses Establishment Hotel, is a stylish multiplex (not two words I ever thought I'd write together) for grown-ups and it works. You could, in theory, live within its four, five – I don't know how many – walls and pretty much do or eat something different every night for a week. If ever Sydney were to come under attack, locals would do well to check in here.

We're both Sydney virgins (you won't find many of them, a witty Aussie later informs me), so obviously Mrs Smith and I want to head to the iconic Bridge and Opera House. We are predictably and gratefully wowed by both. (See how I'm trying to downplay Sydney's unfair advantage over any other city I can name?) We meet up with a friend, who takes us to Bills, owned by chef Bill Granger, where we sit at the communal table and tuck into a brunch of ricotta hotcakes with honeycomb butter and banana.

We then head to Bondi, kick off our shoes and stroll barefoot along the sun-warmed sand. As we vent our envy – comparing this lovely city beach with our local duck pond – we are shepherded towards our next meal at fabulous, low-key North Bondi Italian Food, masterminded by chef Maurizio Terzini. We dine on the terrace, which, if it were any nearer the beach would be a raft, snacking on rosemary-infused olives and tender salami, and sipping chilled chenin blanc as the waves roll in.

I mentioned earlier that this is also a work trip... We are here to launch our company's second office, so of course there has to be a party. Mrs Smith and I smarten up back at the hotel and, after a glass or two from the well-stocked minibar, head to the chosen location – Ivy. Also owned by the Merivale group (which founded Establishment Hotel), this is its latest creation and I have to say that the penthouse (you can rent it out for a mere AU$6,000 a night) is quite a venue. Imagine Hugh Hefner and James Bond got together and created a pad that's showier than an Oscars after-party – a heady cocktail of style and sophistication, shaken not stirred with a little excess. With a terrace hot tub and views over a palm-flanked pool, it feels like Sydney has had an LA love child and Ivy is her name.

A glamorous evening moves on to a new modern Chinese restaurant called Spice Temple, owned by chef Neil Perry (I promise this is work). The menu is takeaway-cliché-free – the pancakes lamb and cumin rather than crispy duck. We dine on the tastiest, spiciest food I've ever had the pleasure of eating. By midnight our body clocks have given up and we're giddy from the party: this – mixed with equal parts exhaustion and champagne – is our cue to retire to the hotel. Our jet-lag, however, has other ideas: at 5am we sit up in bed, blinking woozily.

As bleisure trips go, our stay at Establishment Hotel has convinced us we could easily drop the 'b'. Surveying the room, Mrs Smith and I agree Hef can keep the penthouse. Establishment Hotel is just as luxurious, but also somewhere you can feel at home. And any hotel that has the confidence to call itself Establishment deserves to be taken seriously. Luckily, as this Sydney institution moves into its second decade, it's clear that it more than merits the moniker.

REVIEWED BY JAMES LOHAN, THE ORIGINAL MR SMITH

NEED TO KNOW

Rooms 31, including two penthouse suites.

Rates AU$350–$1,250.

Check-out 11am. Check-in, 2pm.

Facilities In rooms: Bose CD/DVD player, large-screen TV with cable, free WiFi, touch-screen room controls, minibar, Bulgari toiletries. Membership to Fitness First gym next door can be organised or a personal trainer can come to you.

Children This sexy city hotel suits couples, given its sophisticated mix of bars and restaurants – leave the kids at home.

Also Robbie Williams, Outkast and the Scissor Sisters have danced, drunk and slept at this achingly hip everything-under-one-roof destination, and it's a hang-out for Sydney's in-crowd. Enter from quiet side street 5 Bridge Lane which gives onto the incense-infused lobby, rather than from George Street, to avoid the walk of shame of wheeling luggage through the bustling Establishment Bar.

IN THE KNOW

Our favourite rooms The flashest options are the top-floor Loft Penthouse with a sleek living room; and the sprawling two-level Duplex Penthouse which has a king-size bed and deluxe bathroom, with a small study downstairs. For the rest of the spacious rooms, choose between two tonal schemes: black floorboards and strong colour, or a softer, more tranquil style. Marble and bluestone bathrooms come with bath, shower and twin sinks.

Hotel bar The iconic Establishment Bar boasts a striking 42-metre pale marble bar, set in a huge, white-columned room decked out with sleek modern sofas and sinuous dark wood lounge chairs. Next door, the Gin Garden serves tasty gin cocktails, infused with lavender, blood orange and lime, alongside other top tipples. Upstairs repair to hyper-colourful Hemmesphere, an ethnic-glam cocktail bar with Moroccan-inspired low seating and exotic display vitrines.

Hotel restaurant There are three choices: est., run by renowned head chef Peter Doyle, does elegant modern Australian fine dining with French and Asian influences; sushi e is an acclaimed Japanese eatery, with Zen-simple styling; and the stunning Gin Garden serves Indian, Thai and Australian dishes, set amid lush, tall plants, neck-craning columns, sexy pendant lamps and raw brick walls.

Top table Tables 16, 40 and 50 at est. have the best views.

Room service Light bites such as burgers and home-made lasagne are available from 11am to 11pm. After hours, you can still get a cheese platter or sandwiches.

Dress code Modern chic. Dress up, not down with outsize sunglasses, big It bag and even bigger attitude.

Local knowledge Sydney's CBD is bustling with retail therapy. Hot Australian stores nearby at 320 George Street include accessories label Mimco (02 9232 2629) and fashion brand Sass & Bide (02 9232 4394).

LOCAL EATING AND DRINKING

Sashay to the white-hot **Ivy** complex created by Establishment's owners Merivale, a one-stop socialising shop spread over 320 and 330 George Street (02 9240 3000). With zingy yellow and white seats and a green lawn-like floor, New York-style grill **Mad Cow** is a top tip for superior steaks, with a menu by super-chef Peter Doyle. For modern Japanese, hit **Teppanyaki**, which serves dishes from 'the wok', 'the teppan grill' and 'the kitchen' and works a luxe oriental vibe. Don't miss the much-fêted **ivybar**, a clean-lined, monochrome watering hole: upstairs, the seductive **ivylounge** cocktail bar has a 1950s feel, with dark wood-lined walls and dusky rattan chairs, and the art deco-inspired den room is an intimate drinking spot sporting plush buttoned sofas, silk ottomans and a mirrored bar.

GET A ROOM!

Use our free online booking service: check availability and make reservations through www.mrandmrssmith.com.

 SMITH CARD OFFER Free VIP access to Establishment's lounge bar Hemmesphere and a Hemmesphere CD.

Establishment Hotel 5 Bridge Lane, Sydney, NSW 2000 (02 9240 3100; www.establishmenthotel.com)

BYRON BAY

COASTLINE Pristine beaches that go on forever
COAST LIFE Chillin' with like-minded souls

Some jokingly refer to Byron Bay as the most northern suburb of Sydney — everything you can find in the big smoke is on your doorstep here too. But there's also a charming 'peace, love and mung beans' vibe about this beach town that attracts stressed-out, well-to-do city folk and backpackers from all corners of the earth. The New Age, eco-friendly lifestyle here has made Byron the yoga capital of Australia, with a smorgasbord of alternative therapies on offer from massage to flotation tanks, plus healthy, organic food to match. If you can tear yourself away from your mellow day spa, there are rolling hills for walking and splendid beaches to swim, dive and surf off. Add to this northern New South Wales town laid-back — yet glam — bars and restaurants and you've got one of Australia's best-loved destinations.

GETTING THERE

Planes Most people fly into Gold Coast Airport at Coolangatta (www.goldcoastairport.com.au) with Jetstar, Pacific Blue, Tiger Airways or Virgin Blue, then drive just over an hour south to Byron Bay. Nearer, though, is the smaller Ballina Airport (www.ncas.com.au), which handles flights from Jetstar, Virgin Blue and Rex, only 20 minutes away.
Automobiles To make the most of Byron Bay's hinterland you'll need a car, as taxis are a pricey way to get around. All the big hire car brands are represented at the airports, including Avis, Hertz and Budget.

LOCAL KNOWLEDGE

Taxis You don't really need a cab to get around the town itself (if you're tired, hail a Cycle Rickshaw) but they can be handy if you want to head further out. To book, call Byron Bay Taxis (02 6685 5008).
Packing tips Designer swimmers, yoga mat, Havaianas.
Recommended reads Robert Drewe's *The Bodysurfers*, a collection of short stories set by the beach, is considered an Australian classic. Pure escapism is how you'd describe *The Bay*, a novel by Australia's best-selling female author Di Morrissey. Legendary surfer Nat Young lives at Angourie, about 100 kilometres south of Byron. His *The Complete History of Surfing* should keep devotees entertained while they're lying on the beach.
Local specialities It's clean and green up here. Casual, too. It's only in the past couple of years that true fine dining has come to Byron Bay, and most people still tend to eat in a more relaxed fashion. You'll find cuisines from around the world, cool cafés serving up country-sized servings, and plenty of options for vegetarians and devotees of organic food. This is, after all, the epicentre of alternative culture. The lush hills of the hinterland are home to tropical crops: coffee, macadamia nuts (superb coated in chocolate) and exotic fruits such as custard apples and lychees.
Do go/don't go During the warmer months (November to March), Byron Bay seethes with life and it's best to

avoid December and January when the area is bombarded by 'schoolies' (teenagers who have just finished Year 12) and families on holiday. It's also peak wedding season in romantic Byron. Though the sea is a little chilly for swimming, winter here (June to August) is perfect: calm, sunny and warm — with far fewer tourists.

Also... Do as the locals do and learn to surf. Black Dog Surfing (www.blackdogsurfing.com) has small-group lessons and provides all the gear, as well as a pro photographer to capture the moment when you catch your first wave. George, the black pooch of the company's name, is a Kelpie/Jack Russell cross who does, indeed, surf!

WORTH GETTING OUT OF BED FOR

Viewpoint Not only will you be able to see a dreamy sunset at Main Beach, you may also have the bonus of musical accompaniment — depending on whether there are any lingering guitarists.

Arts and culture Check out what local artists and makers produce at the Byron Artisan Market (www.byronartisanmarket.com), held in Railway Park each Saturday night from 6pm. Craftspeople and fine artists from the surrounding area showcase their one-off and limited-edition pieces encompassing everything from painting to jewellery and homewares.

Activities Just off the coast is Julian Rocks Marine Reserve, considered one of the best dive sites in Australia. For an unforgettable underwater experience you can glide with manta rays, as the gentle giants congregate here during summer and early autumn. At other times, you'll see the harmless leopard and wobbegong sharks, eagle rays, turtles, moray eels and around 400 different species of fish. Byron Bay Dive Centre (www.byronbaydivecentre.com.au) offers introductory courses that take five hours and include one ocean dive (be warned: you may be hooked for life) or you can just join them for a snorkel.

Best beach Being slightly separated from the main part of town means that Tallow Beach (south of the lighthouse) is often a bit quieter. It helps that it's also seven kilometres long, so there's plenty of space for everyone. Locals walk their dogs along part of the beach and you'll often see dolphins just beyond the break. If it's really windy, make for the north end and Cosy Corner, which is more sheltered.

Daytripper Head inland to the sleepy, picture-perfect town of Bangalow, 14 kilometres from Byron Bay. You'll see every shade of green on the drive through the hinterland, before hitting the main drag, Byron Street, where old buildings have been converted into chic shops and cafés. Shop at Little Peach (02 6687 1415) for Japanese-inspired clothes and collectables; Island Luxe (02 6687 1605) for beach and holiday wear by Australian and European designers; and Wax Jambu Emporium (www.waxjambu.com.au) in the old general store for super-cool clothes, books, CDs and kids' toys. After you've expelled all that energy giving your credit card a work-out, stop for lunch at Fishheads (www.fishheadsbyron.com.au) and enjoy the fresh oysters, grilled scallops on the half-shell or, for crustacean converts, the Ultimate Seafood Plate. There's also a farmers' market on Saturday mornings on Byron Street selling organic produce.

Children If your kids are born entertainers, they'll love Circus Arts (www.circusarts.com.au). There's a full indoor trapeze at the centre, as well as activities for those littlies without a head for heights. The circus class will teach them trampolining, juggling, hula-hooping and low trapeze, and there are adult sessions too.

Walks On the weekend, the traffic jam going up to local landmark Cape Byron Lighthouse is as bad as

any you'll see in a big-city rush hour, so take the walking track instead. It's about four kilometres if you trek up from Clarkes Beach, around the lighthouse and through the conservation park back into town. When you're at the peak, you'll be glad you made the effort.

Perfect picnic Score some fish and chips from Fishmongers Café in Bay Lane (behind the Beach Hotel) – people swear it's the best in Byron – then park yourself on the beach. It's the ideal way to watch the sun go down.

Shopping While not the main reason people come to Byron, there's still a little spending action to be had, particularly around Jonson and Fletcher Streets. Pick up designer gear by Ksubi, Alice McCall, Lover and Karen Walker at Pompidou (www.pompidou.com.au). Sample hot local surfing label 2FOUR8ONE (www.2481.com.au), named after the town's postcode. Looking for a special piece of handcrafted jewellery? Ixtlan (www.ixtlan.com.au) has bold, contemporary accessories featuring semi-precious stones. For something a bit more girly, try on Nicole Sharratt's designs at Sweet Papillon (www.sweetpapillon.com.au).

Something for nothing You've got seven beaches including beautiful Wategos to choose from. Grab a book, a towel and soak it up. Even when it's cold, it's divine. Peckish? Swing by Byron Farmers Market (Thursdays 8am–11am at Butler Street Reserve; www.byronfarmersmarket.com.au), where you can taste local produce for free.

Don't go home without... sipping on a chilled bottle of Ginger Nektar, the handmade drink produced locally from ginger, rainwater, honey and lemon. You can buy it in just about all the cafés and general stores around Byron.

BLISSFULLY BYRON BAY

If you want to realign your chakras, relax with some reiki or blitz your tired bod, this is definitely the right place. Alternative therapists have set up shop all over town, and there are more yoga teachers here, per capita, than anywhere else in the country. Ask for a copy of the *Byron Body & Soul Guide* at the tourist office for tips on local classes and practitioners. For a Balinese-style day spa try Buddha Gardens (www.buddhagardensdayspa.com.au), which has tropical flower-filled grounds, a soothing plunge pool and sauna. Or tune out with massages, aromatherapy and organic facials at Shambala (www.shambala.net.au).

DIARY

Easter For the past 20 years, the cream of the music world has come together in a big paddock just outside of town for four days of mellow sounds care of the East Coast International Blues & Roots Festival (www.bluesfest.com.au). The line-up changes every year but expect the likes of Michael Franti, Xavier Rudd and Jack Johnson on the bill.

July At Splendour in the Grass (www.splendourinthegrass.com) they take their music seriously, although this festival is more indie- and rock-oriented for a younger crowd. The two days sell out quickly, so beg, borrow or steal a ticket.

August At the popular Byron Bay Writers Festival (www.byronbaywritersfestival.com.au) the focus is on Australian authors, as the literati gather for a three-day gab-fest about books, politics and the state of the world.

'The cosy mood of Kukuru House means you don't feel any pressure to impress or even mingle – you can just make yourself a cup of tea and curl up with a good book'

Brooklet

Gaia Retreat & Spa

STYLE Eco-chic retreat
SETTING Rolling hills and rainforest

You can't mention that you're visiting Gaia Retreat & Spa without someone saying 'Olivia Newton-John owns that you know.' Indeed the singer is one of the directors, and I've also noticed that the warm and fuzzy feeling that seems to wash over people at the thought of her is pretty much the same sense of happiness that Gaia delivers. This gorgeous retreat, which has earned itself an excellent reputation since opening in 2005, is set in the lush, subtropical hinterland of Byron Bay. It's positioned atop the highest point in the area, meaning the views are spectacular; just green rolling hills that meet a broad blue sky.

Retreat experiences are different for all I suppose, but I am definitely of the mindset that they are better shared with a good friend than a husband. To me, they are one of the ultimate female bonding rituals. Mr Smith doesn't particularly appreciate it when I bang on for hours about the products used during a facial, ask which variety of tea I should choose, or what colour my toenails should acquire during a pedicure. My friend Ms Smith, on the other hand, has visited many a spa with me. In fact, we consider ourselves connoisseurs. Once, in Thailand, we talked for three days about the reflexology session we'd had. Yes, Ms Smith is the perfect partner for a weekend stay at Gaia.

This isn't a clinical, hi-tech retreat or an over-designed luxury resort. Gaia is much more laid-back than that. A group of bungalow-style villas surround Kukura House, a spacious Samoan-inspired longhouse with soaring ceiling and a large deck that overlooks the gardens and is used for dining when the weather sparkles. This is the central meeting place for guests, housing the reception, the dining area and the relaxation lounge. The decor is a rather haphazard mixture of styles: a little bit Sanskrit, a little bit Pottery Barn. I'm more used to super-slick styling, but after a while I can't help but go with the flow. It's all so unpretentious and comfortable – there are plenty of DVDs, books and board games to borrow if you're one of those people who always needs something to do – that you can't help but relax.

Before long it becomes patently obvious that the majority of guests are women, some in groups but many travelling solo. The cosy mood of Kukuru House means you don't feel any pressure to impress or even mingle – you can just make yourself a cup of tea and curl up with a good book. The overall ambience of Gaia is very female, in an organic sense – the physical landscape is soft and undulating, and statues of nudes and goddesses dot the property. There is an easiness and a friendliness, from all the staff, and from the guests, which is very comforting, and just the ticket when you need to be nurtured.

We also found the bungalows very user-friendly, although the aluminium sliding doors and holiday-house style kitchenettes are a little incongruous considering how upmarket Gaia is. There are a few too many knick-knacks for somewhere soul-soothing – an edit could sharpen up the decor.

That aside, not a great deal of time really needs to be spent in your room, as there is the incredible day spa to enjoy. Warm, pristine and fragrant, this pocket of pampering is located next to a beautiful heated outdoor pool. Given that Gaia is situated in an area of Australia that tends to attract those with an 'alternative' spirit, the hiring process has clearly been stringent. The therapists are wonderful, each chosen for their skills in a particular

field. And there's a particularly impressive esoteric menu, offering treatments as diverse as cupping, reiki, sound healing, astrology and tarot. I opt for the facial release and kidney cleanse. I think it does the trick, but I can't be entirely sure as I was asleep within five minutes of the treatment starting. When I awake an hour later (I hope there was no drooling), the therapist tells me she thinks I'm probably adrenally exhausted, which makes a lot of sense since, at the time, I was super-stressed. But who'd have thought that someone simply placing their warm hands on your kidneys could send you off into space? When I come to, I am both relaxed and refreshed. Ms Smith chooses a four-handed body rub, a hot-oil head massage and a deep-tissue pummelling, all of which she declares as heavenly. That woman cannot be kneaded enough and, since she prefers just a little light exercise, she's the ideal spa buddy.

The staff at Gaia might be professional but there's also a wonderful casualness that lets you explore at your own pace. The gym is unattended, meaning you can just go in and do whatever you feel, whenever you feel like doing it. You can opt to join group activities, such as t'ai chi or cooking classes, or not. You are being watched over,

but don't feel it. On one occasion, I confide in a staff member that I'm booked for a massage during lunch, so did that mean I was going to miss it. 'We are like a plane,' she replies with a smile, 'we won't take off without you.'

I mention lunch because the food at Gaia is wonderful: organic, inventive and delicious. In fact, most of my days are spent looking forward to the next meal. What is it about fresh air and massage that makes you ravenous? Breakfast is spectacular and a good many resorts would do well to follow Gaia's guilt-free guidelines, with a variety of cereals, fruits, grain breads, juices and hot dishes.

It appears Gaia has a pro-choice policy, which I find liberating – you can choose to have wine at dinner or ask for an organic coffee if you so desire. Given that you are in such nourishing surrounds it is highly unlikely that anybody is really going to abuse those particular toxins, but I like the fact you are treated like a grown-up and given the option. Morning meditation on the hill, a deep-tissue massage, an afternoon nap, a bracing walk, a tasty organic meal and a glass of pinot. Did I say bliss?

REVIEWED BY KIRSTIE CLEMENTS

NEED TO KNOW

Rooms 18, including two suites.

Rates AU$912–$1,385, including all meals and snacks. A two-night minimum stay applies. Gaia prefers to offer a range of two- to seven-night packages, which also include yoga and another selected activity daily, a spa gift on arrival, free spa treatments (depending on length of stay) and local airport transfers. Additional treatments cost extra. Call Mr & Mrs Smith's Travel Team for more details.

Check-out 11am. Check-in, 2pm.

Facilities DVD, CD and book library, board games, free WiFi, spa, gym, tennis courts, bikes, walking tracks, day-beds, meditation decks, outdoor heated saltwater swimming pool. In rooms: CD player, free bottled water.

Children This hotel is an adults-only escape – take a partner or a pal.

Also The retreat's award-winning Gaia Day Spa offers over 40 revitalising treatments including facials, reiki and spiritual healing, with options tailored to men and couples. We love the Hawaiian kahuna massage or de-stress with yoga.

IN THE KNOW

Our favourite rooms The one- or two-bedroom Acala Suites are our top tip if you want to combine mod cons with serenity. On the highest part of the grounds with views to match, they include a separate living area, kitchenette, spacious bathroom and deck (with heated spa), and are the only rooms with a flatscreen TV, DVD player and internet access. Our second choice would be the Sura Terrace Rooms, which have slightly bigger bedrooms and bathrooms as they don't offer a living room. Number 16 enjoys the highest vantage point. Co-owner Olivia Newton-John describes Gaia as 'Barefoot meets Armani', which sums up the understated, elegant interiors, where earth tones chime in with the foliage outside.

Hotel bar Gaia doesn't have a bar but organic Australian wines are available after 6pm in gorgeous modern-ethnic dining area Kukura House. Sip them to the sound of world music.

Hotel restaurant Meals are also served in Kukura, a Samoan-style longhouse with floor-to-ceiling silk curtains. Interiors blend eastern and western influences, as does chef Todd Cameron's organic cuisine. Dinner is a gourmet three-course menu emphasising a balanced, locally sourced diet. Options are chosen by the chef daily, but advise Gaia of any dietary needs before your arrival. Breakfast is a buffet, including gluten-free cereals; light lunches feature salads, soups and pastas.

Top table Dine out on the spacious Tevana deck, with tables decorated with flowers and lanterns, and sweeping views.

Dress code Casual, although designer exercise gear won't go amiss. The gift shop does a mean line in kaftans and the latest yoga kit.

Room service Available from 8am to 8pm for AU$20 a day in the Layana Rooms and Sura Terrace; free in the Acala Suites. Help yourself to a range of tea, snacks and organic fruit all day in Kukura House, which doubles as a communal space for reading, playing board games or hanging out.

Local knowledge Gaia's 25-acre subtropical grounds offer lofty views of rolling hills and green valleys – a bonus if you book an alfresco massage or yoga session. We recommend the day-bed behind the property for watching the sunrise or sunset.

LOCAL EATING AND DRINKING

For local, organic food, head for leafy **Harvest Café** (02 6687 2644), in nearby Newrybar. Set in a rambling cottage, it's a lovely spot for alfresco dining on balmy verandas, offering vegetarian and gluten-free dishes. Choose from over 20 boutique wines by the glass, or cocktails if you fancy retoxing. Stop for lunch at **Fishheads** (02 6687 2883), in historic village Bangalow, and enjoy fresh oysters, grilled scallops on the half-shell or the seafood plate.

GET A ROOM!

Use our free online booking service: check availability and make reservations through www.mrandmrssmith.com.

 SMITH CARD OFFER AU$100 spa treatment voucher.

Gaia Retreat & Spa 933 Fernleigh Road, Brooklet, NSW 2479 (02 6687 1216; www.gaiaretreat.com.au)

'After a little too long enjoying the sunshine and the wine, we amble back to Victoria's and immerse ourselves in the spa'

Byron Bay

Victoria's at Wategos

STYLE Classical Tuscan villa
SETTING Coastal tropical valley

As we turn onto the road to Byron Bay, thoughts of past adventures here flash through my mind: beaches, festivals, mud, tents, music, swimming and sunrises (far too many of them the result of not getting to bed). Among all these great memories, however, there are none that belong to specific sleeping arrangements. This time is going to be different; this time it's all about the hotel.

As we head through town, my thoughts turn to another of my Byron obsessions: whales. On all my trips here, I've never seen one, which doesn't stop me from craning my neck as we come over an incline. Nothing. Well, except for our first glimpse of Victoria's at Wategos. Outside the Tuscan-inspired villa, we're greeted – by name, no less – by staff who make us feel as though we've arrived at an old friend's house. They give us a quick tour before taking our bags upstairs and leaving us to enjoy the room. Mr Smith bounces on the bed, while I begin my explorations: fruit plate, fluffy towels by the spa bath, views of the garden and Cape Byron lighthouse, and a decanter of port for that post-prandial tipple. So far, what's not to like?

Lunch is beckoning, so we decide to stretch our legs and head into town. Only we never figured on stumbling across the Byron Beach Café. What starts out as a stop for a quick bite turns into a long affair. How could it not? Our table looks out over the beach, the sun is beating down, the people-watching is stellar, and we have plates of tasty tapas-style dishes, along with a chilled glass of sauv blanc, as the epicurean accompaniment. Our hosts, locals and visitors are all debating the best place to spot whales; to say my interest is piqued is an understatement.

After a little too long enjoying the sunshine and the wine, we amble back to Victoria's and immerse ourselves in the spa. There are no water restrictions here, our phones are turned off and, with the aid of some deliciously scented bubble bath, we doze off with music softly playing.

Downstairs in the lounge, having emerged from our siesta, we feel as though we could curl up on the couch and never leave, but our rumbling stomachs make us flick through the book filled with restaurant recommendations. We snare a reservation at Olivo, more city restaurant than beach café thanks to its smart local art, where we tuck into the specials, with a lovely pinot to match. The drive back to the hotel is an adventure in itself, as we navigate our way slowly past echidnas and bush turkeys.

Waking to a clear blue sky in the morning, I'm intent on continuing my mission to see the elusive whales. The ever-helpful 'Victorians' have suggested a hot-air balloon ride or a boat trip, both of which would hopefully give us a glimpse. I, however, have a fear of boats and Mr Smith is afraid of heights, so instead we decide on a pre-brekkie stroll. After walking along the almost-deserted Wategos Beach, we tackle the stairs to the lighthouse. From this, the most easterly point of Australia, the views are spectacular, but there are no whales.

Back at Victoria's, the tables are set up in a corner of the lounge, overlooking the pool and down towards the beach. We can't resist the aromas of the breakfast: perfect eggs, crispy bacon, feta and home-made chutney. Just when I think it can't get any better, I'm offered a glass of bubbles.

'Just when I think it can't get any better, I'm offered a glass of bubbles'

Without even trying we fit in a lot of local sights during the morning. Twenty minutes away is the Crystal Castle, with its beautiful gardens, walks among mystic statues and a giant stone Blessing Buddha. It might not appeal to all, but the serenity is a welcome break from our hectic lives. On the way back we go via Bangalow, where there's no choice but to explore the boutiques, galleries and antique shops on the main street.

Realising the time, we return to our sanctuary and the in-room treatment that has been arranged. Not being too keen on the whole holistic experience, Mr Smith leaves me with my idea of heaven to visit his: the golf course. He returns to find me luxuriating in my robe on the bed after a 90-minute massage and facial, feeling like I've been replaced by a new model me (ah, the magic of healing hands). With time before we have to meet old friends for dinner, we give the spa another road-test.

The next morning, to combat the indulgences of the past few days, I'm determined to beat my time to the lighthouse on our dawn walk. Mr Smith, meanwhile, lingers on the beach watching the surftastic members of the Byron Bay Malibu Club in action. I've got my head down, focused on pushing on up the hill, when a Japanese tourist rushes past me laden with cameras, squealing with delight. I hear the word 'whales' as she and her companion sprint by. Picking up the pace, I'm on their tail dashing along the path to the lookout. And there they are, just off the coastline, a small group of migrating mammals playing and splashing. For once, I am speechless. They're beautiful. I look back, but Mr Smith is nowhere to be seen. I race back to the beach and grab him. This, after all, is an event that needs to be shared.

REVIEWED BY MR & MRS SMITH

NEED TO KNOW

Rooms 10, including one suite.

Rates Low season, AU$399–$799; high season, AU$499–$899. Breakfast is extra, at AU$35 a person. Minimum stays of two nights apply at weekends (more during special events).

Check-out 10am. Check-in, 2.30pm, but both flexible subject to availability.

Facilities CD/DVD and book library, surfboards, surf skis, binoculars for whale watching, 16-metre outdoor lap pool, spa treatments. In rooms: TV, DVD/CD player, free WiFi, minibar.

Children This hotel doesn't cater for kids – opt for a liberating adult break instead.

Also At Victoria's you can play boules on the lawn or just wander the pretty tropical garden, which includes a water feature with rocks and lilypads – and a gentle, petite pet goanna.

IN THE KNOW

Our favourite rooms The best room depends on your preferred view – request pool and gardens, sea and mountains, or views up towards Cape Byron Lighthouse. The Executive Spa Suites are the most spacious, with king-size beds. All bedrooms have a floaty, feminine feel, with fairy-tale four-posters, antique French-style dressing tables and chairs, chaise longues, muted cream curtains and white walls. Bathrooms are luxe marble with spa baths set between pillars, and pale coral stone floors.

Hotel bar There's no bar, but minibars come fully stocked, champagne is served at breakfast and a decanter of port awaits you in your room.

Hotel restaurant Victoria's doesn't have a restaurant, but a full breakfast is served 8.30am–9.30am on the terrace by the pool. You can also pick up gourmet picnic hampers, if you fancy seaside snacking, and freshly baked treats for tea. In the evening, canapés, a seafood platter or barbecue hamper can be made to order, or the hotel can direct you to recommended places to eat nearby.

Top table Head for the romantic poolside terrace for drinks or snacks with a soothing mix of chill-out music.

Room service Breakfast and light meals are available between 8.30am and 5.30pm.

Dress code A vibrant kaftan and metallic flip-flops for evening (conjure Elizabeth Taylor in the sexy Seventies); stylish swimming costume or yoga kit by day.

Local knowledge You're inches from one of Australia's most gorgeous beaches, Wategos, so grab your Seafolly suit and get in there. The hotel can hook you up with one-on-one surf lessons, or deep-sea fishing charters, whale and dolphin watching tours and even kayaking with dolphins.

LOCAL EATING AND DRINKING

Restaurateurs John and Lisa van Haandel have brought Melbourne-meets-Mediterranean magic to **Pacific Dining Room** (02 6680 7055) at the Beach Hotel, with tapas-style small plates served in a sophisticated, laid-back venue. At **Dish Restaurant and Marvell Bar** (02 6685 7320), there's a relaxed Balinese ambience, with a creative Eurasian seasonal menu. **Olivo** (02 6685 7950) offers contemporary Australian cuisine and fine wine in an inviting space with smart local art. Set in a historic building with a large balcony, the **Balcony Bar & Restaurant** (02 6680 9666) is a mellow port of call for lychee martinis and mojitos. **Byron Beach Café** (02 6685 8400), at Clarkes Beach, has amazing views from its deck and dining room, and serves a mean wagyu burger at lunch.

GET A ROOM!

Use our free online booking service: check availability and make reservations through www.mrandmrssmith.com.

 SMITH CARD OFFER Tropical fruit platter and a bottle of Australian sparkling wine on arrival.

Victoria's at Wategos 1 Marine Parade, Wategos Beach, Byron Bay, NSW 2481 (02 6685 5388; www.victorias.net.au)

CENTRAL COAST

COASTLINE Bushland, beaches and boats
COAST LIFE Strolling, swimming and sailing

Once a sleepy backwater, New South Wales' Central Coast is a burgeoning hot getaway for weekending Sydneysiders, with top tip the Bouddi Peninsula, a boho cousin to the more familiar glam Northern Beaches across the water. Only two hours' drive north of Sydney, the archly dubbed 'Costa Centrale' is luring early adopters – and savvy commuters – with its simple fibro shacks, serene surf beaches, tranquil lakes and beautiful native bushland. Edit out local towns such as Woy Woy, Terrigal and Gosford, and chill out in pretty villages by the sea, explore the coastal Bouddi National Park, sail on Brisbane Waters or walk along pristine bush tracks to find your own, uninhabited strip of sand. What's more, with award-winning chefs cutting a slice of the action at the area's best hotels and restaurants, you won't have to make do with fish and chips.

GETTING THERE

Planes Sydney's Kingsford Smith Airport (www.sydneyairport.com.au), 10 kilometres south of the city, is well served with international and domestic flights, and is the handiest hopping-off point if you're heading for the Central Coast.
Trains CityRail (www.cityrail.info) trains run from Sydney to area hubs such as Woy Woy and Gosford, as well as other Central Coast destinations.
Automobiles The Central Coast is a two hour drive north of Sydney, via the Sydney–Newcastle Freeway.

LOCAL KNOWLEDGE

Taxis Central Coast Taxis (02 4323 6444) operates out of Gosford, or ask at your accommodation about transfers to and from local restaurants and bars.
Packing tips Fishing rod, Helen Kaminski crocheted-raffia sun hat and New Balance trail shoes for getting to those hard-to-access beaches.

Recommended reads Kate Grenville's *The Secret River* is a novel about a former convict who stakes a claim near the Hawkesbury River in the 19th century. Celebrated chef Stefano Manfredi cooks at boutique hotels Bells at Killcare and Pretty Beach House. Find out his culinary secrets in his recipe book *Seasonal Italian Favourites*.
Local specialities Seafood – oysters, crabs, squid and fish – is a much-loved regional favourite. Terra firma too provides edible thrills; the area around the Hawkesbury is one of the state's best food bowls thanks to first-class farms and citrus-sprouting orchards. Expect simple, seasonal cuisine, with the occasional Mod Oz twist.
Do go/don't go Even midwinter is temperate on the New South Wales coastline, although it may be a little cool to swim. High summer – December and January – sees the tiny towns and normally quiet beaches filled with holidaying families.

Also... Fans of the late comedian Spike Milligan may not know that he had close ties to Woy Woy, where his parents and younger brother lived. There's a Spike Milligan Room in the local library and since 2008, a bridge named in the comic writer's honour. A frequent visitor to the town, the Anglo-Irish poet was never particularly kind, calling it 'the world's only above-ground cemetery'.

WORTH GETTING OUT OF BED FOR

Viewpoint The best vantage point for admiring the tiny harbour beaches and towns is actually on Brisbane Waters. Hop aboard the MV Lady Kendall II (www.starshipcruises.com.au), a 32-metre traditional timber cruiser that runs twice-daily pleasure tours, from Saturday to Wednesday, lasting two and a half hours. Upscale boating – now that's how to sightsee in style.

Arts and culture Admire ancient artworks from wooden walkways at the Bulgandry Aboriginal Engraving Site, just off the Pacific Highway in the Brisbane Water National Park (www.cctourism.com.au), which shows rock engravings of ancestral human figures by the Guringai people. Who needs galleries?

Activities Take the Crab 'n' Oyster Cruise (www.crab-n-oystercruises.com.au) along the Hawkesbury River and find out how these popular local seafood delicacies are grown and harvested. Shuck a mighty mollusc, haul in a crab pot, then indulge in a tasty seafood lunch right on the water.

Daytripper Drive to the Lower Hunter Valley to sample the fruits of one of the area's acclaimed wineries. There are about 140 to choose from, but we suggest Bimbadgen Estate (www.bimbadgen.com.au) and Constable Estate (www.constablevineyards.com.au) in Pokolbin, or Margan Wines (www.margan.com.au) in Broke. Chow down after at contemporary eatery Rock (www.rockrestaurant.com.au), at Pokolbin's Pooles Rock Wines.

Best beach Not all of the sandy shorelines around the Bouddi Peninsula are easily accessible, but you can drive your car right up to secluded and beautiful Killcare Beach. There are rock pools for kids to explore and a decent break for learner surfers.

Children Kids will be excited by the Australian Reptile Park (www.reptilepark.com.au), off the Pacific Highway (take the Gosford exit). There's an array of creepy critters on display including crocodiles and spiders

as well as cuties like koalas and wombats. Watch the Galapagos tortoises being fed, learn about Tasmanian devils or pose with a python.

Walks From the southern end of Pearl Beach you can follow a fire trail through the Brisbane Water National Park to Patonga. It takes about two hours and you get to observe, at close quarters, two of the Central Coast's most exclusive enclaves. You might even spot a celeb.

Perfect picnic Toowoon Bay has won awards for being the country's cleanest beach, and is protected by an offshore reef so swimming is safe. There's a grassy reserve behind the beach that's made for sand-free munching once you've paddled to your heart's content.

Shopping This isn't the go-to place for designer shopping, but you can meet some of the area's food producers at the Entrance Farmers Market, held on the third Saturday of every month at Memorial Park. A new organic farmers' market is also being held at Ettalong every Sunday, offering delicious local fare, as well as arts and crafts, and entertainment.

Something for nothing From June, try spotting those most beloved of marine mammals with help from the National Parks and Wildlife Service (www.nationalparks.nsw.gov.au), which hosts free whale-watching at Crackneck Look-out in Bateau Bay, to coincide with the peak northern migration of humpback whales. Rangers can give you the inside track on other sea life too.

Don't go home without... hiring a small boat – or 'tinny' if you want to be down with the locals – and taking it out fishing. Try Long Jetty Catamaran & Boat Hire (www.longjettyboathire.com) at Tuggerah Lakes.

COMPLETELY CENTRAL COAST

The Central Coast is a breeding ground for the large, ungainly pelican, and it makes a kooky spectacle even if bird-watching isn't normally your bag. These black-and-white birds with their famously long, pouched bills are so tame they come in to be fed in large numbers to the foreshore at the Entrance every day at 3.30pm. A smaller session happens daily at 3pm opposite Fishermans Wharf at Woy Woy. If you'd prefer a more action-packed close-up, join the Pelican Feeding and Oyster Tasting kayaking tours (www.kayaktours.com.au) on Brisbane Waters.

DIARY

May Gosford Regional Show (www.gosfordshowground.com.au), an annual agricultural event, features equestrian displays, sideshows, food and competitions. **June** Pearl Beach Annual Classic Music Festival (www.pearlbeach.net.au) sees chamber musicians play at the local Memorial Hall over a weekend. At Gosford City Blues Festival (www.gosford citywaterfrontblues.com) fans of jazzy tunes hit town for a weekend of swinging sounds. **September** During the Australian Springtime Flora Festival (www.florafestival.com.au) beautiful native wildflowers are among the displays at this popular plant and gardening event.

'It doesn't take long for our thoughts to shift to dinner because, first and foremost, this destination is renowned mostly for what it serves on a plate'

Killcare

Enjoy

Bells at Killcare

STYLE Classy seaside chic
SETTING Graceful Central Coast gardens

Large white capital letters jutting from the blue wall of the reception area at Bells at Killcare grab you on arrival and command: 'RELAX, UNWIND, ENJOY.' It leaves you in no doubt as to what's expected of guests here. There's nothing Mr Smith and I can do but step up to the mark.

It's not a tough job, of course. There's the place itself, with graceful central manor house and English country estate-style gardens. We're led to our room, a king suite, although 'suite' is a rather misleading term. It's more a diminutive cottage with a spacious living and bedroom area, an iron fireplace resting on exposed brickwork, a fully equipped kitchen and an enormous bathroom with an oversized spa bath. Sydney designer and textile goddess Chrissie Jeffrey is behind the decor, which features a crisp mix of nautical blues, whites and beiges alongside elegant antique furniture, chic rattan and sumptuously comforting fabrics and cushions. Bliss.

Mr Smith and I head directly to the big veranda with a cafetière of chef Stefano Manfredi's rich own-brand coffee, and within a few moments are already getting stuck into the wall instructions that greeted us on check-in.

It doesn't take long for our thoughts to shift to dinner because, first and foremost, this destination is renowned mostly for what it serves on a plate. With Manfredi, an

acclaimed chef at the helm, the award-winning restaurant here has made this quiet spot on the Central Coast a point of pilgrimage for foodies. His menu is a robust take on Italian cooking, backed with considered flavouring and a strong emphasis on local and organic produce. And then there's the wine. Owners Brian and Karina Barry have long been names in the nearby Hunter Valley wine industry and have brought their expertise to an extensive and encyclopedic wine list that offers the best from Italian and local vineyards, with staff only too happy to talk you through the choices.

Decision-making over dinner itself isn't too troubling. It's a simple menu that lets the ingredients speak for themselves and inspires snap 'I want that!' decisions. There's an antipasto of meats and oysters, but Mr Smith and I get straight into the primo courses: crisp pork cheek with mushroom ragu and sweetly buttery spinach and ricotta gnocchi. For secondi we try the grass-fed beef rump and roast rabbit with veal sweetbreads – both are boldly flavoured, hearty portions.

But it's not all about gorging yourself silly or sitting on your behind at Bells we discover – there's plenty to do. The picture-perfect setting of Hardys Bay, a typical Australian coastal village complete with fish and chip shop, is just a few minutes down the road. The sweeping views here treat us to an eyeful of the many small islands, bays and waterways that weave around this part of the coast out to Ettalong Beach and Daleys Point. On the other side of the peninsula is Killcare Beach, a big open crescent marked only with a surf club at one end. We walk across the peachy-coloured sand and enjoy the pounding of the waves. As Killcare is nestled on the edge of Bouddi National Park the lure of bushwalks also offsets any conscience about indulging in Manfredi's dishes and the Barrys' wine selections. We spend a couple of hours traipsing the six-kilometre Maitland Bay Circuit, one of the many walks suggested on a map given to us on check-in and dotted with beautiful views.

Calories burned, back at Bells we settle down on the Manor House terrace, overlooking the grounds with a couple of sundowners, enjoying the dying daylight, peacefully huddled among the fat navy-and-white cushions on the lounge. Marita, one of the many friendly and attentive staff members here, has come to see if she can bring us anything. She tells us that this small haven gets many visitors from all over the world and lots of weekenders from the city. 'It's only a short drive from Sydney,' she says, 'but you could be anywhere.' She's absolutely right. Although Bells is firmly planted in the middle of some of the Central Coast's best beaches and bays, it's rather unique as a coastal resort in that you can't actually spy the water. The sea is just a few minutes' drive away and the nautical decor throughout doesn't let you forget your coordinates, but the leafy privacy afforded here also makes it a country retreat that is truly about getting away from it all. 'We're anywhere and nowhere at the same time,' sighs Mr Smith, 'and it feels heavenly.'

With the flush still in our cheeks from all that salt-air-kissed strolling, we head to the inviting embrace of the main dining room. The blue-striped walls (another fitting seaside touch) and larger-than-life mirrors are especially seductive when teamed with chic chandeliers and flickering tealights. Pre-dinner drinks are soon in our clutches, and we flop into the large Chesterfield sofas in the cosy bar, olives and crumbly caper-and-parmesan biscuits to hand. Home-made simple-but-delectable bread is our next treat, along with an olive oil that's so deliciously light and flavoursome I'm tempted to drink it. As romantic as the setting is, it's the menu of two courses and a glass of wine for AU$39, served as a special offer on Tuesday nights, which has us enraptured. Salt cod soup gets both votes as does roast pork belly with savoy cabbage and chestnuts. Hey, it may be corny, but when our waiter, Hayden, brings our dishes, it's the line he delivers with them that captures our sentiments about Bells at Killcare in a nutshell. 'Enjoy!' he smiles.

REVIEWED BY SARAH THOMAS

'Pre-dinner drinks are soon in our clutches, and we flop into the large Chesterfield sofas in the cosy bar'

NEED TO KNOW

Rooms 11, including nine suites and two villas.

Rates AU$500–$600, with gourmet breakfast hamper; packages start from AU$250 (often this includes a minimum two-night stay, plus dinner).

Check-out 11am, but for AU$100 this can be extended. Check-in, 2pm.

Facilities Gardens, free WiFi in the main house, CD, DVD and book library, day spa and pool. In rooms: pre-loaded iPod and dock, flatscreen TV, CD/DVD players.

Children Bells is best for grown-ups; kids are allowed in the restaurant only, but there's no special menu.

Also Stainless-steel Tucker barbecues grace private furnished verandas; the perfect opportunity for Mr Smith to hone his cooked-breakfast skills. If Mrs Smith fancies some pampering, in-room beauty and spa treatments can be arranged.

IN THE KNOW

Our favourite rooms All Bells' boudoirs are set away from the Manor House through pretty English-style gardens, secluded from the gastronomic bustle of the restaurant. The two Deluxe Spa Villas make you feel even more independent, with their upstairs bedrooms, double spa baths and French-windowed balconies. Get north-west facing number 10 for sleeping off lunch in the afternoon sun. Or opt for a King Suite with a spa bath.

Hotel bar As well as a super-extensive Italian wine list, Bells serves many of the best regional wines. The glass-walled, temperature-controlled wine cellar is a key feature of the restaurant area, but quaff the stuff in the Chesterfielded bar or more comfy, literature-lined library, where a replica First Fleet rigger takes pride of place. Suitably, Bellinis are the house cocktail.

Hotel restaurant The grand main dining room, overlooking the gardens, is the spiritual heart of Bells at Killcare. Vivid blues, strong stripes and shell motifs create a relaxed coastal feel, smartened by white linens and stylish banquettes. The veranda is great for larger parties while two private dining rooms – the Wine Room and the Garden Room – offer secluded spaces inside. But you'd be happy eating chef Stefano Manfredi's food anywhere – robust duck and pork ragus, pan-fried veal, home-made gelati and antipasto plates that would feed a family. Italian heritage is overlaid with rigorous local and organic product sourcing, such as Hawkesbury River oysters.

Top table Pick a table on the terrace, but any of the windowside tables for two will do if it's too hot or cold to be outside (number 23 is lovely).

Room service Antipasto platters can be enjoyed in your room – just order in advance.

Dress code TM Lewin shirts and RM Williams moleskins for lunch; stretch pants for after.

Local knowledge To justify further gourmet indulgence, fossick around Bouddi National Park or any of the nine local beaches. Bushwalking maps are provided and tasty picnic hampers, backpacks and guides can be arranged. The more adventurous can swim or surf at Killcare Beach, charter a yacht or go whale watching.

LOCAL EATING AND DRINKING

Yum Yum's Eatery (02 4360 2999), in Hardys Bay, has gentle water views and a smart, simple menu – a great place to slum it after the foodie delights back up the hill. Try beer-battered barramundi or king prawn linguini. Nearby the **Fat Goose Restaurant & Bistro** at Hardys Bay RSL (02 4360 2345) serves burgers, seafood and kangaroo if you really want to savour the local flavours.

GET A ROOM!

Use our free online booking service: check availability and make reservations through www.mrandmrssmith.com.

 SMITH CARD OFFER An exclusive chef's tour of the kitchen gardens, with guidance on seasonal produce.

Bells at Killcare 107 The Scenic Road, Killcare Beach, NSW 2257 (02 4360 2411; www.bellsatkillcare.com.au)

'We enter another world:
just three pavilions, looking
back through lush bushland to
the oyster farms'

Pretty Beach

Pretty Beach House

STYLE Luxe modern-rustic guesthouse
SETTING Bouddi hilltop bush

The moment we creep up the black-run-steep driveway, leaving the modest fibro shacks of the 'Costa Centrale' (Central Coast to the locals) behind, we have entered another world. Pretty Beach House is a private – extremely private – retreat, and there's not a sheet of compressed cement to be seen: just three pavilions, high in the trees and looking back through lush bushland to the oyster farms of the sparkling Brisbane Waters. It's a true sanctuary, and the pampering starts the minute we open our car doors. Staff are gracious, spunky, switched-on and utterly charming. Their passion is palpable and contagious.

We are led along a slatted wooden pathway through beautiful native gardens and gracious gums to Hideaway Pavilion, our seductive new love nest. Ms Smith can barely control a gasp. An enormous bed beckons a few steps above the main living area, which in turn is surrounded by glass doors and a huge deck. Meticulous attention to detail rules throughout, with soothing contemporary furnishings in muted tones. Natural materials abound – polished sandstone, bamboo walls, recycled timber buttresses, twig screens, twine balustrades – but this is ravishingly refined rustic.

As Ms Smith and I pause on the sofa, it's so damn cosy we never want to leave. Thankfully, she swings into action and makes the perfect vodka tonic, complete with lashings of fresh lime, from the fully stocked bar, although perhaps the ambience has a teensy bit to do with it tasting so good. After a quick test of the outsize bed, the request for a softer pillow is met immediately as a staff member delivers three different pillows to choose from (I'm all for a pillow menu). Equally impressive is the enormous bathroom, complete with a heated pebble stone floor. It's a decadent touch, and our feet love it.

Rising steam contrasts against a darkening sky over the treetops as we frolic in the heated plunge pool on the outdoor deck. Eventually hunger overcomes us, so we dress for dinner and head to the main house, where a table pour deux is set by the open fireplace. The menu

here is overseen by acclaimed Italian chef Stefano Manfredi, and focuses on local, uncomplicated flavours. The best part is the luxury of choice. You can dine at any time, anywhere on the property and on almost anything you crave. We feast on steamed white asparagus with generous shavings of new-season winter black truffle, perfectly cooked fish and beef, and a delicious mandarin pudding. Different wines are chosen from the cellar for each course, and they, like the menu, change daily. Boredom is not an option.

The next morning, after a leisurely breakfast in bed – the granola, bread, sausages, chutney and jams all house-made – we take a walk through the untamed coastal bushland that surrounds the property. Guessing our independence (you can have someone accompany you on a hike if you so desire), the hotel manager organises a backpack with water bottles, insect repellent and a map before we set off. We discover the look-out, a canopied day-bed perched at the southern perimeter of the grounds, and decide this is the ideal place to

'It feels as though you're completely cut off from the rest of the world, floating amid views of bush and water'

take morning tea (they bring it to you, of course). It's all rather civilised, particularly since it feels as though you're completely cut off from the rest of the world, floating amid views of bush and water. Back at the main house, lunch might be an antipasto plate or something more substantial: rabbit and pearl barley stew or pizzas from the wood-fired oven. The most difficult choice is where to have it: oh, to lunch lounging on our deck or alfresco by the emerald-green infinity pool? Decisions, decisions.

To complete our weekend of relaxed indulgence, we've booked massages. Our therapists knock on the door late Sunday afternoon, set up tables in the living area and apply their magic touch. It's raining cats and dogs outside but we agree that there's no better place or state to be in. We've hit the jackpot.

After just two days, Ms Smith and I have concluded that Hideaway will be our new weekender, easily reached from our Sydney base when we want to rekindle our romance (with PBH, as well as each other). She was cheeky enough to write in the visitors' book that she'd taken ownership and it was simply no longer available. This is one very special escape, where we could happily stay for quite some time without leaving the compound. When we return, a quick dip in the surf at nearby Killcare Beach will be our first task. Chased up with Stefano's strawberry brioche tarts with vanilla gelato and gooey chocolate pudding...

REVIEWED BY CHRISTINE MANFIELD

NEED TO KNOW

Rooms Three one-bedroom pavilions.

Rates AU$1,700–$2,750 including meals, afternoon tea, snacks, wines and champagnes, and guided bushwalks.

Check-out 12pm, but later subject to availability. Check-in, 2pm – also flexible.

Facilities Free WiFi throughout, CD/DVD library, infinity pool. In rooms: pre-loaded iPod and dock, flatscreen TVs and DVD players, LI'TYA toiletries, private decks, day-beds and heated plunge pools.

Children Under 12s are only permitted with exclusive use of all three pavilions. Free cots and extra beds for older children can be provided, and babysitting with a local nanny can be arranged with 24 hours' notice.

Also Don't miss the day-bed perched high out of sight on the edge of the property.

IN THE KNOW

Our favourite rooms All three pavilions are a knockout, but head to Hideaway for maximum privacy. Attached to the main house, Treetops is set over two floors, with a bathroom each for Mr and Mrs Smith, including a freestanding bath. All pavilions feature dressing rooms, fireplaces and king-size beds. Decor is a soothing mix of natural fabrics, recycled timbers, luxe furnishings and local art.

Hotel bar An intimate cocktail bar sits tucked away on a mezzanine level off the main living area, and has a white mini grand piano if you fancy tickling the ivories. There's also a great wine cellar for quaffing the older stuff. We recommend the signature apéritif, with campari, gin, fresh lime and cranberry juice.

Hotel restaurant Vintage leather chairs, fine Belgian linen, chic Riedel glassware and a huge Arthur Boyd await you in the main dining area. Chef Stefano Manfredi's menu is classic modern Italian – fresh, seasonal, elegant, hearty. Expect bread baked daily, local crayfish with garlic mayonnaise and veal shank with farro. Meals can be served à deux on your private deck, anywhere in the three-hectare grounds, or communally in the main house.

Top table Eating on the timber deck by the infinity pool offers dress-circle views.

Room service Fruit, biscotti, cakes, tarts and antipasto can be brought to your room 24 hours a day.

Dress code Well-pressed linens, outsize resin jewellery and designer clogs.

Local knowledge For the full Jackie O treatment take Pretty Beach's skippered CABO 38 Express sports cruiser out for a spin on Brisbane Waters or seek out hidden, empty beaches where you can swim, snorkel and fish. Best of all, take a Manfredi picnic hamper. To stretch your pins, try a guided walk through the Bouddi Peninsula or stroll over to private Tallow Beach, home to a tempting surf break.

LOCAL EATING AND DRINKING

With fabulous all-inclusive food and drink on tap, you're unlikely to wander beyond Pretty Beach House's boundaries. **Bells at Killcare Restaurant**, at the nearby boutique hotel of the same name, is the exception, with cooking by chef Stefano Manfredi, who also oversees Pretty Beach's menus. Food is seasonal, featuring fresh local oysters and seafood, and Italian-inspired, and has already bagged a coveted chef's hat (02 4360 2411).

GET A ROOM!

Use our free online booking service: check availability and make reservations through www.mrandmrssmith.com.

 SMITH CARD OFFER A signed copy of chef Stefano Manfredi's cookbook *Cook for All Seasons* or a PBH backpack and water bottle for coastal bush walks.

Pretty Beach House Pretty Beach, NSW 2257 (02 4360 1933; www.prettybeachhouse.com.au)

LORD HOWE ISLAND

COASTLINE Peaks, palms and pristine beaches
COAST LIFE The life aquatic

With its soaring volcanic peaks, turquoise lagoon, unspoilt beaches and rare plants, birds and marine life, ruggedly beautiful eco-retreat Lord Howe Island should bring out your inner David Attenborough. This crescent-shaped South Pacific sanctuary, 700 kilometres north east of Sydney, is only 11 kilometres long, 2.8 wide and is bordered by the world's most southerly reef. With just 350 locals, and visitor numbers restricted to 400 at any one time, you're almost guaranteed to have one of its seductive beaches all to yourself. So whether you're into swimming, snorkelling and scuba diving, or more mellow boating, birdwatching and bushwalking, this subtropical paradise should feel like your own personal Garden of Eden.

GETTING THERE

Planes Unless you're a seafaring Smith with your own yacht, the only way to get to the island is by air. QantasLink (www.qantas.com) operates a 32-seat Dash 8 service from Sydney most days, and from Brisbane on weekends. A seasonal weekly service is also available from Port Macquarie from February to June and September to December. Flight time is two hours (it's the closest island getaway to Sydney) and the 14kg luggage allowance is strictly enforced.
Automobiles Walking or cycling is the best way to get round the island, but you can rent a car from Wilson's Hire Service if you prefer four wheels to two (contact michele.wilson@bigpond.com).

LOCAL KNOWLEDGE

Taxis There are no cabs on Lord Howe, and not many regular cars, but your hotel can help with transport (most offer airport transfers).
Packing tips Binoculars for close-ups of rare birds, hiking gear, and a pair of old trainers for reef-walking.

Recommended reads Ian Hutton, a local naturalist, has written several books including *Birds of Lord Howe Island Past and Present*, *Rambler's Lord Howe Island*, *Marine Life of Lord Howe Island* and *The Australian Geographic Book of Lord Howe Island*, which cover all of those geeky eco questions.
Local specialities Freshly caught local fish graces plates here, especially lip-smackingly tasty kingfish, and be sure to have a barbecue on one of the many blissful beaches. Due to the island's remote location and limited agricultural land, most food arrives by ferry from the Australian mainland once a week, which can make it pricey. A small amount of vegetables and fruit is grown locally and there are some beef cattle.
Do go/don't go September to May has the best beach weather, with water temperatures hitting 25 degrees from February to April; cooler days from June to August attract hikers and an older crowd. Lord Howe Island has a perpetual spring climate, though, so any season is a good time to visit.

And... Lord Howe is Australia's top twitching destination, with 14 species of sea birds breeding here in their squawking thousands as well as over 130 other species of resident or migratory winged wonders, including the oddly named muttonbirds, sooty terns and masked boobies.

WORTH GETTING OUT OF BED FOR

Viewpoint A gruelling eight-hour round-trip hike will take you to the top of the island's highest peak, Mount Gower. Your reward? Views of the entire island and Ball's Pyramid, the world's tallest sea stack, 26 kilometres offshore. If that sounds too strenuous, try the easy two-hour return walk up to the lookout tower on Transit Hill for 360-degree views. From Clear Place, an hour-and-a-half round-trip, you'll also get a glimpse of Ball's Pyramid.

Arts and culture Ogle the skeleton of an extinct giant horned turtle at the must-see Lord Howe Island Museum (www.lordhoweisland.info/museum.htm), which has quirky displays on the island's history and World Heritage-listed environment, as well as a shop and café. Go potty for fronds at the Kentia Palm Nursery (www.kentia-elite.com), which offers an hour-long tour every Friday at 10.30am giving the inside track on this endemic species, now exported worldwide. Pick up an original souvenir at Ginny's Shed, which sells bold island-inspired tropical prints on calico by local artist Ginny Retmock (02 6563 2076).

Activities Lord Howe is a great spot for budding Jacques Cousteaus to flex their scuba-diving muscles. Pro Dive (02 6563 2253) offers daily boat dives including Ball's Pyramid, weather permitting, with regular introductory dives and open-water scuba courses. If you're not a diver then glass-bottom boat or snorkelling tours are operated by Lord Howe Island Environmental Tours (02 6563 2326). For more sedate thrills, play lawn bowls with the locals every Thursday from 4pm or golf on Friday (12 holes from 2pm on Sunday, 18 holes from 1.30pm). Chase 'n' Thyme Island Tours (02 6563 2247; or book at the post office) offers small groups an interesting look into life on this rugged and remote island, first settled in the 1830s.

Best beach The island's 11 beautiful beaches are often deserted so you can play castaway with your other half. Lovers Bay is a secluded little cove perfect for snorkelling or watching the sunset with a magical view of twin peaks Mounts Gower and Lidgbird. Neds Beach and Old Settlement Beach are also ace for snorkelling. Surfers in search of breaks should head to the outside of the coral reef bordering the lagoon (hire boards on the island).

Daytripper When the waters are calm, go fishing around the striking sea spire Ball's Pyramid, south east of the main island, which is the best place to catch large (and tasty) green-backed kingfish. Marine Adventures runs day trips for AU$200 a person (www.marineadventures.com.au).

Children The island's sheltered lagoon is ideal for kids to paddle or swim in; sea kayaking is also easy and fun, and snorkelling here is like swimming in a tropical aquarium that's dotted with colourful coral. Many local walks are child-friendly and kids should go gaga for the brilliant bird and marine life.

Walks The island is criss-crossed with walking trails of varying grades, all of which are well signposted with approximate trek times. Malabar Hill and Kims Lookout is the most popular walk. During the five-hour round-trip you'll not only have cor-blimey views but you may also see the red-tailed tropicbirds doing their back-flip mating dance (September to May). The eight-hour round-trip climb up Mount Gower is one of Australia's best day treks, but you'll need to be fit and hire a licensed guide (call Cindy or Jack on 02 6563 2218 or Dean on 02 6563 2214). The vertiginous views and

rare bird and plant life will sweeten the exercise pill though. Ramblin' Ronnie offers a three-hour walking tour during which you'll learn about Lord Howe's unique flora and fauna as well as snippets of colourful local history (to book telephone Wilson's Bike Hire on 02 6563 2045).

Perfect picnic Many of the island's beaches have picnic tables and wood-fire barbecues, so take your pick from seductive shoreside spots.

Shopping Save your shopping dollars for the mainland. There are only two general stores which sell basic supplies and a liquor store on Lord Howe. Larrup's on the main street sells surf gear and accessories and some swimwear.

Something for nothing Grab some stale bread and head to Neds Beach where you can hand-feed the metre-long kingfish, wrasse and silver drummer that are ever-present in the shallows. This feasting frenzy is not to be missed.

Don't go home without... spotting endemic species such as the Lord Howe woodhen, a flightless bird saved from extinction and not found anywhere else in the world.

LISTED LORD HOWE ISLAND

One of only four island groups possessing World Heritage status for the global significance of its natural beauty, flora and fauna, Lord Howe Island's dramatically diverse landscape is home to many indigenous species of bird, marine and plant life. Hundreds of thousands of migratory sea birds nest here and on nearby Ball's Pyramid, the tallest sea stack in the world.

DIARY

January The height of summer sees lots of sea bird activity, with many species either laying or hatching their eggs. Loads of the island's flowers are also in full, fragrant bloom. **February** Colourful coral spawning adds to the underwater thrills. **March** Witness squillions of providence petrels arriving for their winter breeding season. They wander around the island as though drunk, toppling over and allowing humans to pick them up. **October** Catch the finish of the Gosford to Lord Howe Island Yacht Race (www.gosfordsailingclub.com.au), and the red-tailed tropicbird doing its bizarre breeding dance.

'Keen to explore the World Heritage-listed island, we're offered the use of a buggy. Everyone waves as we pass by'

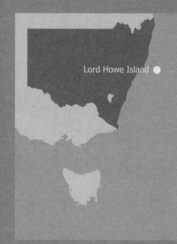

Lord Howe Island ●

Capella Lodge

STYLE Sophisticated beach house
SETTING Subtropical island idyll

Capella Lodge

On approach to Lord Howe, a two-hour flight from Sydney, our Dash 8 pilot shows his true colours: reliable yet somewhat sneaky. He does an impromptu lap of the island, perhaps knowing that I need a suitable distraction before landing on its tiny airstrip.

One sandal on the tarmac, and our friendly hosts Mark and Libby greet us. Leaving our luggage to be claimed, we're led to a waiting vehicle to head south to Capella Lodge. To our left is a belt of undulating green, the island's golf course; on the other side two towering pine trees overlook Lovers Bay. I am mesmerised by the world's most southerly coral reef lagoon, with its turquoise and shades of blue upon blue. Suggesting that it beckons for a dip, Mr Smith agrees on 'the sort prefixed by the word skinny'.

Not 25 minutes after landing we're enjoying a freshly squeezed watermelon, orange and pineapple juice on Capella's main terrace. It affords an uninterrupted view of twin peaks Mount Lidgbird and the taller Mount Gower along with spectacular ocean vistas. Chic day-beds and deckchairs near a plunge pool make this the place to begin our long overdue escape. While we wait for our room to be readied we're invited to breakfast in this serene setting. A maximum of only 20 guests stay at the lodge at any one time, and we meet two other couples – one duo here for their honeymoon, the other returning for the twelfth time.

While I'm relieved there is wireless access for the odd business check, there's no mobile reception. Capella Lodge politely insists that our metropolitan instincts take a break. The team here is super-friendly and gives first-name, impeccably timed service. They possess a delightful ability to anticipate our 'wouldn't it be nice to's', before we have even been able to articulate them.

Upon entering our room, a Lagoon Loft, the first thing to catch my eye is a tray of mini lemon meringue tarts. There's a generous pile of plush pillows in duck blue, cream and cool stripes, wooden furniture, and boat portholes mounted on the white, panelled walls. Fresh South Pacific air seeps through the timber louvre door and windows. Upstairs there's the all-important king-size bed facing huge glass doors that open to an outdoor deck with day-bed and mountain views. A red lighthouse lamp created by Mambo artist Bruce Goold keeps a watchful post in the corner. It's just one of the many pieces of artwork and fabric commissioned for the chill-out zones of Capella.

We're the first guests to enjoy the newly refurbished basalt stone bathroom, replete with bespoke Capella Lodge products (by Small Indulgences), including a heady lavender and mint hand wash. Our fridge is full of San Pellegrino, fruit juices and soft drinks, all complimentary. I'm most pleased with the selection of T bar teas, while Mr Smith is happy to introduce his iPod to the Bose sound system.

Keen to explore the World Heritage-listed island, we're offered the use of a new electric buggy. Everyone waves as we pass by. There are many titles LHI can claim but we can't fathom unfriendly ever being one of them. As

we head out, a woodhen (a species saved from near extinction, which is only found here) plays 'chicken' with our vehicle, sprinting across the road. With a blanket 25 kilometre per hour speed limit on the island, he's convinced we're not going to run him over.

On Libby's recommendation we walk along Malabar Hill before heading down to Neds Beach for a spot of beachcombing and scrambling across the rocks. We're still talking about hand-feeding a school of giant kingfish here. They swim without fear around our knees, greedily snapping bits of bread we've brought from the lodge. Steve Irwin would have been proud.

At dinner Mr Smith opts for grilled Yamba cuttlefish, green lentils, capers, saffron and garlic aïoli, while I treat myself to a local yellowtail kingfish ceviche with tomato and lemon myrtle oil to start. Suppressing a slight pang of guilt, we hope we haven't just taken a bite of one of our recent Nemo friends' relatives. The main course arrives and our bellies are subjected to another round of decadent dining. Feeling a little tipsy, Mr Smith suggests we repair to the adjacent Kentia Lounge. A room dedicated to board games and reading, it's also home to a teak wall and open fireplace. Tonight it's our private space to polish off our shared desserts: hazelnut torte with espresso cream and a farmhouse cheese plate.

The next day we set off on Capella bikes with a packed gourmet lunch. It's been some time since I've felt salty sea air on my face and let it knot my hair without a care. Despite overcast weather we tackle the challenging hike up to Goat House Cave. Capella Spa's post-climb feet therapy is a suitable reward for the effort. Using LI'TYA products, it starts with a soak and finishes with a foot mask of Tasmanian kelp and native pepperberry applied as warm basalt stones are placed between your toes. Mr Smith and I also acquaint ourselves with the hot tub, used equally for relaxing weary muscles and inveigling intimacy.

Returning to our room we quietly implore the weatherman to allow us a snorkel in the morning. He must have been in the mood to meet our wishes – freakish winds prevent any planes from coming in to or taking off from Lord Howe. Stranded, we surrender to paradise for an extra day.

REVIEWED BY CARRIE CHOO

'The main course arrives and our bellies are subjected to another round of decadent dining'

NEED TO KNOW

Rooms Nine suites.

Rates Low season, AU$1,180–$1,980; high season, AU$1,300–$1,980, including breakfast, soft drinks, sunset apéritifs and canapés, three-course dinner with matching wines, and airport transfers.

Check-out 10.30am. Check-in, 2pm.

Facilities Free WiFi throughout, DVD, CD and book library, board games, outdoor infinity-edge swimming pool, Jacuzzi, day spa, gardens. In rooms: flatscreen TV, DVD player, Bose music system (with MP3 input), signature Capella Spa toiletries, minibar.

Children Kids aged six and over are welcome at the lodge (age 12 and over at the Lidgbird Pavilion), which can provide rollaway beds at standard extra guest rates.

Also Blending in with the landscape in bleached wood and glass, Capella Lodge is set at the southern end of Lord Howe Island, with romantic views out over the jagged mountains, turquoise lagoon, coral reef and sea. The hotel provides free bikes for getting around, or hire a buggy for the day (a buggy is included in Lidgbird Pavilion rates; pre-book the other one).

IN THE KNOW

Our favourite rooms We're partial to Room 2, a Lagoon Loft with stunning views – enjoy them from the comfy bed on the mezzanine. If you want to push the boat out, the recently revamped flagship Lidgbird Pavilion now has a second level with wraparound verandas, a plunge pool and outdoor stone bath under the frangipani trees, and offers private dining as well as its own free bar. Bathrooms throughout feature sexy dark basalt stone, baths and rain showers.

Hotel bar The Capella Bar boasts a good selection of boutique wines and great espressos. Complimentary sunset cocktails and canapés are served daily on Gower's Terrace, where you can soak up breathtaking views from chic loungers; or relax on ample banquettes in the Kentia Lounge, with blissed-out beats as a backing track.

Hotel restaurant The open-plan Capella Restaurant has a laid-back yet luxurious coastal look, with dramatic floor-to-ceiling windows for stellar skylines. Fans of modern Pacific cuisine will enjoy chef Phil Woolaston's daily-changing offerings, including locally caught fish, house-made pasta, boutique farmed meats and island-grown tropical fruit and veg. Lunch costs extra, and the lodge can also supply picnic and barbecue packs, for AU$18 and AU$30 a person respectively.

Top table New arrivals are always placed at tables 1, 2 or 3 by the window on their first day, and guests are then rotated so that everyone gets a ringside seat. The fab landscape is still visible from most tables though.

Room service Not available as Capella offers a traditional lodge experience where guests come together to dine, but between the restaurant and bar you should be well catered for.

Dress code Sophisticated neutrals – why compete with the view?

Local knowledge Pamper yourself at the intimate Capella Spa, which uses Aboriginal LI'TYA products in its dreamy treatments. Lagoon kayaks and snorkelling gear are available for exploring the island's marine ecosystem. Picnic tables and wood-fired barbecues dot scenic spots nearby too if you'd rather stay on dry land.

LOCAL EATING AND DRINKING

Breakfast and dinner are all-inclusive at Capella, but for a snack or lunch call in at **Palmsugar** (02 6563 2120) on Skyline Drive for coffee and cake (it's closed Sundays). **Pinetrees** (02 6563 2177) on Lagoon Road, is ringed by a veranda and offers a canvas-covered dining area – perfect for eating under the stars. The fish-fry buffet dinner is a weekly highlight.

GET A ROOM!

Use our free online booking service: check availability and make reservations through www.mrandmrssmith.com.

 SMITH CARD OFFER A gourmet picnic or barbecue lunch for two.

Capella Lodge Lagoon Road, Lord Howe Island, NSW 2898 (02 9918 4355; www.capellalodge.com.au)

Victoria
AUSTRALIA

VICTORIA

MELBOURNE
The Bloomfield
Lyall Hotel and Spa
The Prince
THE GRAMPIANS
Royal Mail Hotel

MELBOURNE

CITYSCAPE History and high-rises
CITY LIFE Culture, cuisine and couture

Known for its sporting passion, cultural edge and cool take on music, fashion and food, Victoria's capital beats Sydney to the crown of Australia's most liveable city. The NSWer may have a sexier location, but Melbourne steals it on attitude (and affordability). Life here is more about being, than doing, but if you are going to do something, make sure you're clutching a latte, humming an indie tune and wearing black – the default sartorial setting. The cityscape is a quirky clash of elegant Victorian houses, skyscrapers and gardens, but beneath the polite façade you'll discover hidden laneways brimming with hip bars, graffiti-strewn galleries, grungy clubs and one-off fashion and vintage stores.

GETTING THERE

Planes Melbourne Airport (www.melbourneairport.com. au), 22 kilometres north-west of the centre, services domestic and international flights. Smaller Avalon Airport (www.avalonairport.com.au), 40 minutes west of the city, handles some Jetstar flights.
Trains Melbourne's main railway hub is Flinders Street Station in the CBD, just one stop away from Southern Cross Station where trains depart for rural Victoria and interstate destinations (see www.vline.com.au).
Automobiles Skybus (www.skybus.com.au) operates a shuttle service from Melbourne Airport to Southern Cross Station in the CBD for AU$16 single or AU$26 return. Melbourne's compact grid and network of trains, trams and buses means you won't need wheels; to ride on any metropolitan public transport pick up a Metlink ticket (www.metlinkmelbourne.com.au) at newsagents, train stations or on board trams. If you're roaming further afield, the usual car hire firms are on hand at the airport.

LOCAL KNOWLEDGE

Taxis Cabs can easily be flagged down in the street or found at ranks in the CBD. Can't see one? Call Silver Top Taxis (13 10 08), and one will come to you.

Packing tips The Crowded House song 'Four Seasons in One Day' was written about the city's ridiculously changeable weather. Bring clothes for all meteorological possibilities – and don't forget your umbrella.
Recommended reads Bearbrass: Imagining Early Melbourne by Robyn Annear is a classic account of the city's history; for a more provocative modern take, Christos Tsiolkas' award-winning The Slap probes multicultural middle-class Melbourne, and the fallout of a man slapping someone else's child. Chopper by Mark Brandon Read, made into a film starring Eric Bana, is the Melbourne-based autobiography of one of Australia's most notorious criminals – now living free in the city.
Cuisine Melbourne is arguably the culinary capital of Australia, whether you want startling modern meals, high-quality comfort food, killer cocktails in hidden locations or great ethnic cuisine at a snip. Head to Richmond for Vietnamese, Footscray for African and Carlton for Italian. Coffee is the city's second religion (football is the first) and you haven't really been to Melbourne until you've sipped a latte in a laneway café.
Do go/don't go There's a carnival atmosphere in summer (December to February) with plenty of free

activities on offer. Winter (June to August) may be a little cold and wet but clear skies suit wine tours in the nearby Yarra Valley or Mornington Peninsula (www.visitmorningtonpeninsular.org).

WORTH GETTING OUT OF BED FOR

Viewpoint The vertiginous 92-storey Eureka Tower at Southbank, Melbourne's tallest building, offers 360-degree views of the city (www.eurekaskydeck.com.au).
Art and culture The flourishing Southbank arts precinct houses the Melbourne Recital Centre (www.melbournerecital.com.au) and Melbourne Theatre Company (www.mtc.com.au). Down the road, the Malthouse Theatre (www.malthousetheatre.com.au) presents contemporary drama. Across the way, the Australian Centre for Contemporary Art (www.accaonline.org.au) curates edgy exhibitions. The studios of modern dance company Chunky Move (www.chunkymove.com) are next door, with classes available if you fancy throwing some shapes. Art lovers should make tracks for the National Gallery of Victoria: International on St Kilda Road, for global works, and the Ian Potter Centre: NGV Australia in Federation Square for homegrown talent (www.ngv.vic.gov.au). Opposite Fed Square, the Forum Theatre (www.forummelbourne.com.au) hosts bands. For more idiosyncratic and indigenous art, check out Flinders Lane, between Spring and Swanston Streets.
Activities Treat yourself to a sunset barbecue on the banks of the Yarra River. Take your prawns to Birrarung Marr park, adjacent to Fed Square, where you'll find cooking grills, a kid's play area and fab views. Joggers should head to the Tan, a 3.9-kilometre track around the beautiful Royal Botanical Gardens. Rent an old school bike from the Humble Vintage (www.thehumblevintage.com). Popular routes include following the Yarra Trail north-east or pedalling bayside towards St Kilda. Bicycle Victoria (www.bv.com.au) has all the info you'll need.
Daytripper Indulge in some wine tasting in the picturesque Yarra Valley – an hour's drive from the city and home to some of Australia's best producers. If you're interested in this land's unique wildlife, don't miss Healesville Sanctuary (www.zoo.org.au/Healesville Sanctuary). Just 90 minutes north-west of Melbourne, the natural mineral springs in Daylesford and Hepburn Springs (www.visitdaylesford.com.au) have enticed city visitors for over a century. Neighbouring Castlemaine

(www.maldoncastlemaine.com), a former gold rush town, is now renowned for its lively arts community.
Children The iconic Luna Park fun fair (www.lunapark.com.au) opened in 1912, and its enormous laughing-face façade has become one of Melbourne's most recognisable symbols. Entry is free, but the rides are not. Bugs and dinosaurs are the stars at the Melbourne Museum (www.museumvictoria.com.au) in leafy Carlton Gardens. Children will also love Melbourne Zoo (www.zoo.org.au/MelbourneZoo) and the Melbourne Aquarium (www.melbourneaquarium.com.au). There's more aquatic action every night at sunset when Phillip Island's little penguins parade to shore (www.penguins.org.au), a worthwhile 90-minute trip out of town.
Walks The Golden Mile Heritage Trail explores how the discovery of gold shaped the city. Walking tours depart from Fed Square – or buy a guide and go it alone. For insight into the city's indigenous roots, wander around the Birrarung Wilam, an installation celebrating Aboriginal communities in the Birrarung Marr park. Or to uncover more of Melbourne, take a Lanes and Arcades tour (www.hiddensecretstours.com).
Perfect picnic Dubbed 'the garden city', Melbourne is flanked on all sides by lovely gardens and parks. Pick up supplies from the Queen Victoria Market (www.qvm.com.au) then stroll or take a tram to Carlton Gardens, Fitzroy Gardens or the Royal Botanical Gardens.

Shopping You can lose hours browsing the lovely designer boutiques on the laneways that criss-cross the CBD. Flinders Lane is a mine of couture excellence. Also try Little Collins Street – home to Assin and Marais (edgy but exquisite mens and womenswear), and Shag (great vintage pieces). Discerning gents should call on luxe men's boutique Harrolds (www.harrolds.com.au) on Collins Street or Chiodo on Russell Street (www.chiodoonline.com). Make for RG Madden (www.rgmadden.com.au), on Little Bourke Street, for designer gifts, accessories and homewares, or Melbourne's GPO (www.melbournesgpo.com), a glam renovated post office on the corner of Bourke and Elizabeth Streets, for impressive international and local labels, including Gorman. For quirkier one-off fashion, vintage and interiors finds, mosey north to Gertrude, Brunswick, Johnston and grungier Smith Streets in Fitzroy. **Something for nothing** Melbourne is renowned for its live music scene, and most nights you can catch a band for free at any one of the city's pubs. Head up to bar-lined Brunswick Street in the boho enclave of Fitzroy and see what catches your eye. Further south, St Kilda's Esplanade Hotel (www.espy.com.au) is a rock 'n' roll institution. **Don't go home without...** seeing an AFL (Aussie Rules) or cricket match at the MCG (Melbourne Cricket Ground) in East Melbourne. Regarded as one of the great stadiums of the world, it can hold 90,000 sports-mad Melburnians.

MARVELLOUSLY MELBOURNE

Trams were introduced to Melbourne in 1885 and the city now has the largest network in the world. It's the only place where cars are required to perform a 'hook turn' – a manoeuvre designed to give trams priority. The trams contribute to the city's distinctive character and are held in great affection by Melburnians.

DIARY

January The year starts with a bang – well, more the thump of tennis balls – at the Australian Open (www.australianopen.com) in Melbourne Park. **February** The St Kilda Festival (www.stkildafestival.com.au) includes a free street party. **March** The Melbourne Food & Wine Festival (www.melbournefoodandwine.com.au) serves up gourmet events across the city. Also, the Australian Grand Prix (www.grandprix.com.au) brings Formula 1 to Albert Park, and out on the Great Ocean Road, the classic Rip Curl Pro surf festival makes waves at Bells Beach (www.ripcurl.com). **July** The Melbourne International Film Festival (www.melbournefilmfestival.com.au) is a chance to catch the latest flicks. **September** Melbourne Spring Fashion Week (www.msfw.com.au) is a sexy showcase for the city's top designers. **October** The Melbourne International Arts Festival (www.melbournefestival.com.au) is the city's flagship cultural event.

'If the Bloomfield were a woman,
she'd be Anita Pallenberg,
the glamorously ageing
Stones muse'

Melbourne

The Bloomfield

STYLE Vintage popstar pad
SETTING Parkside South Yarra mansion

A vintage Rolls-Royce is parked slightly wonkily outside the Bloomfield, as if it has just disgorged a sozzled Patsy and Edina, and I immediately wish we'd arrived at the hotel in this, its resident chariot, instead of a mundane Melbourne taxi. A rock 'n' roll retreat demands a theatrical entrance. Never mind; Mick Jagger still greets us in reception – or at least the equally arresting spectacle of a floor-to-ceiling 1973 photo of him prancing in crotch-crippling pants.

Our home for the weekend is half of an unlikely marriage between a heritage-listed Victorian mansion and a 1960s motor inn. These mismatched buildings, side by side on a leafy South Yarra street, were bought by former fashion magazine editor Sally Bloomfield and her husband Ian Robertson in 2006 and represent two takes on their vision: a hip shrine to music and fashion. It all used to be called the Albany, but now that's just the motel bit. The renovated mansion has become part of the Bloomfield, a more upscale annex to its budget-boutique other half, with an exclusive rooftop pool. They share reception, restaurant, bar and staff.

Arrival is refreshingly fuss-free. Perhaps accustomed to volatile rock-star relationships, a receptionist with skilfully smudged black eyeliner checks if Mr Smith and I would still like to share a room. We giggle, she giggles too and restaurant manager Matthew Stipanov offers a drink. We decide to settle in first, like the squares we are.

We turn left and move from motel to mansion, past more Stones photos and along a scarlet-carpeted, smoochily lit corridor that gives way to soaring ceilings, the battered beauty of original floor tiles and a grand foyer. A giant antique mirror hangs beneath a contemporary lampshade fashioned from tangled coral. It's a beguilingly louche mix of vintage and modern. If the Bloomfield were a woman, she'd be Anita Pallenberg, the glamorously ageing Stones muse.

We're in room five, a Mansion Suite. Sunlight streams through the bay window, bathing eggshell-blue walls, white painted floor and an original fireplace. A modern bathroom has been added and, to avoid disturbing the room's heritage features, it doesn't reach to the ceiling. Covered in the signature black-and-white wallpaper, it

resembles a huge striped gift box set down in the corner. A zebra-skin rug, white roses and retro wicker furniture complete a look Mr Smith rather uncharitably refers to as 'grubby chic'. But I know what he means. The room is stylish but also just a little scuffed, as if a rock band partied here. And they might have. Bono once enjoyed the two-bedroom Bloomfield Suite upstairs.

Mr Smith appears disconcerted by the bedhead, a monochrome mural of movie stars and models, with George Clooney at its centre. Sensing the inhibiting implications of the world's top male heart-throb in our bed, I discreetly cover George with a squishy pillow.

We plan our weekend with the help of the cheeky but thorough in-room literature, which flags the nearby Chapel Street fashion stores, the two parks between which the hotel is sandwiched, restaurants and a beauty salon for short-notice bookings 'if you arrive and suddenly realise you are as hairy as a yeti'. It also tells us that: 'Bloomfield adores cocktails in any way, shape or form.'

Inspired, we go back to the Bloomfield Bar & Bistro, a relaxed mishmash of black leather booths, wicker lounge chairs and cast-iron garden furniture. Wine list highlights are chalked up over the bar. We note plenty of Victorian stars amid a strong, mainly domestic cast and choose a bottle of Crittenden 2007 pinot noir from Mornington Peninsula.

The wine inside and winter outside convince us to stay for dinner. Anthony Siketa, formerly chef/owner of Melbourne's renowned Sel de la Terre, runs the kitchen and his dishes are hearty and Italian-inspired. Steaks are a speciality and my premium eye fillet is tender, flavoursome and a perfect medium rare. Mr Smith's eyes light up at the generous proportions of his Scotch fillet. He's too full to help me revel in a warm, gooey chocolate pudding. I feign sympathy.

It's late and we retire to our room's giant hug of a bed. We sleep soundly, but the morning traffic on Toorak Road rouses us earlier than expected. Heritage rooms don't come with double glazing. They're also prone to grumpy plumbing.

All is forgiven at the breakfast table, where there's plenty to service a rock star's hangover, including Bloody Marys.

I tuck into a stack of pancakes, while Mr Smith sets about an omelette packed with tomato and chorizo.

The Bloomfield's fleet of two vintage Rollers and one Bentley are for hire to ferry you about. For AU$100 we've booked the white 39-year-old Silver Shadow for an hour. It's not stuffy chauffeuring – driver Kieran wears his own casual gear (although he suits-up on Friday and Saturday nights). It's very much in tune with the Bloomfield's laid-back glam and is a stylish way to arrive at Melbourne's city centre.

The Bloomfield is close to a clutch of this city's enviable restaurants and on our second night we try the culinary institution France-Soir. It's as splendid as promised; classic French cuisine served by charismatic waiters.

Next morning, the staff farewell us like friends. I glance one more time at the omnipresent Stones and it strikes me that we've spent the weekend dining with Jagger and sleeping with Clooney, which is really as rock 'n' roll as it gets. But I think it best not to mention this to Mr Smith.

REVIEWED BY AMY COOPER

'It strikes me that we've spent the weekend dining with Jagger and sleeping with Clooney'

NEED TO KNOW

Rooms 32, including four suites.

Rates AU$129–$400. Breakfast is extra, from AU$6.50.

Check-out 12pm, but flexible subject to availability. Check-in, 2pm.

Facilities Heated outdoor rooftop pool, free WiFi in the reception/bistro. In rooms: free broadband, flatscreen TV, minibar and Kevin Murphy toiletries. In-room massages can be arranged.

Children Welcome: the hotel can provide free cots for tots and extra beds for older kids (AU$20 a night). Babysitting can be booked with a local nanny.

Also On Friday and Saturday nights (6pm–10pm), commandeer the hotel's chauffeured Rolls-Royce for drop-offs in the CBD; or hire it any other time to cruise the neighbourhood in style. Owner Sally Bloomfield is the former Melbourne editor of *Harper's Bazaar*, so can give you savvy tips for hot local shopping.

IN THE KNOW

Our favourite rooms The light, high-ceilinged Mansion Suites are suitably chic, with fireplaces, chandeliers and carefully edited vintage furniture in the spacious sitting area. Room 5 has beautiful white floors and a zebra-print rug. Or stay in your own two-bedroom apartment at the sexy black, white and red Bloomfield Suite.

Hotel bar The hotel was a hang-out for musicians in the 1970s and is fast becoming a hub for muso and fashion types today, with the bar interiors capturing the boho vibe perfectly and an iPod mix of tunes from the era providing the soundtrack. Check out the framed offerings on the wall: posters, letters, photographs and ticket stubs, then grab a booth or one of the rattan armchairs and order a Bloomfield Bellini – cinnamon and peach purée topped with sparkling wine.

Hotel restaurant At the Bloomfield Bar & Bistro, chef Anthony Siketa serves modern French- and Italian-style dishes from Thursday to Saturday nights. A laid-back breakfast is rustled up daily.

Top table The three booths are in demand. Snaffle one near the window.

Dress code It's all about understated cool: Tod's moccasins for strolls; Prada tote for shopping.

Room service There's a short in-room 'Heat 'n' Eat' dinner menu, including burgers, fries and dumplings, from Sunday to Wednesday, 6pm–11pm (handy for attacks of the munchies). Late-night room service is available 11pm–5am daily.

Local knowledge Go walkabout in the Royal Botanic Gardens and, in summer, catch a twilight movie at its Moonlight Cinema (www.moonlight.com.au). Watch the city wake up with Balloon Flights Over Melbourne (03 9427 0088), which meets at the gardens for flights over local landmarks, followed by breakfast back on terra firma at the Observatory Café. For swish shopping, amble down Toorak Road and Chapel Street, or browse design store RG Madden (www.rgmadden.com.au).

LOCAL EATING AND DRINKING

Head for Domain Road, where the **Botanical** (03 9820 7888) kicks off with breakfast pastries and stays open all day, serving rustic yet elegant Mod Oz-meets-Italian dishes as well as drinks in the see-and-be-seen Bubble Bar. Fish fans should visit **Bacash** (03 9866 3566), a simple, grown-up venue, where chef Michael Bacash is famed for his grilled oysters. **Oriental Tea House** (03 9826 0168) at 455 Chapel Street serves delicious teas and modern yum cha: try the prawn and pea leaf dumplings. For classically Gallic fare trot along to **France-Soir** (03 9866 8569) on Toorak Road, which sports faux-arrogant waiters and an excellent wine list.

GET A ROOM!

Use our free online booking service: check availability and make reservations through www.mrandmrssmith.com.

 SMITH CARD OFFER Either afternoon tea, including freshly brewed loose-leaf T2 tea with cakes, or a choice of white or red wine and nibbles.

The Bloomfield corner Toorak Road and Millswyn Street, South Yarra, Victoria 3141 (03 9866 4485; www.bloomfieldgroup.com.au)

'Boy, this was bliss:
attentive treatment from caring
and knowledgeable staff in a
serene space, all sleek marble
and high ceilings'

Lyall Hotel and Spa

STYLE Modern art, Asian heart
SETTING Shop-filled South Yarra

'You look like you've been on holiday for weeks,' says Mr Smith, as I waft back into our room. The truth is I've just spent a couple of heavenly hours in the Lyall Spa having a Sodashi facial and Lyall Luxury Pedicure in preparation for the rest of our weekend away. It was bliss: attentive treatment from caring and knowledgeable staff in a serene space, all sleek marble and high ceilings. Flicking through magazines and sipping a fragrant T2 tea as my nail colour dried, it occurred to me that I could spend all weekend here – if Mr Smith wasn't beckoning.

The spa is the embodiment of the entire low-key yet luxurious Lyall Hotel experience. Even its location – a tree-lined South Yarra street among elegant suburban residences, yet only minutes from the city – is the epitome of understated class.

On arrival earlier that day, we were greeted by one of the lovely reception team, whose talent seemed to be making guests feel like a friend returning home. As our weekend progresses, one of our favourite aspects of the hotel becomes the personal attention of the staff. You get the feeling you are part of an intimate, special experience, rather than staying in an anonymous hotel chain. Perfect.

Our suite – actually, it is more like an apartment – has the wonderful bonus of tall windows, a balcony to sit on and French doors that lead out onto the terrace, overlooking the trees below. We waste no time flinging them open to let in the natural light and fresh air. It seems like a rare treat since a lot of hotels these days feel like sealed air-conditioned boxes. The separate granite kitchen has a stove and large fridge, lots of amenities, and the option of a stocked pantry if you can't make it to one of the many stores or restaurants around the corner. Fresh fruit is provided on the dining room table. The bed is huge and heavenly, with crisp white sheets and gorgeous plump pillows, and a pillow menu if you want more choice. The bathroom has a heated tiled floor and toiletries from the hotel spa. There is even a television – one of two in our room – positioned so you can watch it from the spa bath. Free broadband is another generous-spirited gesture. Yes, you could

definitely spend quite a lot of time holed up in this suite without feeling the need to emerge – pass me the 'do not disturb' sign, Mr Smith.

On the first morning of our Melbourne break, Mr Smith and I go downstairs to the intimate Bistro Lyall for breakfast. We take the papers out onto the terrace to read in the sunshine, although the room, like the rest of the hotel, is incredibly inviting. The decor is classic contemporary: all browns, taupes, blacks, moss greens and silver, with tall mirrors, dark woods and cosy-meets-seductive enclaves throughout. The library is especially come-hither with its appealing armchairs, array of newspapers, fresh orchids and soft jazz soundtrack. If I wasn't all ready won over, the jelly beans on the reception counter would be the clincher.

Our weekend-away agenda includes a stroll down Toorak Road and into Chapel Street. This is such a renowned retail precinct that the hotel even provides a special shopping privilege card for its guests. I drag Mr Smith along, stopping at Cose, Scanlan & Theodore, AG Arthur Galan and TL Wood among others. We refuel at the Pound, a cute café

'Mr Smith takes to soaking away the day's efforts in the sybarite-beckoning bath'

tucked away off Chapel Street, and finally arrive back at the hotel, where Mr Smith takes to soaking away the day's efforts in the sybarite-beckoning bath. It seems a spell at Lyall has even made a proselyte of this spa addict's other half.

That night, we have a pre-dinner drink in the Champagne Bar (not for the first time this weekend it dawns on me that Lyall is begging to have me back for a girls' getaway), before heading off to Da Noi, an intimate Italian restaurant – chef Pietro Porcu designs a set menu each day based on the produce he's found at the markets – just down the street.

We spend the rest of the weekend enjoying the neighbourhood around Lyall: Harveys next door for brunch, a short stroll up the hill to the beautiful Botanic Gardens and then down to the Yarra River. We even contemplate taking a couple of the hotel's bicycles for a spin, but decide instead to relax on the terrace back at the hotel. Lazy? Deliciously so.

I notice, while we take our breather, that every request a guest makes is met with an 'of course' or 'certainly'. Nothing, it seems, is too much trouble for the staff. In fact, they seem to take real pleasure in their work, and feel a personal and proud connection to the hotel and its owners. Even as we are checking out, they seem to have a twinkle in their eyes. It makes us sad to say goodbye.

REVIEWED BY LIANE ROSSLER

NEED TO KNOW

Rooms 40 suites.

Rates AU$525–$2,625, including newspaper and 24-hour gym use. Continental breakfast is AU$20; à la carte, AU$30.

Check-out 10.30am, but flexible if available (from noon you'll be charged 50 per cent of your room rate; after 5pm, for an extra night). Check-in, 2pm.

Facilities DVD, CD and book library, free WiFi throughout, spa, gym. In rooms: two flatscreen TVs, cable channels, CD/DVD players, iPod speakers on request, kitchen with fridge and washer-dryer, minibar, terrace.

Children Welcome: kids can stay for free if using existing bedding, or the hotel can supply baby cots or rollaway beds for AU$30 each. Babysitting can be arranged with a nanny for a minimum of three hours for AU$80, then AU$20 an hour.

Also Zap your stress at Lyall's rated destination day spa, a serene, white three-storey space scented with ylang-ylang and mandarin. We recommend the Lyall Signature Spa Ritual, a two-hour massage and facial. There are two steam rooms and an indoor-outdoor area for relaxing.

IN THE KNOW

Our favourite rooms You can swing several cats in the vast two-bedroom Platinum Suite, dubbed the Platinum Blonde Suite after past celeb guests, including Gwen Stefani, Pamela Anderson and Paris Hilton. It sleeps four and comes with a separate living room, two ensuite bathrooms, a double spa bath, iPod speakers, graceful fireplaces, a kitchen (ideal for longer stays) and an airy terrace with rooftop views. We'd be content in one of the spacious one-bedroom suites though, which still resemble deluxe city apartments.

Hotel bar Cool your heels after all that South Yarra retail therapy at the small but sexy Lyall Champagne Bar, to the right of reception, which offers intimate tables and bar stools for sociable perching. Signature drinks include the Lyall Cranberry Champagne Cocktail and the addictive Apple Crumble Martini, or just enjoy an afternoon latte (the bar opens from 3pm till midnight). Expect jazz or easy listening tunes, not a thumping DJ.

Hotel restaurant At the ground-floor Bistro Lyall, chef Robert Keeler serves up light and healthy cuisine, such as chicken sandwiches and tasty hamburgers. Pop in for breakfast, lunch or dinner (the space morphs into the Champagne Bar by night). Decor is restrained, with moss green upholstered chairs, dark wood and smart mirror details.

Top table If it's sunny, grab a table outdoors on the shaded terrace.

Room service A full menu of modern, multicultural dishes is available 24 hours a day.

Dress code Labels, darling. You won't go wrong with finds from local fashion stores Mimco, Alannah Hill, Collette Dinnigan or Scanlan & Theodore (find their boutiques on nearby Chapel Street).

Local knowledge Arm yourself with Lyall's exclusive Shopping Privilege Card, which offers guests 10 per cent off at over 20 hand-picked local stores, such as fashion boutique Cose and shoe store Ebony M. Upscale Chapel Street and Toorak Road are the must-visit shopping drags nearby. Sally forth on a free guest push-bike – if you can balance all those store bags on the handle bars.

LOCAL EATING AND DRINKING

Beside Lyall on Murphy Street, **Harveys** (03 9867 3605) offers decadent delights, such as truffle scrambled eggs, or savour sushi at **Jamon Sushi** (03 9804 5710). Make for the Toorak Road for deliciously rustic Sardinian fare at **Da Noi** (03 9866 5975). **Caffe Veloce** (03 8080 9995) at 9–11 Claremont Street is set in a swish car showroom; the paninis and pastries are as classy as the gleaming machines. Drop by the **Pound** (03 9826 1114) on Chapel Street for a latte lift.

GET A ROOM!

Use our free online booking service: check availability and make reservations through www.mrandmrssmith.com.

 SMITH CARD OFFER A bottle of Chandon NV (Australian sparkling wine) on arrival.

Lyall Hotel and Spa 14 Murphy Street, South Yarra, Melbourne, Victoria 3141 (03 9868 8222; www.thelyall.com)

'One of Melbourne's best restaurants and most luxurious spas; and a boho mix of sophisticated vodka bar, divey saloon and iconic live-music venue'

The Prince

STYLE High-drama design, art deco grace
SETTING Cosmopolitan St Kilda

SHALLOW · NO DIVING · Depth 0.3m

airport for an LA and Aspen 'honeymoon'. The Prince is that kind of hotel – great for life's Big Events. It's certainly sleekly theatrical on arrival, with its minimalist double-storey reception backed by colour-lit floor-to-ceiling fabric and black staircase floating grandly upwards to the spa, pool and accommodation floors.

Welcomed back with minimal fuss, we are taken to our room, a balconied bolthole on buzzing Fitzroy Street with views down to the water. We all know that when it comes to ocean views Melbourne can't compete with its dramatically harboured sister city to the north, but with the low sun streaming through the plane trees outside and the faint sound of clattering mastheads making it up from the marina, it's hard to complain.

Tonight's plan is simple: quick shower (the Aesop products are always a treat), dress for dinner and a vodka pre-prandial at Mink Bar in the basement. The rooms are fairly spacious at the Prince and have an uncluttered masculine style – dark woods, chocolate-grey carpets, simple white bedlinen with obligatory mohair throw – which we love but some find a little cold. The hotel is such a phantasmagoria of amenity options, though, you're unlikely to want to plump up the pillows and watch cable anyway.

I have to say Mr Smith the Just Younger has scrubbed up very nicely for his birthday treat. He's often told he looks like Charles Dance (mostly by his mother), but tonight it's more casually suited rock star; there's a cheerfully futile ruffling of plumage from a glamorous table of tanned and lithe St Kilda girls as we enter. We toast them from our clubby high-backed chairs and remember last year's chance encounter in the small hours of the morning with the charming and bespectacled creator of *Harvie Krumpet*, Oscar-winning Australian animator and local boy Adam Elliot. We can't remember who was more drunk. The Prince is that kind of place, too.

A Mai Tai and some neat Zubrowka under our belt, we wander back upstairs for dinner. Circa has been a Melbourne, and personal, favourite since it opened in the late 1990s. Current Crown Prince of the Melbourne food

Everyone needs a hometown hotel. There's something deliciously extra-indulgent about ringing down for room service or getting your socks tidied up when, just a couple of blocks away, your own bedroom looks burgled and the fridge festers with a mouldy jar of pesto and a parmesan block so hard you could repel intruders with it. It's even more life-enhancing when the said hotel is home to one of Melbourne's best restaurants, most luxurious spas and a boho mix of sophisticated vodka bar, divey public saloon and iconic live-music venue. So it is that St Kilda's deco delight, the Prince, is a local love shack for this particular Mr & Mr Smith.

We arrive today, on a balmy and even more illicit mid-week evening, to celebrate Mr Smith the Just Younger's forty-something birthday. It's one of those perfect late summer afternoons – a hair-rustling breeze off the bay, light sharp enough to cut paper and a temperature in the high 20s I have learned to call mild.

It's a little over a year since the last time we were here, sleeping for a nanosecond between a riotous civil partnership and a hung-over early-morning dash to the

scene (and fellow Smith tastemaker) Andrew McConnell once presided over the kitchen and it's been winning awards and chef's hats ever since. We're lucky to get in tonight – the restaurant is about to have a refit for its own, tenth, birthday. We take in the graceful art deco lines of the room and signature diaphanous black and mauve tulle curtains and wonder what it will look like in the spring. We're pretty sure the Asian- and Pacific-accented Australian plates will taste and look just as good. This evening it's exquisite barramundi and celebratory Tasmanian sparkling that hits the spot. Supremely well fed and slightly tipsy, we call it a night.

Luckily, tonight's not a gig night and there's work on the tram tracks outside, so the screeching and rattling so familiar to Melburnians is soothingly absent. We sleep like babies, in other words, and after a quick coffee and beautifully buttery croissant at downstairs Il Fornaio (Circa does its own, knockout breakfast, but the more relaxed streetside café is our local anyway), we are ready for our next and last treat at the generous Prince kampong: the Aurora Spa Retreat.

Ushered to the upstairs lounge, overlooking an expansive deck through Moroccan-inspired steel screens, we're soon supping green tea in fluffy mushroom-hued robes and being introduced to our softly spoken masseurs. I opt for a good old Bliss Massage, which doesn't disappoint, but I've booked a special detox treat for Mr Smith the Just Younger: a hydrotherapy Rainshower Treatment that takes place in a private steam room. A good thing too, it turns out, since the treatment involves standing upright against the wall in your underpants and being sprayed by a high-pressure water hose. It's very exhilarating apparently, as well as exfoliating.

Too soon, then, our little steal-away birthday treat comes to an end. We check out as late we can, have a final coffee at Il Fornaio and postpone our five-minute journey home to pop in to yet another Prince offshoot, the Prince Wine Store; it's one of the few places in Melbourne where you can buy our favourite tipple, Beaumes de Venise. The culture-forming pesto and parmesan concrete need company in the fridge. We'll be back soon of course; the Prince is our hometown hotel.

REVIEWED BY MR & MR SMITH

NEED TO KNOW

Rooms 40 rooms.
Rates AU$270–$850, including breakfast.
Check-out 11am, flexible if there's availability. Check-in, 2pm.
Facilities CD/DVD library, free WiFi in the foyer, indoor swimming pool, spa. In rooms: TV, DVD player, free broadband, Aesop toiletries, minibar, radio alarm clock.
Children Baby cots are provided for free and rollaway beds for kids for AU$50 a night. The concierge can book a babysitter for a minimum of three hours, price on application.
Also Check the dates of the ear-splitting Australian Grand Prix if you're planning on staying at the hotel in March. The Prince is only a five-minute stroll from Albert Park, where the Formula 1 race is held annually. The hotel's respected Aurora Spa Retreat gets booked up well in advance, so bag a treatment when you reserve your room.

IN THE KNOW

Our favourite rooms All the rooms have a different layout. We love high-ceilinged Room 413, a Premier Suite, which comes with a separate living area, an Arne Jacobsen Egg chair and a freestanding Philippe Starck tub in the bathroom. Its private balcony offers wonderful vistas of Port Phillip Bay and the Melbourne city skyline. We also like Room 315, a Superior, for its sheer size and great views.
Hotel bar Treat yourself to an espresso martini in the sexy and intimate Circa Bar, which throngs until around midnight, especially on a Sunday. The hotel also has three other watering holes: quirky underground vodka bar Mink; the Prince Bandroom (which hosts top gigs); and the grungier Prince of Wales Public Bar.
Hotel restaurant Chef Matthew Wilkinson has been awarded two hats (the Aussie equivalent of Michelin stars) for his seasonal menu in the stunning Circa, the Prince's destination restaurant which has recently had a glam revamp.
Top table A corner banquette for the best people watching.
Room service Snacks and drinks are available 24 hours a day.
Dress code Dress to impress – the Prince attracts a sartorially sussed crowd.
Local knowledge Rollerblading along the esplanade is popular in summer, and you can stop along the way for a drink, an ice-cream or a swim. Hire blades from Rock 'n' Rollin at 22–28 Fitzroy Street (03 9525 3434). Luna Park Funfair, on the Lower Esplanade, opened in 1912 and its enormous laughing-face façade and rollercoaster structure is a National Trust-protected icon of St Kilda. Entry is free, but you have to pay for rides.

LOCAL EATING AND DRINKING

A great place for a coffee and cake or a snack at its pavement tables, low-key café-bakery **Il Fornaio** (03 9536 1111) at 2 Acland Street, is also perfect for picking up picnic supplies. Its fridge is full of ready-prepared, take-home items such as tarts, frittatas and sandwiches made with home-baked bread. Next door at 4 Acland Street, **Lau's Family Kitchen** (03 8598 9880) offers delicious Cantonese food in a laid-back yet sleekly seductive contemporary space. A cosy little tapas bar in a birdcage-type enclosure inside the George Hotel complex, **Mockingbird** (03 9534 0000) at 129 Fitzroy Street, is ideal for after-dinner cocktails. Also in the George, the **Melbourne Wine Room** (03 9525 5599) serves upmarket modern Italian food with wonderful whites, reds and rosés by the glass and bottle. Down on St Kilda Beach, **Donovans** (03 9534 8221) at 40 Jacka Boulevard, whips up gorgeous food in an elegant yet homely setting.

GET A ROOM!

Use our free online booking service: check availability and make reservations through www.mrandmrssmith.com.

 SMITH CARD OFFER A bottle of sparkling wine and free car parking.

The Prince 2 Acland Street, St Kilda, Melbourne, Victoria 3182 (03 9536 1111; www.theprince.com.au)

THE GRAMPIANS

COUNTRYSIDE Mountains, cliff faces and bushscapes
COUNTRY LIFE Hiking boots and sparkling wines

If the striking geography of this sandstone mountain range in Victoria doesn't take your breath away, an on-foot sampling of its mighty trails should. Craggy mountains, gushing waterfalls and impossibly cute wildlife vie for your attention whether via a low-geared stroll or a strenuous hike through bush or up rock. While it's easy to tap into the magic of this national park with 150 kilometres of scenic calorie-burning trekking at your feet, the Grampians isn't just beguiling to adventure hounds. Tasty local produce, celebrated wine and critics-choice restaurants create a vibrant après-walk scene that allows the gastronomy of this area of outstanding natural beauty to be just as pulse-raising.

GETTING THERE

Automobiles It takes around three hours to drive from the Victorian capital of Melbourne to the Grampians, with scenic views en route.

LOCAL KNOWLEDGE

Taxis Cabs are few and far between in the Grampians, and distances are significant, so fares can be pricey. In hub town Halls Gap itself, Halls Gap Taxi Services (03 5356 4774) might be useful if you've imbibed too much local wine with dinner. Nearby operators include Ararat Taxis (03 5352 2283), Stawell Taxis (03 5358 4207) and Horsham Taxis (03 5381 1223).

Packing tips Hi-tech designer-label outdoor apparel is the clobber of choice in the Grampians, even for less sporty types. Hiking boots, Gore-Tex and polar fleece are everywhere and you can wear your thermals with pride. Whether rambling or rock-climbing, make sure you're properly prepared with all-weather clothing and water, and take a map, compass and food for longer campaigns.

Recommended reads Most books on the area are based around activities, such as *Walking the Grampians* by Garry Van Dijk, and *Discovering*

Grampians-Gariwerd by Alistair Paton. *Grampians – Selected Climbs* by Simon Mentz and Glenn Tempest is one of several excellent rock-climbing guides.

Local specialities The regional foodie scene features superb beef, lamb and dairy products artfully prepared at gastropubs and high-end restaurants by some of the country's best chefs. Another Grampians speciality is tricked-up gourmet bush tucker – kangaroo, crocodile, barramundi, bush tomatoes and desert seeds. Western District cool-climate wines consistently win awards (see www.grampianswine.com.au) or make for nearby Mount Zero Olives (www.mountzeroolives.com), Australia's premier olive producer with a café and farm-gate sales.

Do go/don't go Spring (September to November) and autumn (March to May) are the best times to visit the Grampians. Spring brings the blooming wildflowers and orchids, and autumn provides long mild days, which are perfect for walking and climbing. Summer days (December to February) can be oppressively hot, while winter (June to August) tends to be cool and wet, with night-time temperatures sometimes falling to zero.

Also... If you prefer something less gung-ho, there are some fine art galleries in Horsham (www.horshamartgallery.com.au), north-west of Halls Gap, and Hamilton (www.hamiltongallery.org), not far from Dunkeld.

WORTH GETTING OUT OF BED FOR

Viewpoint The Grampians are peppered with panoramic look-outs – wherever there's cars and a gathering of people you're almost certainly going to find something special to see. Highlights include Reed Look-out, an easy two-kilometre return walk from the carpark, and Boroka Look-out, 100-metres return. Watch out for vertigo.

Arts and culture The must-see Brambuk Aboriginal Cultural Centre (www.brambuk.com.au) in Halls Gap is one of the country's most important storehouses of indigenous art, showcasing traditional tools and artefacts alongside cutting-edge multimedia exhibits on the local Jardwadjali and Dja Dja Wurrung people, their relationship to the landscape as well as white European settlement. It is in equal parts inspiring and sobering. Brambuk is free, open 9am–5pm daily, and also exhibits and sells traditional and modern artworks.

Activities It's all about the great outdoors – camping, walking and hiking, four-wheel driving, fishing, canoeing, mountain biking, rock-climbing and abseiling, and horse riding. Parks Victoria manages the National Park and has an office at the Brambuk cultural centre issuing maps, brochures and fishing licences. The Grampians page of its website (www.parkweb.vic.gov.au) has links to oodles of organised activities, or call into the Halls Gap visitor centre (www.grampianstravel.com) for more info on things to do. In Halls Gap, Grampians Personalised Tours & Adventures (www.grampianstours.com.au) is inside the general store.

Daytripper For nearby excursions, check out historic towns such as Stawell, Horsham and Hamilton that boomed on 19th-century gold-rush money and squattocracy, and the tiny rural settlements of Dunkeld, Pomonal and the Wartook Valley. If you're looking for something a little further afield, point the bonnet south and head through Dunkeld to Warrnambool and the mighty thrashing Southern Ocean about two hours away.

Children With lots of bush, fresh air and gentle but spectacular walks, kids love the Grampians. There's wildlife everywhere but if you want to handfeed the critters head for the Halls Gap Wildlife Park & Zoo (www.hallsgapzoo.com.au) where kangaroos, wallabies, wombats, emus, possums and koalas are joined by exotic animals, reptiles and farmyard friends.

Walks You'll find walking tracks to suit all abilities in the Grampians. Halls Gap is a good base, with scenic options in the surrounding Wonderland Range, from an easy half-hour stroll to Venus Bath to a tougher five-hour walk up to Pinnacles Look-out. From the Zumstein picnic area north-west of town you can also hike to the impressive McKenzie Falls.

Perfect picnic If you fancy an alfresco meal, there are popular facilities – tables and chairs, water and sometimes toilets, shelters and free electric barbecues – throughout the National Park. For somewhere far less crowded, try the Red Rock area in the Southern Grampians on the banks of the Glenelg River, which is rich in birdlife and blooming wildflowers in spring.

Shopping There's no shortage of tourist tack and souvenir clothing touted in the region's shops, so your money's better spent on the more select (and authentic) wares at the Brambuk National Park and Cultural Centre. Or buy some of the tasty local wines and gourmet foodie produce on offer.

Make the well-worth-it trip to Red Rock Olives (www.redrockolives.com.au), or get some deluxe body treatments using natural plant, earth, sea and mineral products at Blaze Rock Retreat (www.blazerock.com.au) on the Halls Gap–Ararat road.

Something for nothing Wander the area's walking tracks, creeks and rivers, where you can spy platypuses swimming and koalas napping in the treetops.

Don't go home without... walking the Nerve Test. At the end of the Pinnacle Walk is this unsigned lumpy sliver of narrow rock that falls away perilously on each side. Whether you're testing your machismo or showing off your sure-footed beam-gymnastics, there are no second chances.

GLORIOUSLY GRAMPIANS

Also known as Gariwerd to the local Jardwadjali and Dja Dja Wurrung Aborigines, the Grampians have been a sacred place for millennia. For aeons, Indigenous Australians have made their indelible marks amid the area's brooding mountains and cliffs, leaving behind extraordinary ancient rock art. Visit sites at Gulgurn Manja Shelter and Ngamadjidj Shelter, in the Northern Grampians near Mount Stapylton; Bunjil's Shelter near Stawell; or the Billimina and Manja Shelters to the west.

DIARY

February The popular Grampians Jazz Festival draws crowds in Halls Gap (www.grampiansjazzfestival.com.au). **Easter weekend** Australia's most prestigious, and lucrative, foot race is the Stawell Gift (www.stawellgift.com) held in Stawell. It's a handicapped event run over 120 metres. **May** Gourmands tuck into excellent food and wine at the Grampians Grape Escape (www.grampiansgrapeescape.com.au), with more than 80 stalls offering foodie fare and cooking demonstrations with celebrity chefs. **September** Wildflowers are celebrated at the Halls Gap Wildflower and Arts Show (www.grampianstravel.com). **November** Cinephiles gather for the Halls Gap Film Festival (www.grampianstravel.com).

'The evening heralds a
mesmerising meal of culinary
wizardry as Hunter's team moves
like a corps of ballet dancers'

Dunkeld

Royal Mail Hotel

STYLE Gourmet-stamped pub
SETTING Southern Grampians panorama

As grey kangaroos graze among the grass trees below our bedroom window, the last of the sunlight dances over the two monolithic mountains that act as full stops to the Southern Grampians. Rain squalls skid across a landscape recently transformed from russet to emerald and there's a sense of renewal afoot in the small farming town of Dunkeld. It's inspired in part by the Royal Mail Hotel, which is quickly gathering cult status among serious foodies.

We stayed at this pub turned boutique inn primarily to eat a 10-course extravaganza by chef Dan Hunter, who returned to Australia from Spain's Mugaritz, one of the world's top 10 restaurants. This tasting menu is spectacular, and the Royal Mail also has a superb wine list, from local back vintages of Best's Great Western to some of France's finest drops.

A three-hour drive from Melbourne, the Royal Mail is truly a destination restaurant. With its art deco façade, it sits on the main drag, right before we'd usually hit the accelerator to head further west, Mount Sturgeon looming dramatically behind. This isn't an old Federation place with rooms above – the accommodation has been purpose built away from the hotel, tucked into gardens that seem like a botanical library of Australian natives, from Sturt's desert pea to various banksias.

The aptly named Mountain View Rooms offer mesmerising panoramic vistas, framing the landscape (although the windows could do with a bit of a clean, as they're speckled with dirt, like the face of a jackeroo on a weekend bender). Welcoming gestures such as a half-bottle of French sparkling and handmade chocolates (offered with some packages) warmed our cockles, but given this is a gourmet retreat, UHT milk came as a bit of a curve ball. Surely there's a cow handy on the adjacent farm, owned by the same family, where a reputed 170 different vegetables, herbs and edible flowers are grown in the kitchen garden?

Trivial quibbles aside, the Royal Mail's rooms rise above the usual pub egalitarianism, with decor that's more rural pragmatic than city slick, subdued olive tones suggesting the colours of the landscape. This is a nonetheless comfortable setting, right up to the point where Mrs Smith tries to shower and the water remains stubbornly cold. Pity the man – or tap – that tries to get between a woman who's just been in the car for hours on end and a hot wash. But sometimes things go wrong in ways that leave you wondering if the Grampians hosts gremlins, if not mischievous bunyips. It happens twice, but an understanding reception calms Mrs Smith with the offer of another room while the problem is fixed. The receptionist jokes later about *Fawlty Towers*. There's a good-humoured warmth and professionalism to all who work here. Stuff happens. We don't mind and they know how to soothe the bumps with unruffled generosity.

The evening heralds a mesmerising meal of culinary wizardry as Hunter's team moves like a corps of ballet dancers around the open kitchen, placing tiny veggies and herbs on plates with tweezers. Each small dish is a complete picture that manages to be simultaneously ethereal and rooted firmly in the earth, from the opening gambit of a pretty smoked tuna consommé with sardines, jamon and radishes, to the follow-up: a nutty, malty mix

of toasted rye with legumes and a sensual, runny egg yolk. Hunter produces a remarkable parade of contrasting textures and flavours, none more so than eel with beef tendon, the latter ingredient slippery and gelatinous, as if impersonating an eel. The following day, while visiting Brambuk, the Aboriginal Cultural Centre in Grampians National Park, we discover that slippery snakey fish was a staple food of the original inhabitants of the region, adding resonance to the dish.

Dinner at the Royal Mail is one of the finest experiences I've had in a long career of eating out professionally. Crisp, wise service and a galaxy of glorious wines only add to the lustre.

The following day we explore, heading to the Great Western wine region, home of two legendary labels, Seppelt and Best's. We buy a bottle of Seppelt Silverband sparkling shiraz as a memento of Mrs Smith's and my earlier walk to the pretty Silverband Falls in the National Park. Alas we're too late for a tour of the 19th-century underground tunnels that form the Seppelt cellars, but it leaves time to visit Best's, home to one of Australia's finest shiraz wines, the Bin 0. Mrs Smith takes a shine to the pinot noir rosé and several cases are shipped home.

After a day venturing into the jutting and jagged sandstone landscape of the Grampians, we've worked up an appetite, which leads us excitedly back to the Royal Mail. The same kitchen knocks up a mean bar menu as well as fine dining, while its bistro fare straddles the middle ground. It sits right next door to the posher space, the demarcation being a lack of tablecloths and slightly less polished, yet equally sartorial, black-clad waiters.

After tapas-style plates of tuna empanadillas and small pigeon pies – both delicious, but Mrs Smith has a fear of pastry overdosing – comes the serious business of a smoked pork belly with spiced plums and maple syrup starter, then a main of slow-cooked lamb with stewed eggplant. The portions are as expansive as the countryside and this is rustic yet no less clever fare; the wines are equally deft.

We retreat to our room, the complimentary wireless keeping us in touch with an outside world we're in no hurry to embrace. I'd like to stay one more night, if only for a game of pool in the bar and a wagyu burger. Hell, I'd stay in a bark humpy to eat here again; mercifully though, the Royal Mail offers slicker head-resting options for the pleasure.

REVIEWED BY SIMON THOMSEN

NEED TO KNOW

Rooms 20.

Rates AU$180–$250, including newspaper and continental breakfast.

Check-out 10am. Check-in, 2pm. Both flexible subject to availability; a further charge may apply.

Facilities Free WiFi throughout, gardens, heated outdoor pool. In rooms: flatscreen TV, balcony.

Children Welcome; but book a local nanny for dinnertime. The kids might get fidgety during the four-hour tasting menu.

Also With over 150 varieties of heirloom vegetables and herbs sourced from the hotel's own extensive kitchen gardens, cuisine here is hyper-local and organic.

IN THE KNOW

Our favourite rooms Don't settle for anything except the aptly named Mountain View Rooms, where full-width, floor-to-ceiling, glass sliding doors frame postcard-perfect aspects of Mount Sturgeon and the Southern Grampian Ranges. Interiors are clean-lined, contemporary and fairly no-frills, but it's pretty special drinking premium wine on a private sun-drenched veranda, so who's complaining? Ask for the more private room furthest from the restaurant and bar.

Hotel bar The Royal Mail Hotel Public Bar is more pub than cocktail lounge, but it's the real thing. Foodies from all over Australia rub shoulders with locals and there's the occasional live band.

Hotel restaurant Winner of a fistful of foodie awards, this is, quite simply, one of Australia's best restaurants. Headed up by Dan Hunter (former head chef at two-Michelin-starred Mugaritz in San Sebastian), it fuses fresh, local and seasonal ingredients with essence-enhancing technology to create tummy-tickling flavours. This is molecular gastronomy with an Australian accent, mixing lamb and liquorice, or pigeon and white chocolate. The Royal Mail Cellar, the country's leading collection of Burgundy and Bordeaux wines, has also garnered gongs. A gourmet bistro alongside the formal dining area serves refined Spanish-inspired dishes, including tapas, and there's a sunny outside courtyard.

Top table Bag a discreet corner table; or sit closer to the fire in the thick of things.

Room service A short in-room menu, including wagyu burgers, is available daily between 6pm and 9pm.

Dress code Wide-brimmed Akubra hat for hiking in the hills; low-necked little black dress for seducing over dinner.

Local knowledge Pick up a map marked with eight walking trails from the hotel and work off lunch with a stroll to the Dunkeld Arboretum or stone Chinese Wall on Mount Sturgeon – take a Hiker's Hamper to avoid gourmet withdrawal. Further afield, discover deserted look-outs, Aboriginal rock art, waterfalls and lakes in the National Park itself, visit Hamilton's fine regional art gallery, or play a round at the 18-hole Grampians Golf Club – just don't hit the emus or wallabies wandering the greens. If you'd rather chill, relax with an in-room massage or get bendy at local yoga retreat, Griffins Hill (www.griffinshill.com.au).

LOCAL EATING AND DRINKING

Head for Halls Gap if you fancy eating out. Part of Brambuk, the National Park & Cultural Centre, **Bushfoods Café** (03 5361 4000) serves up Aboriginal bush tucker and native foods, such as kangaroo, emu and crocodile. Another stalwart, **Quarry Restaurant** (03 5356 4858), offers Mod Oz fare with a nod to gourmet bush tucker (wallaby steaks, barramundi and tiger prawns). Set in a historic timber mansion, the **Balconies Restaurant** (03 5356 4232) is the place to go for globally inspired dishes spanning Thai green curry and French lamb cutlets, with live jazz on Saturdays.

GET A ROOM!

Use our free online booking service: check availability and make reservations through www.mrandmrssmith.com.

 SMITH CARD OFFER A copy of photographic journal *A Dunkeld Portfolio* by Richard Crawley.

Royal Mail Hotel 98 Parker Street (Glenelg Highway), Dunkeld, Victoria 3294 (03 5577 2241; www.royalmail.com.au)

UNDER
DOWN

Tasmania
AUSTRALIA

TASMANIA

HOBART
The Henry Jones Art Hotel
The Islington Hotel
LAUNCESTON
Quamby Estate

HOBART

Incredible coastlines, lush valleys and ancient peaks comprise Tasmania's geography, so add to this a unique heritage, succulent seafood and famous wildlife and you can't imagine a seasoned traveller asking for more. This southern isle is staggeringly beautiful, awash with an artist's palette of natural colours spanning cerulean seas and skies, white sandy shores, verdant valleys and sun-kissed hops. The island's intimate capital, Hobart, is especially enticing, with its historical harbour and tempting restaurants, backdropped by the looming Mount Wellington. It's unlikely that Hobart's earliest European inhabitants – convicts shipped over by the British Empire – appreciated Tassie's coastal expanses, volcanic peaks and fertile orchards though. Instead, their relentless graft culminated in the capital's prized 19th-century architecture. Two centuries on, Hobart is a feelgood destination for all.

GETTING THERE

Planes Hobart International Airport (www.hobartairport.com.au) is about 17 kilometres east of the city centre. Regular flights are available from most major cities in Australia (Melbourne's an hour away) with Qantas (www.qantas.com.au), Jetstar (www.jetstar.com) and Virgin Blue (www.virginblue.com.au). A taxi from the airport to the city is AU$25–$30.

Boats Ferries to Tasmania from the mainland are provided by Spirit of Tasmania (1800 634 906; www.spiritoftasmania.com.au). Its service operates year-round, with daily departures between Station Pier in Port Melbourne and Devonport on Tasmania's north coast. On-board accommodation ranges from functional airline-style seating to private deluxe cabins.

Automobiles Most major car hire companies can be found at Hobart Airport or in the city itself, including Hertz (www.hertz.com.au), Avis (www.avis.com.au) and Europcar (www.europcar.com). Although Hobart is small enough to navigate by foot, it's definitely worth getting a car to explore the surrounding sights.

LOCAL KNOWLEDGE

Taxis Nicknamed Slo-bart, the city makes for pleasant walking. Cabs are easily hailed though, or call United Taxis (03 6274 3120) for a reliable service around Hobart and the surrounding areas.

Packing tips Binoculars for devil spotting, a sou'wester for fly fishing and trainers for scaling rocky outcrops.

Recommended reads The Fatal Shore, by Robert Hughes, chronicles the transportation of 160,000 convicts from Britain to grim prisons in Australia, aboard ships bound for an unknown world. Wild Rivers, by photographer Peter Dombrovskis and Greens Senator Bob Brown (both of whom were instrumental in saving Tasmania's Franklin River from being dammed), gives a flavour of the island's spectacular wilderness.

Local specialities Tasmania's seafood is among the finest the southern hemisphere has to offer. Take your pick from plump oysters, silky-smooth scallops, luscious lobster, deep-sea trevalla, abalone, wild trout and succulent salmon. Sample white cherries from

New Norfolk, Coal River Valley venison and have a tipple of Pepperberry Bush Liqueur, produced in Tasmania from the alpine berries that grow all over the highlands. Wine worshippers rejoice; locally produced pinot noir, chardonnay and riesling make for refreshing and delicious drinking.

Do go/don't go Foodies should head to Hobart in November or December to reap the fruits of Hobart's harvest; in these months, farm shops sell rations for your day's adventures by the roadside: juicy berries, fresh juices, creamy yoghurts, just-baked breads, cheeses and other goodies. Avoid Hobart in winter (June to August) when the island is lashed with rain and the Roaring Forty winds.

WORTH GETTING OUT OF BED FOR

Viewpoint At a knee-wobbling 1,270 metres, Mount Wellington, and its surrounding parkland, guarantees dazzling photos for even the least camera-capable. Head for the top if you dare and admire the incredible view. Layer up though – there's a bone-battering wind chill on gusty days. If you're feeling lazy, admire the mountain's heady heights from Hobart's harbour, while lapping up sea views (and fish and chips).

Arts and culture Historians should head to Port Arthur and examine the craggy remains of Australia's first penal settlement (www.portarthur.org.au). Hobart also has a rich hop-growing history, so visit the nearby Derwent Valley's timber oast houses. Hops are still grown in the area; in autumn, the valley turns an intense amber gold, bathed in light. There are plenty of galleries dotted around Salamanca Market, or take the half-hour drive to the serene suburb of New Norfolk and browse the antique shops (www.newnorfolk.org).

Activities Hire a bicycle and explore magnificent Mount Wellington. Brake Out Cycling Tours (03 6239 1080) has a range of bikes and even provide a lift (in a van) to the top. The scenery on the way down is stunning and you barely need to pedal. Feeling thirsty? Head to the HQ of premium beer Cascade (03 6224 1117; www.cascadebrewery.com.au) for their guided tours and tastings. The brewery is set in a beautiful historic building surrounded by the gorgeous Woodstock Gardens; drink in the view, as well as the brew. Bored of being a landlubber? Take a luxury cruise from Hobart along the scenic waterways past North Bruny Island. Try Hobart Cruises (1800 751 229; www.hobartcruises.com).

Day tripper It's only a short drive to the historic, sandstone village of Richmond where Australia's oldest bridge spans the pretty Coal River. The bridge was built in the early 1800s by – you've guessed it – convicts. Wander the antique shops, art galleries and boutiques, then finish off with a tasting of Tasmania's superb cool-climate wines in one of the wineries of the beautiful Coal River Valley wine region. Meadowbank Estate (03 6248 4484; www.meadow bankwines.com.au) produces fabulous wines and has a restaurant where you can linger over delicious shared platters and drink in the vineyard views.

Children To give your kids their very own golden ticket, take them to the Cadbury Chocolate Factory in Claremont (1800 627 367). Daily tours explain the history of cocoa and how the good stuff is made – but let's cut to the chase: yes, there's a shop at the end. Little ones who prefer wildlife to Wonka will love platypus-spotting: these elusive, bizarre-looking creatures are best seen in the morning or early evening when they are feeding. For a guaranteed sighting, head to Something Wild (03 6288 1013; www.somethingwild.com.au), a sanctuary for orphaned and injured animals.

Walks Tasmania's spectacular landscape is a walker's dream. Choose from Mount Field, Lake St Clair, the Styx Valley (home to some of the world's tallest hardwood trees), Tasman National Park and the spectacular Wineglass Bay, named for its curving shoreline (www.parks.tas.gov.au).

Perfect picnic In the Margate area of Hobart, Bicentennial Park has spectacular coastal views, rolling expanses of open grassland and playgrounds. There are also picnic and barbecue facilities, walking trails and secluded seating.

Shopping Hobart's Salamanca Market (www.salamanca.com.au), Saturdays 8.30am–3pm, is ideal for gifts and souvenirs. Peruse locally produced arts and crafts and edible artistry: jams, honey, relishes, smoked fish, meats and delicious cheeses are all there for the tasting. It's framed by historic Georgian warehouses filled with galleries, bars and coffee shops; allocate a day to potter around and admire the dockside setting. Make sure you sample some scallop pie – a Tasmanian speciality – from the Flatheads stall.

Something for nothing For free live music on Friday evenings (5.30pm–7.30pm), hightail it to the courtyard of the Salamanca Arts Centre (03 6234 8414; www.salarts.org.au) at 77 Salamanca Place. Wander artists' studios, galleries and shops, and grab a mulled wine. To discover more about the island's Aboriginal and colonial past, visit the Tasmanian Museum & Art Gallery (03 6211 4177; www.tmag.tas.gov.au).

Don't go home without buying a wooden trinket from Salamanca market. The market showcases beautiful, locally crafted woodwork made from Tasmanian timber such as Huon pine, myrtle and blackwood.

HABITUALLY HOBART

Keep your eyes peeled and ears pricked for a Tasmanian devil. The island's most famous – and deceptively cute – species resembles a cross between a bear cub and a dog. Look out for its distinctive black fur, emblazoned with a crest of white, and beware its piercing screech. If you're lucky enough to spot the endangered nocturnal marsupial, don't get too close: powerful fangs aside, it releases a pungent pong when panicked. Catch them at Bonorong Wildlife Centre, 25 minutes' drive from Hobart (www.bonorong.com.au).

DIARY

February The Clarence Jazz Festival is held in Bellerive, Hobart (www.ccc.tas.gov.au). **March** Don't miss the Southern Vineyards Open Weekend, when the wineries welcome the public for cellar-door tastings and sales (www.winetasmania.com.au). A Taste of the Huon is a two-day celebration of the region's fine food, wine, arts and crafts (www.tasteofthehuon.com). **October** Revel in all things nautical including shanties, seafood and grog at the Seafarer's Festival on Bellerive Boardwalk (www.ccc.tas.gov.au). **December** The state's largest food and wine festival, the Taste Festival (www.hobartsummerfestival.com.au), is held on the picturesque Hobart waterfront.

'Old beams, rough-hewn
convict stonemasonry – the
history of this reinvented
1820s jam factory is tangible'

The Henry Jones Art Hotel

STYLE Happening heritage
SETTING Historic Hobart harbourside

A rainy Southern Ocean squall blows across Sullivans Cove as we peer out through the windows of the harbour-front Henry Jones Art Hotel. The sassy young receptionist smiles wryly and offers a huge red-and-white striped umbrella. Winter in Tasmania is something to endure, but a season the locals learn to love. Like other cold, rainy cities (Seattle, Oslo, Wellington) far-flung Hobart looks inwards for inspiration. This attitude is distilled at the Henry Jones, where contemporary art, local interior design, Australian history, immaculate service, and fine food and wine create spark-flying chemistry.

We checked in yesterday afternoon, warming up inside the hushed lobby with its art-spangled sandstone walls, massive recycled timbers, leather loungers and inexplicable sense of homecoming. The vibe here is nonchalant yet embracing, and more refreshingly unsnooty. We feel like we've finally been granted membership to that coveted, secret clubhouse, sidestepping the formalities.

Moving towards our room through low-lit corridors peppered with industrial remnants — old beams, rough-hewn convict stonemasonry — the history of this reinvented 1820s jam factory is tangible. Mrs Smith muses she can almost smell boiling vats of blackberry jam and hear conveyor belts rattling past. Rugged textures and earthy tones from the past are emphasised by ranks of contemporary Tasmanian art (all for sale, some very affordable). Plush-carpeted suites feature yet more pieces, and humongous beds striped with wine hues and piled with soft pillows. Luminous against brick-and-sandstone walls, the ensuites are brilliantly conceived, translucent-glass boxes with neck-deep baths and heated floors for chilly Hobart midnights. Minibars are stocked with boutique Tasmanian beer and shortbread. Gazing through the windows, views draw the eye beyond the crayfish boats in Victoria Dock to the sombre, dolomite flanks of Mount Wellington or, at the back of the hotel, into the arch of the atrium, spanning the café and gallery courtyard below.

If last night's dinner at Henry's Harbourside Restaurant was anything to go by, we've no doubt Henry Jones, an entrepreneur from the turn of the last century, loved his nosh. Baby Smith is accompanying us and the maître d' handled our kid-centric requests — an early booking, highchair and tactical table location — with aplomb. Mrs Smith and I sipped G&Ts as he adroitly guided us through chef Andre Kropp's menu of Tasmanian delights. Our starters soon arrived: polenta infused with Tasmanian truffle oil, and a dozen piquant local oysters (with a flavour more 'splashed at the bow' than 'dumped by a wave'). For our main course we opted for butter-fried Southern Atlantic salmon on parmesan mash, and roast eye-fillet with braised ox cheek, sluiced down with a deliciously dry bottle of Bay of Fires pinot gris from the island's north-east. Afterwards, our cheese platter (wedges of local King Island brie, blue and parmesan, with house-made fruit paste, wafers and fig-and-walnut bread) was delivered to the leather couches in the lobby, but we could easily have opted for the adjoining bar or our room. Nowhere, it seemed, was at all inconvenient. We sat back and watched a wedding party arrive, in formal silks and satins, and sip their cocktails at the bar. None of them seemed to be present at breakfast the following morning — fools! They've missed out on a relaxed, custom-cooked affair with bottomless coffee. If the measure of a good breakfast is the hollandaise, this was a very smooth production indeed. We ordered eggs Florentine and Benedict, then lingered over pastries, fresh fruits and another latte.

Henry's unflappable service standards are upheld by staff across the board, most of whom are young and urbane. They're all well-informed about Hobart, Tasmania and local activities: so grill them on cycling, fly-fishing and bushwalking. Free valet parking is swift and efficient, your bags loaded before you even notice they're gone. Also on call is a dedicated staff historian, Warren, who runs free Art and History Tours of the hotel every Friday evening with art curator Christine, kicking off with a glass of wine at the bar. To our surprise, when we arrived at this hotel we received a list of convicts with our surnames who were transported to Tasmania in the early 1800s (did my great, great grandfather really meet my granny on a prison hulk?). Even if there's no direct lineage, it makes for a titillating crime-tinged read.

Outside the rain seems to be easing, but we grab an umbrella anyway and head out. Over near the orange hull of the Antarctic vessel Aurora Australis, Hobart's iconic Saturday-morning Salamanca Market is kicking into gear. We spent too long there yesterday evening, bending elbows at Knopwood's Retreat, a sea-salty corner pub, so instead opt for a short walk into the city to snoop around a few shops: the chic toy store Ruby's Room and bespoke boutique Love & Clutter are both welcome additions to Murray Street. Then maybe we'll drive up to the snowy summit of Mount Wellington, 1,271 metres above sea level, or munch some lunchtime fish 'n' chips from the floating Flippers Fish Punt on Constitution Dock. An afternoon session with the hotel's in-house masseuse is a definite, before a pre-dinner drink at the snug, sophisticated IXL Long Bar. Prime Minister Kevin Rudd was propping up the bar here recently, and we feel it's our duty to grill the staff about his drink of choice: a local Cascade Pale Ale perhaps, or a parochial Queensland XXXX Gold? A sensible cup of tea? Regardless, whether you're prime ministerial material or just here to cast your vote on Hobart, the Henry Jones is the very portrait of artful hospitality and consummate diplomacy.

REVIEWED BY CHARLES RAWLINGS-WAY

'We've no doubt Henry Jones, an entrepreneur from the turn of the last century, loved his nosh'

NEED TO KNOW

Rooms 56, including five suites, Standard, Superior and Deluxe Spa Rooms and Artist Studio Lofts; most have a choice of harbour or atrium views.

Rates AU$260–$950. Breakfast is extra, at AU$25 a person (included in some packages).

Check-out 10am, but flexible (although a cost may apply if you're more than a half-day over). Check-in, 2pm (or earlier if your room's ready).

Facilities Commercial gallery, art and history displays, DVD library, spa. In rooms: flatscreen TVs, cable TV, DVD/CD player, broadband internet (from AU$6.50 an hour), minibar, Melle Beauty amenities.

Children If you'd drag your kids around the Tate Modern, or they like the History Channel, bring them along. If they're plug and play types, leave them with the in-laws.

Also Built across seven historic wharfside warehouses, and once home to Tasmania's oldest and Australia's largest jam factory, the Henry Jones takes its history, as well as its art, seriously. It has even got a full-time History Liaison Officer, the erudite Warren, who, depending on your name, will give you a print out of all the 19th-century convict arrivals who share your moniker. Not the place to check-in as Smith. Book a private Art and History Tour with Warren, or join his regular Friday evening hotel tours for no charge.

IN THE KNOW

Our favourite rooms We love the two beautiful Oriental Suites for their Japanese styling, extra space, double showers and oh-so-decadent SOK overflowing spa baths; one even has a little rooftop garden with views of Mount Wellington, while the other Suite has harbour vistas. All Deluxe Spa Rooms have glass-pod bathrooms.

Hotel bar The IXL Long Bar mixes rough-cast sandstone walls with red plastic bar stools creating the unlikely scenic love child of *Sex in the City* and *The Perfect Storm*. Pleasure your palate with cheese and wine tastings and cocktail-mixing classes. Styling includes the iconic IXL jam labels from the factory's heyday.

Hotel restaurant Sup under canvas sail at Henry's Harbourside Restaurant, the hotel's sleek eatery, although other cafés and a wine bar operate in the atrium during the day. Chef Andre Kropp conjures up modern Australian fare using local produce with exotic twists – duo of Huon rabbit with a Tunisian brik, or liquid apple and spice-cured salmon with wasabi marshmallow and turmeric foam. There's even light music from local pianists or Tasmanian Symphony Orchestra duo, Strings on Fire.

Top table Anything in the 40s for quieter tables for two, or catch the last light in the atrium during summer evenings.

Room service A range of grazing options are available from 7am until 2.30am, including salads, focaccias and sweets.

Dress code Blend in with Jim Thompson silks and nautical flourishes.

Local knowledge Watch out for the 2010 opening of the expanded Museum of Old and New Art (MONA; www.mona.net.au), the largest privately held collection of conceptual contemporary art and antiquities in Australia (it's been carved out of the cliffside at the Moorilla Winery, 15 minutes north of Hobart).

LOCAL EATING AND DRINKING

Head across the marina drawbridge to foodie hotspot Salamanca Place: local favourites **Monty's** (03 6223 2511), **Piccalilly** (03 6224 9900) and **Smolt** (03 6224 2554) are all within five minutes' walk. Alternatively, amuse yourself at veggie-friendly **Machine Laundry Café** (03 6224 9922) watching people do their washing. The true gourmet pilgrimage is to the **Agrarian Kitchen** (03 6261 1099) in bucolic Derwent Valley – but you'll need to put your pinny on and take an organic cooking class to enjoy it. Or head to Sandy Bay for upmarket Chinese at **Me Wah** (03 6223 3688).

GET A ROOM!

Use our free online booking service: check availability and make reservations through www.mrandmrssmith.com.

 SMITH CARD OFFER A bottle of Tasmanian wine.

The Henry Jones Art Hotel 25 Hunter Street, Hobart, Tasmania 7000 (03 6210 7700; www.thehenryjones.com)

'A classic English garden setting,
augmented by exotic Australian
birds flitting through native flora.
Add to that a postcard-perfect
view of Mount Wellington'

Hobart

The Islington Hotel

STYLE Hip Regency guesthouse
SETTING Herb-scented ridge-top gardens

Six months into the year and Mrs Smith and I have the horrifying realisation that we haven't been on a single break. This, we decide, has to change. To the Apple Isle, immediately. Smith Jr at home in capable hands, this trip is about getting away from *everything*.

Arriving at Hobart Airport, Mrs Smith decides we need to eat – and fast. A lazy lunch, she figures, will get us into the swing of this trip. Panic creeps in when we can't get hold of the friend we hail as 'Tasmania's all-knowing expert on where to eat'. As we're due to check in at the Islington Hotel, we tap the hotel on where to go for a relaxing meal. Lisa, one of the hosts, sends us confidently in the direction of Meadowbank Estate.

Detouring off the freeway, we motor down a gorgeous country road flanked by cherry blossoms and vineyards. We arrive at the recommended winery 15 minutes from Cambridge, and the view from the dining room's floor-to-ceiling windows swallows our attention. French provincial-style tucker, great wine and the vision of mist swirling around the mountains are what the doc ordered; we leave hours later in a new state of mind, officially relaxed.

Hobart is a pretty city: situated on the coast, split down the middle by the Derwent River and backdropped by Mount Wellington. For us it's shrouded in a soft white haze, pierced occasionally by shards of sunlight. Driving through one of Hobart's dress-circle suburbs, we admire gracious old houses, beautiful gardens and river views. As soon as our tyres crunch on the gravel of the Islington Hotel driveway, Lisa and Thomas rush out to welcome us. Their friendly, confident approach sets the mood. We're in safe hands.

Originally built in 1847, the architecture is resplendent in Regency notes. These days as a hotel it houses lounges, a dining room and four bedrooms. A double-height, glass-and-steel conservatory comprises a new extension, where we find a fireplace-flaunting bar, open kitchen and the offer of informal dining, and six rooms up for grabs. Beyond the buildings, the hotel is lovingly couched in an acre of gardens designed by Andrew Pfeiffer, a landscaper celebrated in London, Istanbul and Buenos Aires for his green-fingered Midas touch.

From foliage to soft furnishings, we give the decor in the public areas a thorough once-over. It exemplifies the popular anything-goes aesthetic of mixing old and new, antique and à la mode, Asian and Euro – held together elegantly in this instance by the owners' art collection. Contemporary local artists hang alongside Brett Whiteley and walls are festooned with travel memorabilia and artefacts reflecting both familial and local history. Seeing another person's passion boldly on display reminds me of why I love to travel. Our room, located in the contemporary wing, is beautifully understated, modern but far from minimalist. Outside is the classic English garden setting, augmented by exotic Australian birds flitting through native flora. And add to that a postcard-perfect view of Mount Wellington.

After a pinch-me-it's-paradise afternoon of napping, reading and garden perusing, we're ready for dinner. Dressed for the occasion, we head to the rose-tinted drawing room where Thomas uncorks a bottle of champagne. Sinking into a sofa, Mrs Smith and I have a long catch-up while Thomas attends to every need, topping up glasses and

plumping cushions. We've ordered tasting plates matched with some of Tasmania's finest wines. In that stunning show kitchen, the chef creates a beautifully balanced menu harnessing the region's bounty – impossibly fresh oysters, delicious ocean trout and succulent lamb – cooked with precision and care. And, of course, imbued with passion.

The next morning, over breakfast, we plan our Derwent Valley attack. Before whetting your appetite for wanderlust, let's get you salivating again. If only every day I could tell a chef how I'd like my eggs. Home-made granola and poached fruits are followed by organic scrambled eggs and house-cured gravlax. The only possible gripe? No espresso machine. Coffee connoisseurs will be relieved to know one's on order.

Lisa takes the reins of our day, arming us with directions, bookings, re-bookings and more bookings – all of it with a smile. We set off first to explore antique stores in New Norfolk, then in the opposite direction for lunch. Peppermint Bay overlooking Bruny Island is a wonderfully of-the-moment providore with a tempting restaurant and bar. Great service, first-class local produce and crayfish, and a fabulous wine list prove that having Lisa play architect to our excursions outdoes relying on our all-knowing mate.

Back at the Islington, the sun disappears behind the hills and our afternoon segues to evening with another bath, another siesta and another bottle of bubbly. Tonight we're off to Hobart hotspot Piccolo, an Italian eatery and bar. Post-carbs, bed beckons, but instead we're sidetracked by the Islington's conservatory and its cocktails. Looking up through the glass roof, the stars are twinkling so brightly it's as if we're in the country.

Another heavenly sleep in the bespoke Angel beds (custom-made locally) and our perfect escape is at an end. But we got what we came for: pampering, relaxation and a deluge of great food. Just before we leave, Mrs Smith reads a quote from the in-house brochure: 'It feels like you're staying at a rich friend's house,' she shares. 'It's better than that though,' she suggests. 'It's as though your mates have gone away and left all their staff at your disposal too'. Now there's a service that really trumps that in-the-know Tasmanian pal of ours.

REVIEWED BY ANDREW MCCONNELL

'Contemporary local artists hang alongside Brett Whiteley and walls are festooned with travel memorabilia'

NEED TO KNOW

Rooms 11, including five rooms in the original 1847 house and seven garden rooms in the modern extension.
Rates AU$300–$550, including breakfast and minibar soft drinks.
Check-out 10am; check-in, 2pm, but both flexible, subject to availability.
Facilities Library, music room, outdoor pavilion with open fire and barbecue, free WiFi throughout. In rooms: flatscreen TV, in-house movie and cable channels, DVD/CD player with library, iPod dock, minibar, Basic Earth Botanicals and Beauty & the Bees toiletries.
Children This is more of a couple's retreat – no under-16s allowed.
Also Spend some languid downtime in the Andrew Pfeiffer-designed gardens, shaded by the 100-year-old willow.

IN THE KNOW

Our favourite rooms Tucked away at the back of the new extension, smart and simple ground-floor Rooms 6 and 7 have the best views, but stay in the old house to feel cocooned and connected – 3, the Louisa Anne Meredith Room, named after the first female chronicler of Tasmanian life, is generous, elegant and airy. Room 5, named after early postmaster John Collicott, is a small, tastefully cluttered room with views through its original casement window to the conservatory below.
Hotel bar An extensive honour bar, featuring all-Tasmanian wines, beers and local gin, whiskey and vodka, is available for guests whenever they fancy a tipple. The Asian-themed and darkly lush rose-hued drawing room is a soothing place for a late-night glass of tawny port, or house-speciality martini.
Hotel restaurant The main dining area and fireside snug are housed in a two-storey sandstone conservatory with a chequered black-and-white marble floor and huge, fern-filled urns. The Islington's talented chef cooks up a delicate but flavour-packed storm, with a mix of Mod Oz and European influences. Local produce reigns – Cressy lamb, Highlands wild rabbit, fresh-from-the-water fish – to be paired with a selection of superbly swillable wines.
Top table Nab the corner table overlooking the reflective infinity pond with its ghost-white Murano glass stalagmites, or ask for a private dinner at the grand colonial table in the library.
Room service You can order dishes from the main menu to enjoy in your room during breakfast and dinner hours, and light snacks such as cheeses and soups are available at other times. Picnics can be arranged in summer.
Dress code Understated but well-pressed and designer.
Local knowledge Pop down to nearby Battery Point and wander the waterfront lanes of this old maritime quarter of quaint cottages, cafés and pubs.

LOCAL EATING AND DRINKING

In North Hobart, chef Alex Jovanovic dishes up tasty Italian-meets-Tasmanian fare at **Piccolo** (03 6234 4844) on Elizabeth Street, where gnocchi, calamari and tiramisu should tempt you. A short drive from Hobart on Richmond Road in Cambridge, **Meadowbank Estate** (03 6248 4484) is a rated winery restaurant, with flavoursome sharing plates and wines served by the glass. Further afield, team a catamaran cruise with a trip to **Peppermint Bay** (03 6267 4088; www.peppermintbay.com.au) on the waterfront at Woodbridge, where local crayfish, oysters and fish are the star attraction (it's a 35-minute drive from town, if you'd rather stay on dry land). The **Source** (03 6277 9900) at the Moorilla Estate winery serves up seasonal produce from local suppliers and beautiful views over the Derwent Estuary. **Piccalilly** (03 6224 9900) in Battery Point is a good bet for imaginative fish, Euro-style small plates and wine.

GET A ROOM!

Use our free online booking service: check availability and make reservations through www.mrandmrssmith.com.

 SMITH CARD OFFER 20 per cent off dinner (including drinks).

The Islington Hotel 321 Davey Street, Hobart, Tasmania 7000 (03 6220 2123; www.islingtonhotel.com)

LAUNCESTON

CITYSCAPE Historic Tamar-hugging town
CITY LIFE Colonial charm, contemporary crafts

Lush and leafy, Launceston wears its colonial history with puffed-up civic pride. Indeed, with graceful Georgian estates peppering its West Country farmland surrounds, this is as Jane Austen as Australia gets. Tassie's second largest city is also more than just country meets town – Launceston has a maritime spring to its step too, thanks to its position on the banks of the winding Tamar River. Huge, four-metre tides breathe in and out of the city twice a day and ships bigger than the Spirit of Tasmania dock in its modern-day port. Mucking about on the river, Ratty and Toad style, is de rigueur, but the hilly latticework of streets also hides gourmet, craft and fashion treasures. Or tickle your tasting tonsils with a visit to nearby Tamar Valley, carpeted with some of the best-credentialled cold-climate vineyards in the world.

GETTING THERE

Planes There are no international flights that service Tasmania, but there are connections with mainland cities via Jetstar (www.jetstar.com.au), Qantas (www.qantas.com.au) and Virgin Blue (www.virginblue.com.au).
Boat A fun but time-consuming way to get to and from the island is on the Spirit of Tasmania (www.spiritoftasmania.com.au); two ferries ply the waters nightly between Melbourne and Devonport, taking nine to 11 hours shore to shore. It's then a 90-minute drive to Launceston. Book a cabin with a queen bed and ensuite. However, the Bass Strait is renowned for its choppy waters, so if you get lily-livered, stock up on the ginger.
Automobiles A car is a must-have when travelling around the island. Bring your own on the Spirit of Tasmania boat or hire one from Launceston Airport (www.launceston airport.com.au), which has most of the big-name rental companies on-site.

LOCAL KNOWLEDGE

Taxis Launceston's largest fleet of cabs is Taxi Combined (13 2227; www.taxicombined.com.au). A ride from the airport into town costs around AU$32.

Packing tips Waxed anoraks for the water; portable spittoon for the wine.
Recommended reads Property is the new porn, so ogle the region's smartest homes in *Country Houses of Tasmania* by Alice Bennett and Georgina Walker. Most are still privately owned; all come with colourful stories of the arriviste, ex-convict or blueblood colonials who built them. To engage with the island's recent and Aboriginal history, as well as a personal story of lost relatives and new loves, try Nicholas Shakespeare's *In Tasmania*.
Local specialities To love Launceston is to leave it, but only for the short drive into the Tamar Valley (www.winetasmania.com.au), the oldest wine-growing region on the island. It's noted for crisp sauvignon blancs, chardonnays and rieslings, but it's the sparklings that really, well, sparkle – especially with the infusion of French talent through the Jansz partnership of Louis Roederer and local group Heemskerk. Tamar Ridge, Pipers Brook and Stony Rise are regularly garlanded producers.
Do go/don't go Come for mists and mellow fruitfulness in autumn or manageably balmy summers away from

the desert and tropical heat of the mainland. The island can get a little closed-down during winter, but the fires are toasty even if the winds are Antarctic.

Tasmania has come a long way since dubbing itself the Apple Isle, and you're just as likely now to stumble across a saffron farm as a pear orchard. Despite the 75 kilometres that separate the city from the sea, Launceston's broad Tamar River has also been bringing munificent ocean harvests to town to rival more maritime state capital Hobart. Round it all off with extensive dairy farming – Launceston's cheeses are legendary – and you've arrived in gastronomic nirvana.

WORTH GETTING OUT OF BED FOR

Viewpoint With gabled tearooms and a bandstand worthy of a Tolkien novel, the Basin at the end of Cataract Gorge (www.launcestoncataractgorge.com.au) is a Rivendell-like place of quaint Edwardiana and craggy bushland. Clamber aboard the world's longest single-span chairlift for vaunt-worthy views.

Arts and culture The city's Queen Victoria Museum and Art Gallery (www.qvmag.tas.gov.au) is an old-fashioned cornucopia of Australian colonial art, contemporary craft and design, Tasmanian history, zoology, and 19th-century industrial railway workshops. By contrast, the Design Centre (www.designcentre.com.au) offers a sveltely Scandi-like survey of sculptural and practical wood design, much of it harnessing local Huon pine and blackwood.

Activities A cruise on the Launceston riverfront – from industrial-sized dry docks to lush Cataract Gorge – is a lazy-day must. Tamar River Cruises (www.tamarrivercruises.com.au) runs a number of watery jaunts on both a modern catamaran and more traditional long boat, the Lady Launceston. If you'd prefer to be airborne, hang glide the easy way – strapped on to a wire – at Cable Hang Gliding (www.cablehanggliding.com.au), over nearby Trevallyn Dam. Or just drink beer at Boag's Brewery (www.boags.com.au), while feigning interest in the hop-fermenting process.

Daytripper The National Trust properties surrounding Launceston are some of the best preserved in Australia and give a fascinating insight into the pretensions and perils of early colonial life. So grab a three-ticket pass at any of them, and play the visiting squire and his mistress at settlers' homestead Entally (www.entally.com.au), grand mansion Clarendon (www.nationaltrusttas.org.au) and Woolmers Estate (www.woolmers.com.au), all within 30 minutes of each other to the west and south of town. Woolmers is perhaps the most engaging, barely changed in 200 years, with its long, low-backed veranda sweeping steeply from an Italianate façade.

Children After a 50-minute drive north to Beauty Point, you'll be rewarded with the wonderful Seahorse World (www.seahorseworld.com.au), a cool conservation project dedicated to saving the little ocean equines. Mini Smiths will love the touch pool, where they can play with underwater starfish, crabs and welks. The seahorses live next to their friends the platypuses – Platypus House (www.platypushouse.com.au) is just down the road. Back in town, distract the nippers with the Japanese Macaque monkeys in City Park or, just outside, with bigger critters at Tasmania Zoo (www.tasmaniazoo.com.au), where there's a breeding programme for the near-extinct and suitably scary Tasmanian devil.

Walks Local art gallery 1842 (www.1842.com.au) hosts an hour's leisurely ramble through the old Lonnie streets, spinning yarns about the rogues, rascals and ratbags who once frequented them.

Perfect picnic Stock up on gourmet goodies at the Mill Providore at Ritchies Mill, 2 Bridge Road (03 6331 0777), tucked away in the old grain mill by the town's main bridge, and drive out to Egg Island Reserve at Hillwood, about 20 minutes north-west. Experience estuarine ecstasy as you watch swans glide over the water.

Shopping The handmade thing of beauty is king, so track back to the Design Centre shop (www.designcentre.com.au) for rolling pins as smooth as babies' bottoms or ornate, inlaid music boxes. The one-stop designer shop is Cocoon on George Street (www.cocoonlaunceston.com.au), or bigger wooden furniture can be found at 1842.

Something for nothing Launcestonians are justly proud of Cataract Gorge (www.launcestoncataractgorge.com.au), their wilderness retreat only 15 minutes walk from the city centre. Do the straight line from the Gorge entrance to the Basin or wander further from the madding crowd and go bush. Preening peacocks and scurrying marsupials abound.

Don't go home without buying Clothbound Pyengana Cheddar Cheese from fourth-generation cheesemaker Jon Healey. Made traditionally – think wood-fire milk-boiling, slatted pine shelves for 12-month maturation, weekly turning and wiping – it's crumbly, hard, nutty, complex and the cheese equivalent of liquid gold. Available from the farm door (Pyengana Dairy Company, St Columba Falls Road, Pyengana; 03 6373 6157), an hour east on the St Helen's Road, or at Delicacy Delicatessen on Canning Street (03 6334 8911).

LITERALLY LAUNCESTON

Launceston loves its relative antiquity, and it rains fairly frequently, so it's little surprise there's an Old Umbrella Shop at 60 George Street (03 6331 9248). Run by the National Trust, this is small-town eccentricity at its best: hand-painted cardboard advertising signs, original blank receipts, and, you guessed it, old umbrellas, take on the aura of Dutch Master museum exhibits, alongside potted histories of the multi-generational Shotts, North Tasmania's pre-eminent brolly-selling dynasty.

DIARY

February The Lonnie year kicks off with Festivale (www.festivale.com.au), three days of eating, drinking, performing and clapping in the town's City Park. **April** Too much exertion all round with the Three Peaks Race (www.threepeaks.org.au) as paired teams sail and run from Beauty Point to Hobart and scale Mounts Strzelecki, Freycinet and Wellington on the way. **October** The Royal Launceston Show (www.launcestonshowground.com.au) brings the district's loveliest livestock and oversize veggies to town. Don't miss the auxiliary Tasmanian Whipcracking Championship **November** Push back with the Launceston Blues Festival (www.ozblues.net/lbc) where performers get together to jam.

'We stare out the French doors at magnolia trees, rose bushes and, further afield, the grazing sheep'

Hagley

Quamby Estate

STYLE Historic 1820s homestead
SETTING Tree-lined Tasmanian gardens

At Launceston Airport, the air is fresh and the grass around the airport so green and luscious that I want to run the gauntlet of security and throw myself into it. Maybe later.

This is our first time in Tasmania, and we've been dreaming of long rural walks, rugged up in scarves and Barbour gilets, for weeks now. Already I can feel my deadline-fried mind turning to more relaxing thoughts: drinking glasses of wine overlooking rolling pastures, eating hearty meals of local produce, rambles around the countryside, long drives along narrow lanes. Quamby Estate, here we come.

Twenty minutes later, as we motor up the driveway lined with hawthorns, elms and oaks, the sun peeks through the clouds and, not for the first time today, I feel a smile spread across my dial. We pass the old Georgian stables (now converted to the base camp for both Cradle Mountain Huts and the Bay of Fires Walk) and pull up to the homestead – an unusual blend of Anglo-Indian architecture that gives this otherwise rather English bucolic scene a touch of the old Raj.

The front door opens, and host Liz Frankham issues a warm welcome. Stepping onto the slightly uneven cobbles, we feel as though we've drifted back into colonial times. Everything from the neatly placed lovers' seat on the wide veranda to the purple agapanthus growing in the garden is bathed in sunshine and dazzling.

Inside, we step across the traditional-style black-and-white chequerboard floor tiles and down the central hallway with its ornately decorated high ceilings. As we move into the drawing room it becomes obvious that, while there are contemporary touches everywhere, much care has gone into maintaining the character of the original building, completed in the 1830s. Gold detailing remains on the ceiling and marble mantelpieces hold up lavishly framed mirrors; it's been given a more modern spirit with billowing white curtains and furnishings in dove grey with splashes of lime green. 'You could definitely sit in here with a pile of magazines and a cup of tea,' says

Ms Smith, as we stare out the French doors at magnolia trees, rose bushes and, further afield, the grazing sheep. I file that particular activity on my mental to-do list, and wonder where I can pick up a couple of copies of *The Lady* or *Horse & Hound*.

The billiard room, Liz informs us, was once the house's ballroom. The magnificent volume of the space makes my imagination soar: I see men in dinner jackets and women in rustling ball gowns moving across the floor to music supplied by a string quartet.

Finally, we climb a tiny staircase to our room. It lends the charming sensation that we've been shrunk down to doll's house dimensions. (There's also only one other room in this part of the residence, and it's used for massages.) It is like a loft, with of-the-moment furnishings and luxurious touches – local woollen throws and waffle blankets are piled high on the king-size bed – and is probably just a tad too romantic for a girls' weekend away. (At this point, I'm seriously starting to wonder if I've chosen the right companion for this mini break.) In the middle of our room – just a hint, bring your slippers during winter as the floors can be freezing – is a freestanding, pod-shaped

'Local woollen throws and waffle blankets are piled high on the king-size bed'

bath. I immediately want to fill it to the brim and soak my troubles away in Molton Brown bliss, but Ms Smith and I have to draw up some kind of bubbles roster since it's all a bit out-in-the-open.

It is, however, almost time for dinner, so we tame the gentle bickering about who gets to bathe first. Down in the communal kitchen – open all hours for tea and coffee, and the setting for breakfast – the chef offers us a small menu from which to choose, before we're led to what feels like our own private dining room. We feast on hearty, tasty fare, and by the time we reach dessert we're truly sated.

The next day, we ponder the different local options – the Tamar Valley Wine Route, antiquing in nearby Deloraine or visiting the National Rose Garden at Woolmers Estate (the final two definitely fit with the weekend's English country house vibe) – but instead these Smiths decide to swing. As in golf clubs. Quamby Estate has its own nine-hole, par-76 course. Ms Smith and I like to think we looked the part when we got out there, but the divots on the beautifully manicured greens tell another story. Still, the hours spent soaking up the sun and swinging away to our hearts' content leaves us happy if a little sore. Now, to enlist someone to get to work on us in that little room we found. As in a post-golfing massage, in case you thought I was suggesting it really was time to throw our keys in.

REVIEWED BY MR & MRS SMITH

NEED TO KNOW

Rooms Nine.

Rates Low season, AU$300–$450; high season, AU$420–$590, including breakfast. Quamby's Georgian stables are the base for its Cradle Mountain Huts and Bay of Fires walks, which can be teamed with a stay here at special rates.

Check-out 11am. Check-in, 2pm.

Facilities DVD, CD and book library, internet access, massage room, tennis court, golf course, drawing room, billiard room, gardens. In rooms: flatscreen TV, DVD player and iPod dock.

Children The hotel can provide extra beds for kids up to age 12 in Deluxe Rooms for AU$60–$80, including breakfast. Infant cots aren't available but babysitting is, with hotel staff (price on application).

Also Go clubbing at the hotel's nine-hole golf course, complete with lakes, cascades and tricky bunkers (fees apply; hire clubs and buggies). Beware the eighth hole (at 576 metres, the longest par 5 in Tassie).

IN THE KNOW

Our favourite rooms Each unique bedroom blends restored heritage features and furniture with original art and modern bathrooms. Deluxe Room 9 is our top choice for romance, with a bold black rug, European-style furniture and a minimal freestanding bath opposite the bed. Sky-blue toned room 10 has a gorgeous tub beside low windows so you can sit back in the bubbles and enjoy impressive views.

Hotel bar Help yourself from the homestead's 24-hour honesty bar, which offers local Tasmanian and Australian wines – then sip them in the chic colonial drawing room. Or pop over to the Quamby Estate Golf Club for a drink at weekends.

Hotel restaurant Savour modern Australian dishes – such as rack of lamb with butternut pumpkin purée and rosemary butter – for dinner in Quamby's simple dining room, a crisp mix of black chairs, white linen and vibrant artworks. Breakfast is served around a communal table in the kitchen, or take it out on the homestead's sandstone veranda. Lunch is only available Friday through Sunday, from noon until 3pm.

Top table In the dining room, cosy up with a table by the fireside. For a nostalgic *Gone with the Wind* mood, it's hard to beat the wide flag-stoned porch, where you can take in the pretty park-like grounds.

Room service Quamby doesn't offer room service, but staff can advise you on places to eat lunch or tea while you're touring the area.

Dress code Understated luxury, as befits this trad-modern Tasmanian treat.

Local knowledge Tasmania has some of the best wild trout fishing in Australia. While staying at Quamby book a one-, two-, or three-day course with well-known guide Daniel Hackett and his team at RiverFly Tasmania (www.riverfly.com.au).

LOCAL EATING AND DRINKING

'Quamby' is an Aboriginal word meaning 'a place to camp, settle and rest', but if you can bear to leave the lodge, you'll find some fine local dining. Book ahead for award-winning **Stillwater** (03 6331 4153) in Launceston, which serves gourmet Euro-Asian lunch and dinner in a renovated flour mill by the Tamar River. Choose between a six-course tasting menu or à la carte dishes, washed down with Tasmanian wines. Or detour to restaurant **Daniel Alps at Strathlynn** (03 6330 2388), at Ninth Island vineyard at Rosevears, for striking views and tasty local produce from the Tamar Valley wine region.

GET A ROOM!

Use our free online booking service: check availability and make reservations through www.mrandmrssmith.com.

 SMITH CARD OFFER A round of golf.

Quamby Estate 1145 Westwood Road, Hagley, Tasmania 7292 (03 6392 2211; www.quambyestate.com.au)

South Australia
AUSTRALIA

SOUTH AUSTRALIA

BAROSSA VALLEY
The Louise
CLARE VALLEY
North Bundaleer
KANGAROO ISLAND
Southern Ocean Lodge

BAROSSA VALLEY

COUNTRYSIDE Valleys, vines and vales
COUNTRY LIFE Sublime food and wine

A breezy road-trip north-east of the capital of South Australia (take the scenic route via the Adelaide Hills), the Barossa Valley dukes it out with NSW's Hunter Valley for bragging rights as the most celebrated grape-growing region in Australia. The patchwork valley hillsides sustain more than 80 vineyards, producing over a fifth of Australia's wine – mostly big, ballsy reds. A distinct local foodie culture has evolved alongside the drinkables, with cool cafés and sexy restaurants extolling regional fare with a doff of the cap to the valley's Germanic heritage. Fleeing religious persecution, Lutheran immigrants came to the Barossa in 1842, bringing with them hardy vine cuttings. Historic stone-wall towns like Tanunda, Bethany and Angaston are infused with Teutonic tastes: admire gothic church steeples and brass band festivals and rifle through food stores for smoked wurst, pretzels and sauerkraut. Guten appetit!

GETTING THERE

Planes The Barossa is a one-hour drive (on a good day) north of South Australia's capital city, Adelaide. Domestic flights from all other Australian capitals and many regional centres fly into Adelaide's international airport (www.aal.com.au).
Automobiles The Barossa is compact – 25 kilometres end-to-end – but you'll need a motor to get there and access back-road cellar doors and townships off the main tourist trail. Hire a car at Adelaide airport or in the city itself, where all the major rental brands are represented.

LOCAL KNOWLEDGE

Taxis Barossa Valley Taxis (08 8563 3600) runs a 24-hour service throughout the valley. A cab from Tanunda to Angaston costs around AU$20.
Packing tips Leave some room in your luggage for a few bottles of vintage Barossa red, and bring a sun hat for those long afternoons traipsing between cellar doors.

Recommended reads In between appearances on the ABC TV show The Cook and The Chef, Barossa celebrity gourmet Maggie Beer has published some great books, including the superb Maggie's Harvest, zooming in on the best Barossa produce. Barossa Food by Angela Heuzenroeder is also a worthy stomach-centric read.
Local specialities The Barossa is all about that ruby-tinted tipple – cabernet sauvignon, shiraz and grenache – but you can also pick up some fab bottles of riesling, gewürztraminer and semillon if you delight in a great white. There are around 50 cellar doors across the valley, most offering free tastings, so you'll never be short of opportunities to swish, swill and swallow. On the dining front, expect hearty German-style main courses – plenty of steak, schnitzel, chicken and oodles of sausage – in established restaurants, complemented by a new breed of café-style eateries featuring smaller servings with zing. Vegetarians take heart, the local cheese is also a winner.

Do go/don't go Summer in the Barossa (December to February) can be hot and heaving with visitors: better to time your trip during autumn (March to April) when the grapes are being harvested, the days are fresher and the nippers are back at school.

WORTH GETTING OUT OF BED FOR

Viewpoint The back road from Tanunda to Angaston via Bethany winds through some beautiful countryside, tracking up to Mengler's Hill Look-out – a top spot to check out the valley below (just pretend the weird sculptures in the foreground are invisible).

Arts and culture At the Keg Factory (www.thekeg factory.com.au) on the southern fringe of Tanunda you can watch real-life coopers construct and repair wine barrels for the local wineries – an exercise in high art in the hands of such masters.

Activities For a serene, lofty perspective on the Barossa's lanes and landscapes, contact Balloon Adventures (www.balloonadventures.com.au). Daily one-hour flights bob skywards from Tanunda and include a champagne breakfast. No visit to the Barossa would be complete without over-indulging in some wine tasting. Lots of companies can escort you so you don't have to drive: try Barossa Experience Tours (www.barossavalleytours.com), Barossa Epicurean Tours (www.barossatours.com.au) or Barossa Valley Tours (www.barossavalleytour.com).

Daytripper Can't get enough fine wine and good times? The Clare Valley – South Australia's other big-name wine region – is less than an hour's drive to the north. Pile into the car and prime yourself for some pleasing riesling in historic towns like Auburn, Mintaro and Clare itself. Check out www.clarevalley. com.au, or contact the Clare Valley Visitors Centre (08 8842 2131).

Children The Barossa can be a bit of a drag for kids (know any eight-year-old grenache fanatics?) so for more child-friendly fun take them to Kaiserstuhl Conservation Park (www.environment.sa.gov.au/parks) in Angaston, which has some beaut bushwalks, valley views and plenty of wildlife (especially echidnas, kestrels, hawks and kangaroos).

Walks For a fragrant, colourful stroll head for Lyndoch Lavender Farm (www.lyndochlavenderfarm.com.au), where you can wander through several acres of flowering fields, boasting over 90 varieties of the sweet-smelling purple flora. There's also a café, wine tastings and a shop for afters.

Perfect picnic Quite a few of the Barossa's wineries have a sweep of green grass out the front with views over the vines. Pack a hamper from Maggie Beer's Farm Shop (www.maggiebeer.com.au) in Nuriootpa and hit the lawns at Peter Lehmann Wines (www.peterlehmann wines.com.au) in Tanunda. A bottle of Lehmann's Stonewell Shiraz is the perfect partner in crime.

Shopping Most Barossa wineries can arrange shipping, if you fancy taking a few dozen cab sauvs home. Feel the need for a fine feta or cool camembert? The perfectly aromatic Barossa Valley Cheese Company (www.bvcc.com.au) in Angaston sells handcrafted goats- and cows-milk creations. Also worth browsing are Raven's Parlour Bookshop (08 8563 3455) in Tanunda for its stylish range of new and second-hand tomes, while Timeless Books (08 8564 2222) in Angaston also sells CDs.

Something for nothing The bountiful Barossa Farmers' Market (www.barossafarmersmarket.com) in Angaston takes place every Saturday 7.30am–11.30am. It's free to get in and roam the produce stalls, but, who are we kidding? You'll probably emerge piled high with local breads, sausages, fruits and cheeses – all to accompany the local drop.

Don't go home without... listening to the Whispering Wall. The century-old concrete Barossa Reservoir dam's incredible acoustics mean you can earwig a pal's whispered conversation from the other side, over 100 metres away. Seven kilometres south-west of Lyndoch on the way from Adelaide to the Barossa via Gawler, it also makes a scenic stop-off.

BRILLIANTLY BAROSSA

South Australia has half a dozen world-class wine regions, but the Barossa wins hands down when it comes to cultivating an historic, reverent atmosphere. It has a lot to do with the vaulted sandstone tasting rooms, the old European trees and the valley's German heritage (play 'Count the Umlauts' as you drive past winery signs), but it's also about the grape gravitas: weighty, substantial and brooding. This is no fizzy, fun-in-the-sun frolic. This is serious business. The old-school 'Barossa Barons' attract the lion's share of trade and traffic, but sassy young boutique wineries have also carved out a market niche in recent years.

DIARY

January The Tour Down Under (www.tourdownunder.com.au) cycling race wheels through the Barossa – watch 'em fly by. **February** Barossa Under the Stars (www.barossaunderthestars.com.au) and A Day on the Green (www.adayonthegreen.com.au) music festivals see crooners like Shirley Bassey and Chris Isaak charm mature viticultural crowds. Lay out a picnic rug on the winery lawns and soak up the good-times vibe. **April** The week-long Barossa Vintage Festival (www.barossavintagefestival.com.au), in odd-numbered years, is a frenzy of maypole dancing, street parades and music (oh, and plenty of wine). **September** The Barossa Wine Show (www.barossa.com) is a let's-pat-ourselves-on-the-back awards event with tastings for the passing public. **October** The Barossa Music Festival (www.barossa.org) shifts the emphasis from crooners to classical and jazz in intimate venues (tasting rooms, churches, wine vaults). Expect picnics and wine aplenty.

'I'm much more a suitcase and "floor-drobe" kind of guy. But, as I *fold* the last of my underwear *neatly* into the drawer, it strikes me: I am relaxed in this space'

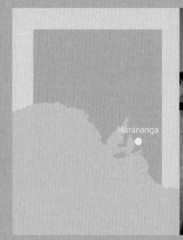

Marananga

The Louise

STYLE Contemporary courtyard chambers
SETTING Hillside vineyard retreat

We don't arrive in Adelaide until the sun is already slinking away. By the time we negotiate the main road north (helpfully named 'the Main Road North') it's coal-black out, the air is mint-crisp and the city's far behind us. We're heading to the Louise in the Barossa Valley, an hour plus some, according to our impressionist map. We pass a Penfolds sign and can almost smell the Grange. A few more turns through the rolling hills and we see the inviting yellow glow of our home in the valley for the next two nights.

It's late but we're welcomed warmly at reception and taken through our booking – a private wine tour has been arranged the next day as has dinner at the hotel's restaurant, Appellation. I'm tasked with filling in the following morning's breakfast order – a job that in my ragged state seems impossibly difficult. I tell our check-in man I'm having a brain freeze as we just somehow gained 30 minutes flying across a few borders. (South Australia is half an hour behind the east coast of Australia.)

We're staying in the Seppeltsfield Suite, one of 15 too-lovely lodgings at the Louise, which we enter through a spacious private courtyard to find a fresh and modern living room. Impressed and excited, we conduct the obligatory opening of drawers and doors – and then something unexpected happens. I unpack my clothes. I can't claim to know other people's habits, but I am much more a suitcase and 'floor-drobe' kind of guy (to the consternation of Mr Smith). But, as I fold the last of my underwear neatly into the drawer, it strikes me: I am already relaxed in this space. I'm not sure what I can pin this on – the rich, restful colours of the room, the country air, the plush, cosy furniture, the sleep deprivation?

Mr Smith runs the cavernous bath and we both soak, fitting comfortably, candles lit, jets pulsing. I'm sure I have a micro-sleep. Towelled off, Mr Smith pours us both a generous glass of the dangerously delicious complimentary port and we snuggle on the sofa, ignoring the lure of the LCD television. We resist a refill and retire to our enormous bed with its peak of cushy pillows.

The next morning we're awoken by our arriving breakfast (I picked well). I try out the espresso machine and it makes a mean latte. We're sorely tempted to stay here, meander through the weekend papers, and laze on the terrace deckchairs that overlook the tapestry of vineyards in more shades of green than a paint chart. However, we're here for the true Barossa experience.

Almost all we know about the Barossa is wine, wine, wine – this is the spiritual home of Australia's bold, brassy reds. And having just finished a month of self-imposed abstemiousness (for charity, for liver), we are more than ready to dive in. First up though, we take in the sights and smells (including dizzying wafts of bacon) of the nearby farmers' market, a showcase of Barossa's non-boozy bounty: artisan cheese, rustic bread, just-plucked veggies. The feel here is genuine and local – it's not (yet) swamped with moneyed tourists.

Bellies full, we swing into action, ticking off some favourites: Henschke, Grant Burge, Charles Melton and Torbreck. Mr Smith is designated driver, and I'm quietly sozzled. We meet up with Sally Kalleske of Kalleske Wines in the early afternoon and get a private tour – arranged

'Still buzzing, we follow the lit path back to our suite and climb into bed, completely satisfied'

through the Louise – where we learn a great deal about wine-making, and we also meet their pet pig Wilbur. The little oinker, named after the rambunctious runt of *Charlotte's Web*, has his hungry snout set on my footwear, so we don't linger long in his pen. Kalleske is an organic, biodynamic winery. The holistic theory I like, but some of the practicalities of such a venture – like preparing soil with a cow's horn stuffed with manure – is lost on me. No matter, the wines are truly fabulous and our host delightful.

Towards the end of a glorious afternoon, we head back to our suite and prepare for dinner at the Louise's award-winning restaurant Appellation, arguably the foodie crown of the Barossa. We start with an apéritif and end – some three hours later, after traversing the local, seasonal, sensational tasting menu – with a bread and butter pudding so awesome I still haven't shut up about it. Other highlights included punchy prosciutto-wrapped pigeon and lamb as tender as mother-love. Still buzzing, we follow the lit path back to our suite and climb into bed, completely satisfied.

Next morning, Mr Smith opens up the shutters to our (we dream) private vineyard and we loll about in bed, reading the paper and inventing unique wine blends. Our flight time ensures we can't lie about forever, so we shower (did I mention it came with a choice of two drenching rain shower heads in a capacious room of its own, with a third shower in a linked outside space?) and hit the road. We're sad to see the Barossa and the Louise fading from our view during take-off but delighted about our shipment of vino arriving in seven days. As we fly across the border, we lose that half an hour again, but at this point I'm not sure that I really care.

REVIEWED BY PAUL MCNALLY

NEED TO KNOW

Rooms 15 suites.

Rates AU$395–$1,082, including breakfast.

Check-out 11am, but flexible subject to availability (charges may apply). Check-in, 2pm.

Facilities Guest computer, outdoor swimming pool, sauna, hot spa, bicycles, gardens. In rooms: free WiFi, flatscreen TVs, DVD player, BOSE Wave CD player, iPod dock, espresso machine, minibar, Vive toiletries, rubber ducks in spa baths, private courtyard with terrace and gate intercom.

Children The Louise can provide cots for infants under two for AU$20 a night, but isn't suitable for children aged two to 14. Babysitting can be arranged with a local nanny with at least 48 hours' notice.

Also Accommodation and dining packages incorporating meals at Appellation (the in-house restaurant) and wine-tasting are also available. The Louise and Appellation close for four weeks each July for upgrades and renovations.

IN THE KNOW

Our favourite rooms We like No 29, a Stonewell Suite, the best of the 10 suites revolving around the entrance piazza – access is via a private courtyard. The living and sleeping areas are an exercise in seductive mod tones (from raspberry to aubergine), leading onto a superb bathroom complete with underfloor heating, walk-in shower, spa tub, recessed candle nooks and an outdoor shower for sub-star shampooing. The terrace is perfect for an evening glass of red overlooking the vines. Suite 33, a Seppeltsfield Suite, is a two-bedroom affair in a separate wing with even more enticing vineyard views.

Hotel bar Adjacent to the restaurant, an elegant modern lounge bar serves pre-dinner drinks, including a heady selection of local wines, spirits, cocktails and beers. Repair to the terrace to watch dusky sunset colours shift over the vine rows.

Hotel restaurant The Louise's award-winning in-house restaurant, Appellation, serves dinner nightly (there's just 48 seats, so bookings are essential). Executive chef Mark McNamara's menus are underpinned by the 'locavore' philosophy, with 90 per cent of the menu's seasonal produce sourced within a 30-kilometre radius (smoked duck, anyone?). Choose between à la carte dishes and a tasting menu, with courses brilliantly paired with Barossa wines.

Top table There's one window seat in each of the restaurant's two zones with views across the vines.

Room service Continental breakfast is served in your suite every morning. A snack menu is available between 11am and 7pm, including pies, salads, terrines and cheese platters.

Dress code Snappy, sassy, self-confident.

Local knowledge The Louise can book you in for 'Breakfast with the Kangaroos' at dawn, where a local guide whizzes you away in a 4WD to a nearby conservation park. After a 15-minute hike, your guide will throw out the picnic rug and plate-up a gourmet breakfast, rousing the curiosity of 'roos who enjoy their own tucker nearby (it's not kosher to feed them). Wine tasting is a Barossa must: ask at reception about local cellar doors, or exclusive tastings by appointment.

LOCAL EATING AND DRINKING

You might have seen South Australian celeb Maggie Beer on *The Cook and The Chef* on ABC TV or tasted one of her successful range of Barossa-made condiments, preserves and pâtés. Swing by the brilliant **Maggie Beer's Farm Shop** on Pheasant Farm Road, Nuriootpa (08 8562 4477), a hybrid upmarket deli and cooking school, for a superb gourmet picnic lunch. On Tanunda's main drag, Murray Street, the 1846 **Tanunda Hotel** (08 8563 2030) is an anything-goes kinda joint: pool tables, big bar meals and live bands twanging. Just down the way, **Keils Fine Food & Coffee** (08 8563 1468) delivers a decent caffeine fix, as well as home-made soups, pies and pita-bread wraps.

GET A ROOM!

Use our free online booking service; check availability and make reservations through www.mrandmrssmith.com.

 SMITH CARD OFFER A bottle of sparkling wine on arrival.

The Louise Seppeltsfield Road at Stonewell Road, Marananga, South Australia 5355 (08 8562 2722; www.thelouise.com.au)

CLARE VALLEY

COUNTRYSIDE Agriculture meets viticulture
COUNTRY LIFE Gimme a riesling

An hour or so north of South Australia's more famous Barossa Valley, the historic Clare Valley in the Mid North district punches well above its weight in the wine stakes. Producing just three per cent of this land's quaffable stock, it still rakes in 20 per cent of the industry's awards. Young, sweet and fragrant, the riesling is really what you're here for. Knock around the Barossa and then roll into Clare, and you'll notice a seismic shift in atmosphere. Gone is the squat German colonial architecture, replaced by refined stone structures built with boomtown mining money. Absent too are the garish signs, swapped for subtle, boutique marketing and discreet cellars. The Clare Valley delivers a personable wine experience with aplomb. And its landscape is tasty too: rolling hills and villages steeped in history.

GETTING THERE

Planes The Clare Valley is a 2.5-hour drive north of South Australia's capital city, Adelaide, which has a shiny new international airport (www.aal.com.au). Domestic flights from all other homeland capitals and many regional centres fly into Adelaide too. There's also a sealed airstrip at Jamestown, just north of the Clare Valley, for charter planes sized up to DC-3 (and believe us, that's hefty).

Automobiles The Clare Valley is long and skinny so you'll need your motor to traverse the cellar doors and townships. Having keys to your own steed will help you discover back-road vineyards off the main tourist trail. Hire a car at Adelaide airport or in Adelaide itself.

LOCAL KNOWLEDGE

Taxis Clare Valley Taxis (08 8842 1400) runs between the towns in the valley.

Packing tips Bring some bike-riding gear – one of the best ways to experience the Clare Valley is on two wheels – and make sure you leave plenty of room in your luggage for a few bottles (or more) of fine Clare Valley riesling.

Recommended reads The Story of the 'Monster Mine' by Ian Auhl tells the tale of Mid North copper-town Burra and the transport route to the coast through the Clare Valley, which founded most of the local villages. Viticulture and Environment by John Gladstones looks at the Clare Valley's microclimates, explaining why the riesling here is so good.

Local specialities Expect farmer-sized food portions (read: huge). Unlike the Barossa Valley, the Clare Valley hasn't gone totally upmarket – any eatery worth its salt will still have a chicken schnitzel and a hefty steak on the menu. The CV may trail the Barossa in gourmet terms, but anything tastes good with a crisp summer glass of that riesling. You'll also find better-than-good bottles of shiraz, sangiovese, pinot grigio, viognier and cab sauv. Most cellar doors have free tastings and open from 10am to 5pm.

Do go/don't go Summer in South Australia (December to February) can be a crazed, crowded and sun-burnt prospect, particularly around this neck of the woods, which is closer to the dry Outback than the more populated regions. A better idea is to visit during

autumn (March to April) when the harvest is on and the days are cooler.

Also... The valley towns vary in size and atmosphere, but most are worth a look: utilitarian Clare is the biggest and busiest, absent of a whole lotta charm. Further south, Mintaro is famous for its slate, and has a gorgeous crop of old cottages. Auburn has a drive-through vibe but a couple of handy places to eat and drink.

WORTH GETTING OUT OF BED FOR

Viewpoint There are few accessible spots to get above the valley and fathom its virtues, but you'll get an intimate perspective from the Riesling Trail (www.southaustraliantrails.com), a level cycling track running around 25 kilometres between Auburn and Clare, following an old train line. Along the way you'll bump into the vineyards, farms and gnarled red gums for which the Clare Valley is famous. For bike hire, contact Clare Valley Cycle Hire (www.clarevalleycyclehire.com.au) or Cogwebs in Auburn (www.cogwebs.com.au).

Arts and culture The Mid North is serious agricultural and wine-making country. The practical, not the arty or whimsical, is what counts here, but Clare does boast the Old Police Station Museum (www.nationaltrustsa.org.au), an 1850 outpost which today houses displays of vintage photos, furniture, Victorian clothing and domestic relics.

Activities Why are you here? No spin through the Clare Valley would be worth much without swishing some of that hallowed vino around your mouth. If you don't want to drive, Clare Valley Experiences (www.clarevalleyexperiences.com) chauffeurs you in a shiny Mercedes, or Clare Valley Tours (www.cvtours.com.au) offers Mid North minibus forays soaking up the Clare wineries and Martindale Hall. If you prefer to have a snoop under your own steam, wineries to look for include Pikes (www.pikeswines.com.au), which has a beautiful cellar door, and Skillogalee (www.skillogalee.com), with a pretty veranda restaurant, both in Sevenhill; and the big daddy of them all, Taylors Wines (www.taylorswines.com.au), in Auburn, which rules the export roost.

Daytripper If you're a history fiend, check out the eccentric town of Burra, around 45 kilometres north east of Clare. It was a copper-mining boomtown from the 1840s to the 1870s, and the visitors centre

(www.visitburra.com) can kit you out with maps and a pass to a slew of historic sites including mines, jails and old dugout houses. It's not quite a ghost town (there are still 1,000 people living here), but the atmosphere is curiously spooky.

Children When the kids grow weary of all your wine sniffing, swilling and spittoon-filling, take them three kilometres south-west of diminutive Sevenhill to the Spring Gully Conservation Park (www.environment.sa.gov.au/parks/sanpr/springully) – a 400-hectare reserve with gushing waterfalls (in winter) and tall stands of red stringybark and blue gum. There are plenty of feathered and furry types here too, plus some long bush trails to exhaust the little ones on.

Walks Sample a section of the 1,200-kilometre long Heysen Trail, South Australia's longest trail dedicated to bushwalking, which passes near Kapunda, Clare, Burra, Jamestown and Spalding in the area (www.environment.sa.gov.au/parks/heysen).

Perfect picnic Pack a hamper and head for the eerily beautiful Martindale Hall (www.martindalehall.com), an amazingly well-preserved 1880 manor just outside

Mintaro. The Hall featured in the classic 1975 Peter Weir film *Picnic at Hanging Rock*, in the guise of Appleyard College. You can tour the lavish innards, but the grounds are just as lovely – roll out your rug on the lawns.

Shopping There's not much to see here in terms of traditional walk-in-and-buy-something stores, but most Clare Valley wineries can arrange shipping, so your two dozen rieslings will be waiting for you when you get home.

Something for nothing If you like old buildings (or can't stomach another winery), pick up a copy of the *Walk With History at Auburn* brochure from the Clare Valley Visitors Centre (08 8842 2131), and stroll around the old stone cottages and backstreets of this small town 25 kilometres south of Clare.

Don't go home without... walking, or even better, cycling, along a section of the Clare-to-Auburn Riesling Trail (www.southaustraliantrails.com).

CLASSICALLY CLARE VALLEY

Touring the Clare Valley you get a sense that before anyone discovered you could grow wine here, the area had an established identity and was a potent place indeed. With the 'Monster Mine' in nearby Burra spewing out copper in the 1840s, the Clare towns evolved along the transport route, with impressive stone properties built in prospering Auburn, Mintaro and Clare. But then in the 1850s someone discovered gold in Victoria and all the miners shipped out – boom went bust. Thankfully the architecture remains – a lavishly optimistic gallery of European-style old buildings.

DIARY

March The Bundaleer Forest Weekend (www.bundaleerweekend.com.au) is an opera-and-symphony spectacular in the Bundaleer Forest near Jamestown. **May** The annual Clare Valley Gourmet Weekend (www.southaustralia.com) is a fab festival of wine, food and song, with tastings, degustation dinners, a black-tie ball and plenty of jazz.
September The Clare Valley of the Vines Race Day (www.racingandsports.com.au) is a horse-racing meet with all the usual thrills and pitfalls (sometimes champagne just goes down too easily...). It's fun for the family, with kids' activities, live bands and competitions. **October** The annual Clare Show (www.sacountryshows.com) is the largest one-day agricultural show in Australia. Expect much mooing of cows, chopping of wood, horse jumping and kids chewing dagwood dogs (for the uninitiated, a sausage on a skewer, battered, deep-fried and dunked in ketchup). Further north, Jamestown Cup Day (www.racingsa.com.au) is also worth a gander.

'It has the power to transform
you into an Austen heroine – until
a family of kangaroos bounds
past and bursts the bubble'

Jamestown

North Bundaleer

STYLE Vintage Victorian homestead
SETTING Wineries and wilderness

'Last night I dreamt I went to North Bundaleer again,' said Mr Smith a week after our two days of pampered relaxing at this gracious homestead. Although it wasn't Manderley, and our own story didn't have quite such a melodramatic conclusion, I knew what he meant; this is a hotel that transports you to another, more romantic, era.

From the hill that crowns 160-hectare grounds – the perfect sundowner spot – the sandstone chimneys of North Bundaleer peek through the blue gums. The house, built in 1901 in the Victorian Queen Anne style, is one of the grandest in the district and has shades of wild folly about it. Above the front door sits a fabulous tower that serves no purpose. At the property's core, there's a ballroom where I could imagine the ladies of Longbourn coquettishly munching ices while waiting for Darcy to ask them to dance.

Evoking English country-house Victoriana on the fringes of the Outback is no mean feat, and it's testament to the owners' imagination that North Bundaleer has the power to transform you into an Austen heroine – until, that is, a family of kangaroos bounds past and bursts the bubble. About six years ago, Marianne and Malcolm Booth bought a crumbling pile and have since turned it into a mansion retreat with every comfort. Today, it's a luxurious hotel from which to explore parts of the striking South Australian Outback, from the Clare Valley to the Flinders Ranges.

With only four rooms, a stay here is inevitably intimate. We were lucky enough to secure the headline act – the Red Room Suite, with its enormous canopy bed. It also has a private, ruby toile-wallpapered sitting room with a Chinese theme (a blanket box is topped with the latest editions of *The World of Interiors* – what more could a decor-obsessed Mrs Smith require?), and a conservatory converted into a modern bathroom. If you're bedding down here, follow my lead and take a leisurely candlelit bath, gazing out through the wall-filling windows at the sky flocked of stars.

The other bedrooms are no aesthetic slouches either. In short, if you're into period furnishings done tastefully, you'll like North Bundaleer – I am, and I do. When we were there, every room showcased vases of seasonal flowers and eucalypts, but I can imagine perfume filling the house when the rose garden is in its full summertime bloom. Stepping eagerly into the ballroom, we were struck by one detail in particular – a restored wallpaper adorned with a winged seahorse, the hippocampus of mythology, now the homestead's logo. Perhaps it was wishful thinking on the part of the original owners that the symbol of a water god should have loomed so large in such a bone-dry place.

North Bundaleer's surrounds are alluring enough, but coupled with Marianne's inspired cookery (son Leo is executive chef) and Malcolm's attention to detail, you have somewhere special indeed. As a guest, I am not without quirks – one of which involves tea. I am a staunch subscriber to the etiquette that a pot should be served alongside milk and hot water for those of us who like their flavours delicate. Most people don't bring it, despite repeated requests. Not here. Delivered to our room with a pot of hot water and a fresh cupcake, my brew was perfect and continued to be, without fail, every time afterwards – heaven for tea purists and exacting guests alike.

Mr Smith and I had stayed at 'hosted accommodation' before with mixed (OK, bad) results, so when we discovered we were to dine with the owners in the grand but austere dining room on the first night, our hearts sank. It was with some trepidation that we joined Malcolm, Marianne and another guest for apéritifs in the drawing room.

At least there was lots of bubbly (all drinks are included in the room rate) and spicy deep-fried olives to get things going. And going they got. To our immense relief our hosts were delightful, managing the meal and conversation with tact and verve. By the end of the first course (a wonderful fresh-from-the-garden stinging-nettle soup) we felt as welcome as family members come home for the holidays.

In fact, we may have felt a touch too at home, if the hangover was anything to go by. We meandered into breakfast to find it was an all-in occasion once again, and I feared for Mr Smith – never his best in the morning. Fortunately for him – and me – the quality of the food soon made us shake off our fug. Everything was home-made: eggs from the chooks, jams from local orchard fruit – and more of that pot-perfect tea. When it came to the day's agenda, we felt that we'd already had more than a fair sampling of the Clare Valley vineyards the previous night, so we planned to walk a small section of the famous Heysen Trail, which passes nearby, and then return to snooze, read, bathe and prepare for the next meal.

Named after Hans Heysen, an early 20th-century landscape artist spellbound by the Flinders Ranges, the Heysen Trail is a 1,200-kilometre trail that stretches from Cape Jervis to Parachilna Gorge. If you have 60 days to kill, you can walk its entirety. Mr Smith and I were less well time-endowed, but a few hours in the crisp air were more than appreciated. The countryside varies from rolling green hills to dry creek gorges, so if you want to see Australia au naturel with minimal effort, this is the way to do it. The trail passes by a property named Never Never – we pondered whether it was called that because it never, never rained there.

While we were getting back to nature, Marianne was busy cooking it; preparing, at my request, supper in our sitting room that night. There we sat at a cloth-covered table for two, napkins white and silver shining, with candles and firelight for atmosphere and a menu that featured the most delicious leek-and-stilton tart. As we ate, we reflected on how we could easily get used to living Marianne and Malcolm's unique brand of Victorian high life. Leaving for Adelaide the next morning, our feelings were confirmed by the present of a cask of home-pressed olive oil packed in our luggage. North Bundaleer: it's that type of place.

REVIEWED BY MARGIE SEALE

NEED TO KNOW
Rooms Four, including one suite.
Rates AU$390–$500, with cooked breakfast. Packages, including breakfast, dinner, tea, coffee, biscuits, canapés and an open bar, start from AU$1,080 for two nights.
Check-out 11am, but flexible subject to availability. Check-in, 2pm.
Facilities Library and drawing room, grand piano, TV room, open fires, espresso machines, free WiFi throughout, gardens. In rooms: Gilchrist & Soames toiletries.
Children North Bundaleer is too romantic (and too packed with antiques) to warrant bringing mini Smiths, although they can be accommodated.
Also With no set in your room, you'll need to head to the indigenous-art-adorned TV room for small-screen entertainment, or to the lavish library to peruse antiquarian books. If you're feeling a bit Piano Man, tickle the ivories in the grand ballroom.

IN THE KNOW
Our favourite rooms The vibrant Red Room Suite has a canopied four-poster, a sitting room with an open fire, and a bath and shower in an airy, window-lined ensuite (it's a former conservatory – cue great views out). The Blue Room boasts a huge bathroom with a freestanding roll-top bath, and the more contemporary African Room has ethnic artefacts and a private shower, which is not ensuite. Our favourite is the William Morris Room where a big brass bed and lavish wallpaper pay homage to the Arts and Crafts genius.
Hotel bar The rates here include a selection of alcoholic drinks from the 24-hour bar, a dedicated nook off the kitchen. Help yourself to fine local wine (Sevenhill, Crabtree and O'Leary Walker), South Australian Coopers beer or a G&T – you can enjoy a tipple anywhere in the homestead.
Hotel restaurant After canapés in the drawing room, supper in the dining room is coordinated by Sydney-trained executive chef Leo Hollingshead, and usually involves four courses in an affable, dinner-party atmosphere. Typical dishes include white asparagus with gorgonzola and truffled honey. The wine flows as fast as the conversation; expect silverware, antique crockery, candles and crisp linen. Breakfasts maintain Hollingshead's high standards. For lunch, order a picnic hamper.
Top table There's only one table in the breakfast room, and another long table in the dining room, so go with the familial flow and get communal.
Room service The emphasis here is on shared meal times with your hosts and other guests, but room service is available all day too. Red Room guests can breakfast or dine in their suite for romantic privacy.
Dress code High-necked frilly blouses for her and a pointy beard and monocle for him wouldn't look out of place amid the Victoriana, but smart-casual attire will do.
Local knowledge Wander the property at dusk to spot mobs of resident roos – there's nothing quite like seeing a dozen big boomers bounding across an open field. Climb up to Maslin' Look-out for sublime sunset views (and a bottle of bubbles) or stroll among ancient pines in nearby North Bundaleer Forest (both the Heysen and Mawson Trails pass through here). If you don't fancy trekking, the Clare Valley boasts around 35 winery cellar doors for chilled-out tastings.

LOCAL EATING AND DRINKING
On a hillside south of Clare, **Salt n Vines Bar & Bistro** (08 8842 1796), at Wendouree Road, serves up sophisticated contemporary fare on a sunny deck. **Kirrihill Wines**' (08 8842 4087) cellar door is also on site for sampling some riesling. **Cafe Cygnets** (08 8849 2030) whips up the best coffee in Auburn, or hit the providore counter for gourmet delights.

GET A ROOM!
Use our free online booking service: check availability and make reservations through www.mrandmrssmith.com.

 SMITH CARD OFFER A gift box of handmade Haigh's Chocolates, an iconic South Australian brand founded in 1915.

North Bundaleer RM Williams Way, Jamestown, South Australia 5491 (08 8665 4024; www.northbundaleer.com.au)

KANGAROO ISLAND

COASTLINE Southern Ocean surf
COAST LIFE Wild times (big nature, not big nights out)

Touting itself as 'Australia's Galapagos', Kangaroo Island (KI) has an amazing proliferation of wildlife – in the sky, the scrub and the sea. Located 13 kilometres off South Australia's coast, it's the country's third biggest island – so there's plenty of space for the local wildlife to do its thing without the 4,250 islanders getting in the way. KI is a remarkable sanctuary, and no trip to the island is complete without encountering some of the hairy, feathery or fishy residents (and no, we don't mean the fishermen). Get up close and personal with kangaroos, seals and penguins, as well as bountiful birdlife. Things here are slow-paced and uncomplicated, a cultural hark-back to simpler days when you slept with the doors unlocked and ate what you farmed on the land or fished from the sea.

GETTING THERE

Planes Pick up a regular 35-minute flight to Kangaroo Island's Kingscote Airport, 14 kilometres from main town Kingscote, from Adelaide's international airport (www.aal.com.au). Rex (www.regionalexpress.com.au) and Air South (www.airsouth.com.au) fly between the two for around AU$160 return.

Boats Sealink (www.sealink.com.au) runs car ferries between Cape Jervis on the mainland and Penneshaw on KI (45 minutes each way). There are at least three ferries each way daily, costing around AU$90 return a person, plus around AU$170 return for a car.

Automobiles There's no public transport on Kangaroo Island so it's worth bringing your own wheels. If you hire a car in Adelaide, be wary that some companies won't let you take hire cars onto KI. Driving from Adelaide to Cape Jervis (the ferry departure point) takes around two hours. Alternatively, Sealink (www.sealink.com.au) runs buses between Adelaide and Cape Jervis (AU$40 return). You can also hire a car on KI with Budget (www.budgetki.com) or Hertz (www.hertz.com.au).

LOCAL KNOWLEDGE

Taxis There are no taxis on the island, but Airport Shuttle Services (0427 887 575) links Kingscote Airport with Emu Bay (AU$18), Kingscote (AU$20), American River (AU$25) and Penneshaw (AU$40). Sealink (www.sealink.com.au) runs town-to-town shuttle buses between Penneshaw and American River (AU$11) and Kingscote (AU$14).

Packing tips Take a hat and sunblock if you're hitting the beaches in summer, or a beanie if you'll be checking out the island's wildlife, clifftops and forests in winter.

Recommended reads Pete Dobré's photographic book *Kangaroo Island* captures the best of KI in gorgeous detail. *Unearthed: The Aboriginal Tasmanians of Kangaroo Island* by Shirleene Robinson digs into the

grim history of the Tasmanian Aborigines who were abducted by white sealers in the early 1800s and brought to KI. Also worth a look is *Kangaroo Island Shipwrecks* by Gifford Chapman.

Local specialities One of the best things about KI is the seafood – abundant, affordable and unfailingly fresh. Make sure you try some American River oysters and some clean-cut fillets of King George whiting. This is also farming country – the local beef, lamb and chicken are superb. There's a nascent cool-climate wine industry on KI too, with a handful of upstart wineries opening up their cellar doors for tastings (sauvignon blanc, shiraz and chardonnay are the mainstays). You'll also find cheesemakers and honey farms on the island.

Do go/don't go South Australian summers (December to February) are always sunny, but when the desert heat swoops down from the north the temperatures can top 40°C for days on end. Surrounded by the sea, KI tends to dodge the worst of the swelter, but time your visit with spring or autumn when it's clear skies, warm days and plain sailing. Winters on the island can be chilly and windswept but beautifully atmospheric. Also... Mobile phone reception on KI is patchy at best, so there's no excuse for bringing the office offshore.

WORTH GETTING OUT OF BED FOR

Viewpoint On the road to Kingscote, 25 kilometres out of Penneshaw, there's a jaunty set of stairs leading up to the top of Prospect Hill. Explorer Matthew Flinders (who named the island) used the hill as a look-out while he was mapping its shoreline. From the summit there are great vistas across to Pennington Bay.

Arts and culture KI has an emerging arts and crafts scene, with local talent hocking their wares in little galleries around the island. But what's really interesting here is the maritime and social history: check out some nautical relics at the Penneshaw Maritime & Folk Museum (www.nationaltrustsa.org.au) and colonial history at the Hope Cottage Museum (08 8553 2656) in Kingscote, a stone cottage built in 1857.

Activities On the south-west of the island, Kelly Hill Conservation Park (www.environment.sa.gov.au/parks/sanpr/kellyhill) is a collection of dry limestone caves named after a horse who fell into them in the 1880s. Tours run daily between 10.30am and 4.15pm. KI is also ideal for sampling one of the six Ss: swimming, surfing, sandboarding, snorkelling, sailing or scuba diving. Little

Sahara is an amazing area of steep sand dunes where you can go sandboarding; hire a board from Vivonne Bay General Store (08 8559 4285) on South Coast Road. Try KI Diving Safaris (08 8346 3422) for local dives with leafy sea dragons, seals and dolphins.

Best beach On the island's north shore there's a string of sheltered swimming beaches, including the sand dune-backed Emu Bay, Stokes Bay (which has a penguin rookery and protected rock pool) and photogenic Snelling Beach. Western River Cove is a small sandy nook flanked by dark stone cliffs.

Daytripper Spend a day wobbling between the island's wineries. Kick things off at quirky Chapman River Wines (08 8553 1371) at Antechamber Bay. Dudley Cellar Door (www.dudleywines.com.au) in Penneshaw bottles up a crisp chardonnay, a shiraz and a pretty good sparkling rosé. Sunset Winery (www.sunset-wines.com.au), on the Penneshaw–Kingscote Road, makes the most of its killer view-drenched hilltop position.

Children The kids will love a visit to the Penneshaw Penguin Centre (08 8553 1103), near the ferry terminal. Tours run at 7.30pm and 8.30pm from April to October; 8.30pm and 9.30pm from November to March. Bookings essential. During the day, head over to Seal Bay Conservation Park (www.environment.sa.gov.au/parks/sanpr/sealbay) on the south coast. Tours of the sea lion colony run between 9am and 4.15pm all year.

Walks Don't miss a walk around Flinders Chase National Park (www.environment.sa.gov.au/parks/sanpr/flinders chasenp/index) at the south-western end of the island, where you'll find the wind-gouged Remarkable Rocks, a couple of ageing lighthouses and Admirals Arch, an impressive span of surf-eroded rock that's a favourite for fur seals. A short drive away, the Ravine des Casoars boasts a striking walking trail by the coast.

Perfect picnic No matter what time of year you visit, you'll be able to find a stretch of beach with absolutely no one else on it. Try the beach near Vivonne Bay on the central south coast; the village has a store for picking up supplies.

Shopping No one comes to KI to shop, but some of the local produce makes worthy (and edible) souvenirs. Try some tasty sheep's cheese from Island Pure Sheep Dairy in Cygnet River (08 8553 9110), some honey ice-cream from Island Beehive (www.island-beehive.com.au) or Clifford's Honey Farm (08 8553 8295) in Haines. Emu Bay Lavender (08 8553 5338) sells biscuits and shortbread enhanced with the sweet smell and flavour of this fragrant flower.

Something for nothing It's not exactly rock 'n' roll, but here's one for history buffs. Near the Penneshaw ferry terminal on Hog Bay, you'll find a replica of Frenchman's Rock, a boulder inscribed by a sailor on French explorer Nicholas Baudin's 1803 expedition to KI. The real rock is at the visitors centre in Penneshaw (08 8553 1185).

Don't go home without... tasting some KI wine and whiting, and sniffing out the seals at Seal Bay.

KEENLY KANGAROO ISLAND

With isolation comes security, a phenomenon KI's wildlife has taken full advantage of. Rummaging through the undergrowth you'll find koalas, wallabies, bandicoots, possums, echidnas, goannas and, of course, those jumping marsupials. Offshore there are southern right whales, dolphins, fairy penguins, sea lions and New Zealand fur seals. Up above you'll catch sight of 243 known bird species, including airborne armadas of glossy black cockatoos.

DIARY

February The annual Kangaroo Island Cup (events@kin.net.au) happens in mid-February at the Cygnet River Racecourse near Kingscote. The horses do their thing, and everyone gets festive and fashionable in the party tents. **May–October** Penneshaw Farmers Market (0412 194 840) occupies Penneshaw Oval the first Sunday of the month, plus sundry other dates between November and April; call for details. **October** The Kangaroo Island Art Feast (www.tourkangarooisland.com.au/artfeast.aspx) at various venues is an annual celebration of all things artsy, craftsy and islander. **November** Kangaroo Island Speed Shears (www.kispeedshears.com) takes place over three days in Parndana, and is Australia's most lucrative sheep-shearing comp. The Shearers & Shedhand Ball kicks things off.

'Before us were craggy cliffs dropping to beaches as white as Brad Pitt's smile and lapped by the porn-star-eye-shadow-blue waters of the Southern Ocean'

Kangaroo Island

Southern Ocean Lodge

STYLE Unspoilt nature, unadulterated luxury
SETTING High above Hanson Bay

The local at the airport car rental asked where we were heading. 'Southern Ocean Lodge,' I replied. 'Lucky bastards,' he said. Ten minutes later, driving through the rolling hills, our serenity was shattered by some crazy hoon tooting and flashing his headlights. Was it a demented yokel going all *Deliverance* on us? Nope, it was the car-rental guy, pulling alongside at 80km an hour and shouting out the window that we'd left the Kangaroo Island map on his counter. 'You'll need it,' he yelled, flapping it out the window more dangerously than Paris Hilton's eyelashes on Spring Break. Given that there's only two main roads on the island this seemed unnecessary, but it came to reflect the unique, nothing's-too-much trouble character of the place.

Now with map, we continued through a spookily sexy forest and were suddenly upon the lodge. Bounding down the walkway came manager Ben, who gave Mrs Smith and I the sort of heartfelt welcome we'd expect at a mate's place. His mesmerisingly sweet wife Louise helped with the bags. Marcus parked the car. Ree offered cold towels, and the chef waved from the kitchen. We'd been there two minutes and already we knew everyone.

The lodge doors opened to the limestone-wrapped Great Room and its IMAX-sized view. Before us were craggy cliffs dropping to beaches as white as Brad Pitt's smile (and just as shallow) and lapped by the porn-star-eye-shadow-blue waters of the Southern Ocean. A glass of champagne and a salmon finger sandwich later, we trailed down the long corridor (we later dubbed it Dead Man Walking for its length and the nightly journey to an abundance of food), past rooms named after different local shipwrecks until we reached ours, Vale. 'Went down twice in one night,' Ben said reverentially. 'If only,' I thought.

Our room, an Ocean Retreat, was like a luxe beach shack, open-plan with endless windows. The timber bed rested on a cosy carpeted floor, which segued into heated limestone then a huge bathroom and Pavarotti-sized rain shower. Down a few steps was a generous lounge room complete with books, music, home-made

lamingtons and an eco-fire. This was a room designed by someone who not only has great style, but also lives like a normal person.

Even at the fanciest-schmanciest hotels, the food can be blah, but that night at dinner Mrs Smith and I thought we'd discovered the world's greatest unsung chef. Matthew Upson's food was simple and honest, impeccably cooked with an inspired imagination. And no request was too great. Mrs Smith didn't feel like steak so they did her a fish. I didn't feel like a souffle so they did me a Sixties-style Milo and ice-cream – and then asked me if I'd like them to mush it up! Even worse, I let them.

We were also surprised to find just how much of the menu came from the island: honey from the local Ligurian bees, lamb from a farm up the road, greens from the market garden over the hill. When I said I wanted the barramundi I assumed it would be an import, but our waiter explained that the local high school had established a barramundi farm. The under-rated benefits of living somewhere where there's not much for kids to do...

Up early the next day, I drew a bath in the two-person tub, pouring in a cocktail of all the local salts on offer.

In a lavender-honey-vanilla daze, I read the in-room book about our shipwreck, and gazed out the window at two eagles nesting in our midst. I'm not really a wildlife junkie, so when I wound up the platypus bath toy I thought that was probably as close to nature as I'd get. At that moment, in the waves right outside, I saw two pods of frolicking dolphins. I immediately woke Mrs Smith who sprang out of bed and onto the terrace. 'Where,' she cried. 'Near that whale?' And she wasn't joking.

Like the lodge itself, Kangaroo Island is all about the environment, so we'd organised a morning tour to see it all, including the Henry Moore-like Remarkable Rocks, a seal colony, a 'rare breeds' farm and a truly extraordinary native bush garden. Again, everyone was so unbelievably friendly and happy to see us. It was like *The Stepford Wives*, but with more dirt. After lunch on the deck it was time to rub the city out of my neck. The spa, on a nearby cliff, delivered a serene massage using local eucalyptus oils that began with an indigenous Dreamtime technique and a welcoming cleansing of smouldering gum leaves in a bowl. I was initially sceptical, but it was performed with such soul I was completely converted.

Over sunset drinks in the lounge, the staff's real pride in the place shone through. One knew the guy who carved the sculpture, another knew the names of all the wildflowers out the window. Lovable nerds, all of them, but real people and that was the secret for making everyone – the chic industrialists from Milan, the cheerily loud Californians, the super-stylish Poms and a diverse array of Aussies – feel so at ease. Back in the room we slipped into the alpaca slippers and snuggled up with chunky woven rugs. The whole place is just so frigging tactile. Then there are all the tiny details that make it perfect, even in the smallest room: the leather toilet-roll holder, mood lighting and timber shelves complete with glass sculpture and a 1974 copy of *Dinkum Aussie Dunnies* with the real inscription 'happy birthday darling Kaye, love Nanna'. This is as special a place as I've stayed in Australia, a new benchmark in how a hotel should not only look, but also feel. The staff made it lovable, the rooms made it liveable and the island made it memorable. As we were leaving, I annoyingly triple-checked with Mrs Smith to see if we had everything. 'No,' she replied. 'I'm going back to steal the hair dryer. Best hotel hair ever.' She was joking ...ish.

REVIEWED BY DAVID GRANT

NEED TO KNOW
Rooms 21 suites.

Rates AU$1,800–$3,600, including all meals, drinks, activities and airport transfers.

Check-out 10.30am, but flexible subject to availability. Check-in, 2pm.

Facilities Destination spa, outdoor plunge pool, wine cellar, library lounge with board games and DVDs, mountain bikes. In rooms: free WiFi, sound system with MP3 input, minibar, LI'TYA toiletries and outdoor terrace with day-bed. Selected suites have flatscreen TVs, DVD players and EcoSmart fires.

Children Only kids over six years old allowed. Extra beds can be provided for AU$350 when a child shares a suite with two adults.

Also There's a minimum two-night stay. Multi-night packages are available, incorporating day-spa treatments, room upgrades and private island charter tours.

IN THE KNOW
Our favourite rooms There are five grades of rooms here and unsurprisingly, top dog, the super-private Osprey Suite, is the pick of the bunch. Jaw-dropping views, separate sunken lounge, freestanding oval handmade stone bath and terrace spa, plus state-of-the-art audiovisual gadgets (including a laptop). On a more affordable tip, we also love the 11 Flinders Suites (which have dreamy day-beds for terrace chilling), and five Ocean Retreats (with fabulous freestanding tubs and fireplaces).

Hotel bar The open-plan bar in the Great Room is a curved wonder next to the restaurant. There's not just a spectacular view to drink up for free – there's also wine, beer and cocktails at your disposal. Aside from the premium cellar list (which includes Penfolds' Grange, Bollinger and Henschke's Hill of Grace), alcohol is included in room rates.

Hotel restaurant Head chef Matt Upson conjures a five-course tasting menu or four-course à la carte employing local South Australian produce and wine. Dine inside in the soothing restaurant or outdoors on the viewtastic deck. Anglers, if you manage to snare something yourself from Hanson Bay, they will also gladly fillet and cook your catch.

Top table Any of the six window-side seats lets you soak up that incredible unfettered view. On a warm night, try the sea-air-kissed terrace.

Room service Light snacks are available on request including soup, local cheese, charcuterie and fruit plates; and in-suite minibars come well stocked.

Dress code Organic linen separates in soothing neutrals will blend well with the photoshoot-fit lodge backdropped by nature.

Local knowledge KI's wildlife is world class, and if you've never seen a kangaroo, wallaby, echidna, possum, koala, goanna or New Zealand fur seal before, this is your chance. Flinders Chase and Kelly Hill National Parks offer a wealth of animal-watching activities. Try a trip to nearby Seal Bay to see its sea lion colony or opt for a Kangas & Kanapés sunset session and sip bubbly while you eyeball those bouncing critters.

LOCAL EATING AND DRINKING
The **Marron Café** (08 8559 4128) on the Harriet Road is the place to try marron, a delicate freshwater crayfish. **Rock Pool Café** (08 8559 2277) runs on a bit of a whim, but when it is open, be assured that the cheery chef will be cooking something local for lunch, such as seafood. **Penneshaw Hotel** (08 8553 1042) on the corner of North Terrace and Thomas Wilson Street is a rough-and-tumble fishermen's boozer that's had a makeover. It's reliable for a pub lunch, a low-key dinner of King George whiting or kangaroo sausages, or a quick beer while you wait for the ferry to Cape Jervis.

GET A ROOM!
Use our free online booking service: check availability and make reservations through www.mrandmrssmith.com.

 SMITH CARD OFFER AU$50 spa treatment voucher.

Southern Ocean Lodge Hanson Bay, Kangaroo Island, South Australia 5223 (02 9918 4355; www.southernoceanlodge.com.au)

WESTERN AUSTRALIA

MARGARET RIVER
Cape Lodge
NINGALOO REEF
Sal Salis Ningaloo Reef
SOUTHERN FORESTS
Stonebarn

MARGARET RIVER

COUNTRYSIDE Coastlines, cabernets and culture
COUNTRY LIFE Wine tasting and wave-riding

If Margaret River didn't exist, someone with an active imagination would have made it up. Just three hours south of Perth, the region mingles natural beauty with phenomenal dining and over 120 wineries that produce a quarter of Australia's best bottles. Your options are endless: the coastline proffers clear waters and world-class surfing, cellar doors are always open, wildflowers are abloom, and an arty heritage spills out of its many galleries. Stir into the mix a host of hearty exploits from sea-air-kissed trail walks to soul-uplifting yoga, and it's easy to see why the allure of this WA getaway is increasingly contagious.

GETTING THERE

Planes Perth Airport (www.perthairport.net.au) is the gateway to Margaret River, servicing international, domestic and regional airlines including Qantas, Jetstar, Tiger, Virgin Blue and Skywest. Air Australia International (08 9332 5011) runs charter flights to the region.

Trains TransWA (www.transwa.wa.gov.au) runs daily trains to Bunbury from Perth, which connects with the Westrail bus service that takes passengers south through Margaret River.

Automobiles Margaret River is about a three hour drive (272 kilometres) south from Perth along either the Coast Road or the South Western Highway, neither of which is a particularly inspiring route. However, a car is invaluable when exploring the region and touring the vineyards. Rentals are available at Perth Airport.

LOCAL KNOWLEDGE

Taxis You're more likely to catch a ride on the Bommy – Margaret River's fast, peeling right-hand surf break – than flag a cab down on the street. Better to book one in advance through the Margaret River Taxi & Tour Service (08 9757 3444).

Packing tips A picnic rug and corkscrew for alfresco ploughman's lunches; a snorkel and mask for exploring the waters; a camera for snapping the surf gods.

Recommended reads The Australian Wine Annual 2009, by one of the land's foremost wine writers and presenters, Jeremy Oliver, will help you tell your semillons from your sauvignons. Ray Jordan's WA Wine Guide 2009 rates and reviews the state's best wines and vineyards.

Local specialities It's only been just over 40 years since the first vines were planted in this region but already the Margaret River wineries are producing world-class premium wine. Chardonnay, cabernet sauvignon and cabernet blends are the region's most celebrated wine varieties but you'll also uncork splendid shiraz and more unconventional varietals like sangiovese and viognier.

Do go/don't go The Mediterranean climate makes the Margaret River an ideal destination year-round. In summer, temperatures rarely creep above 32°C and in winter average around 18°C during the day, although it can be a touch chilly at night. This is a popular holiday destination, which gets very busy at Easter, Christmas and during major events, so book well ahead.

Also... For an alternative view of the area, canoe up the Margaret River with Bushtucker Tours (www.bushtuckertours.com), while exploring Aboriginal culture and feasting on wild foods. Trips depart from Prevelly Beach at the river mouth, running 10am–2pm, and costing AU$80 for adults.

WORTH GETTING OUT OF BED FOR

Viewpoint It's a bit of a drive but the view from Cape Leeuwin Lighthouse, the tallest on mainland Australia, is worth it (www.margaretriver.com). This is where the Indian and Southern Oceans meet and the area is teeming with incredible wildlife including sea lions, dolphins and whales.

Arts and culture All that wine is obviously proving inspirational as the region is peppered with some great galleries representing local and Western Australian artists. Yallingup Galleries (www.yallingupgalleries.com.au) and Gunyulgup Galleries (www.gunyulgupgalleries.com.au) are both excellent and exhibit paintings, prints, ceramics and glass. For contemporary fine art head to the Purist Gallery (www.puristgallery.com).

Activities Margaret River is the surfing capital of Western Australia, so why not learn to cut some waves like the locals? The coastline between Capes Naturaliste and Leeuwin offers clean waters, world-class rips and year-round powerful reef breaks (mainly left handers). There are a number of small beach breaks perfect for inexperienced and novice surfers too. Yallingup Surf School is a good port of call, offering group, private and couples classes, as well as three-day courses (www.yallingupsurfschool.com).

Daytripper Several hundred caves lie within the craggy limestone coastline but only a handful are open to the public. Of these the most famous are the multi-chambered Mammoth Cave, which was first discovered in 1850, and the enormous Jewel and sparkling, crystalline Lake Caves (www.margaretriver.com).

Best beach Margaret River's sublime beaches should tempt you away from winery-hopping. Eagle Bay offers kaleidoscopic snorkelling opportunities, Yallingup Beach has a sheltered lagoon and Meelup, near Dunsborough, is another great swimming spot. Diving here is also excellent, with the purposely scuttled HMAS *Swan* wreck a big draw.

Perfect picnic Pack your picnic hamper with brie and camembert from the Margaret River Dairy Company (www.mrdc.com.au), grab a bottle of your favourite wine and get set for some alfresco dining either on the beach or near the vines.

Walks At 135 kilometres, the spectacular coastal and forest Cape to Cape Walk (www.capetocapetrack.com.au) might be too much of a schlep but there are plenty of access points along the way, so you can join the track for as little or as long as you like; maps are available from the visitor centre (www.margaretriver.com).

Children A handful of wineries such as Xanadu (www.xanaduwines.com) and Cape Mentelle (www.capementelle.com.au) have play areas to keep the kids occupied while you get busy behind the cellar door. The Yallingup Shearing Shed will have everyone oohing and aahing at the baby lambs (www.margaretriver.com), and at the Wonky Windmill Farm & Eco Park (www.wonkywindmillfarm.com.au), little ones can hang out and feed pigs, ponies, alpacas and emus. Lose the kids – temporarily – in the Yallingup Maze (www.yallingupmaze.com.au), a tricky modern wooden tower- and bridge-studded course.

Shopping If there's room in your case after visiting the vineyards then head to the amiable town of Margaret River to check out its galleries and boutiques. At the Natural Olive Oil Soap Factory (www.oliveoilsoapfactory.com.au), watch their feel-good body products being made on the factory floor and snap 'em up afterwards.

Something for nothing This area is a fisherman's dream so the options for catching your own dinner are endless. Cast your rod from a boat, jetty or riverbank and you'll find bream, herring and yellowfin whiting snapping at your line.

Don't go home without... visiting a local winery. Big names such as Leeuwin Estate (www.leeuwinestate.com.au), Xanadu (www.xanaduwines.com) and Voyager Estate (www.voyagerestate.com.au) are here but it's worth exploring the smaller cellar doors too. If you're unfamiliar with the tipples that hail from here, the Regional Wine Centre (www.mrwines.com) can point you in the right direction. Cape Mentelle (www.capementelle.com.au) offers a superb lunch to accompany your viognier, Windance (www.windance.com.au) produces one of the best semillon sauvignon blancs in the region and Amberley Estate (www.amberleyestate.com.au) is worth visiting for the views alone.

MARVELLOUSLY MARGARET RIVER

Despite being one of the great wine-producing regions of the world, the original vines were only planted in Margaret River in the late 1960s. In 1967, Dr Tom Cullity successfully planted the first acres of cabernet sauvignon, riesling, malbec and hermitage on his property, resulting in the birth of the Vasse Felix vineyard (www.vassefelix.com.au). Just four years later the winery won its first award and subsequently released its debut commercial offering, and with that the Margaret River wine industry was born.

DIARY

January–March Look out for open-air concerts at Leeuwin Estate (www.leeuwinestate.com.au). **March–April** Surfers do their thing at the Margaret River Pro (www.drugawarepro.com). **April** Winemakers do theirs during the Margaret River Wine Region Festival (www.margaretriverfestival.com). **April–October** is also the best time to see Western Australia's wildflowers and rare orchids in bloom. **June and September** Humpback and southern right whales pass the coastline during this time. **November** Leeuwin Estate celebrates the end of the pruning season with its annual Burning of the Vine Cuttings celebration.

'All eyes are focused on the ocean, looking for the telltale spouts of water, and it's not long before we see our first whale'

Yallingup

Cape Lodge

STYLE Classic country club
SETTING Elegant lake-studded Eden

Waking up at four in the morning is only ever acceptable when you're jetting off for a dirty weekend. This was to be Mr Smith's and my first trip to Western Australia, and the anticipation of arriving at the renowned Margaret River wine region was enough to keep us in great spirits despite the godforsaken hour of our flight to Perth. By 10am, we've crammed our over-packed case into the tiny rental car, Mr Smith is behind the wheel, the iPod is connected, and I've assumed the role of navigator, a task I always approach with trepidation. With about five different maps scattered around me, including one very large, detailed and thus confusing road atlas, I am ready to guide us to Cape Lodge. I think.

Three hours later we turn into the long driveway – vineyards on one side, tall eucalyptus trees on the other – leading up to the magnificent hotel (ornate entrances seem mandatory around here). Minutes later, we're shown to our Forest Spa Suite and it delivers on every level: it's spacious, with lofty ceilings, a huge bed and underfloor heating in the bathroom. When I discover the Jacuzzi, overlooking the lake and trees, I can't contain my squeals of delight. As I skip out with a smile, Mr Smith plants a G&T in my hand. The getaway has begun.

Our first wine tasting is scheduled for 5.30pm in the hotel's lounge. Visions of a room filled with people fighting to get another sip of free wine have been niggling in the recesses of my mind, so I'm surprised to find Mr Smith and I are the only guests hunkering down in the plush chairs. We're served a Cape Lodge sauv blanc and a shiraz and are left to explore the delicate flavours of the local wines. After a quick dinner at a local restaurant we feel the pull of our king-size bed, and soon enough we're slipping into our luxurious sheets, exhausted but satisfied.

Mr Smith can hardly believe it when the alarm goes at 7.30am the next morning. It's early for a workday, never mind while we're on holiday, but we have big plans. In my humble opinion, the size and quality of breakfast should be inversely proportional to the hour of the day you wake up, and this morning's ticks all the right boxes:

a gourmet experience, classical music in the background and a serene lake view. The only downside was that we had to rush to make an appointment with a whale.

After an hour's drive we arrive at Augusta, where we spot a scarily small boat moored at the jetty. Mr Smith seems ill just looking at it, but then realises it's only taking us out to a much larger boat – one that won't be so easily swallowed by the largest mammal on earth. With 16 people on board, we set off to spot humpback and southern right whales. The swells are quite large, so I fix my gaze on the horizon in an effort to avoid seasickness (we've been branded 'daredevils' by our fellow passengers for taking up a perhaps foolhardy position on the bow).

All eyes are focused on the ocean, looking for the telltale spouts of water, and it's not long before we see our first whale. They're not particularly shy creatures, and soon another curious beastie is popping its head out of the water to take a peek at us. It is as incredible as anything I've ever witnessed. After two hours and eight or nine whale sightings, and with the threat of an approaching storm, we head back to shore. Feeling invigorated by the whales and the sea air, Mr Smith and I agree on the beautiful Leeuwin Estate for some wine tasting and food. Outside on the terrace we fall in love with the oaky Art Series chardonnay, the estate-baked bread served with Olio Bello Leccino extra virgin olive oil, and the chocolate fondant.

Back at Cape Lodge, Mr Smith has secretly organised for an indulgent prelude to dinner: a bottle of champagne in the room. Now, I decide, is the perfect time to rejuvenate in that hot tub with its views of the lake. A bottle of fizz and a very bubbly bath later, we saunter off to eat (again). There is a sophisticated charm to the lakeside restaurant, from the lilting Mozart to the lovely French waiters. We may stand out from the other diners, being the youngest couple here, but this doesn't stop the entire experience being excellent. Mr Smith is hooked on the butter-poached marron (it's a freshwater crayfish farmed locally), and a dish of pork prepared three ways wins me over, as does the accompanying Cape Lodge sauv blanc. A slice of chocolate torte later, and we retreat, ever so slowly, back to our suite, agreeing that the holiday has taken a decidedly gourmet turn.

Breakfast the next morning is a leisurely affair and Mr Smith comments that we've come dangerously close to committing the second deadly sin on this break. Of course, it doesn't stop us from asking if we can take one of the strawberry and dark chocolate muffins for the road. The cherry on our weekend cake is being handed a beautifully tied box with two of the delicious muffins inside. We wind down the windows and drive slowly away, the parcel safely on the back seat – along with a couple of bottles of Cape Lodge wine, of course.

REVIEWED BY MR & MRS SMITH

'A slice of chocolate torte later, and we retreat, ever so slowly, back to our suite'

NEED TO KNOW

Rooms 22, including 17 suites. Or hire out the luxe Vineyard Residence, a three-bedroom private house with a two-bedroom Guest House attached.

Rates Low season, AU$325–$575; high season, AU$475–$695, including breakfast and afternoon tea. Rates for the Vineyard Residence start from AU$1,500 per night; and the Guest House from AU$525 per night. Two-night minimum stays apply at weekends.

Check-out 11am. Check-in, 3pm.

Facilities DVD, CD and book library, WiFi throughout, tennis court, croquet lawn, outdoor pool, 16-hectare gardens, vineyard. In rooms: flatscreen TV, DVD/CD players, minibar, Natural Olive Oil Soap Factory toiletries.

Children This hotel isn't suited to kids, so leave the smalls with grandma.

Also If you're a foodie, take advantage of one of Cape Lodge's monthly gourmet weekends featuring cooking classes and demonstrations, picnics and wine tastings.

IN THE KNOW

Our favourite rooms King-size beds, spa baths, modern decor and artworks in all bedrooms ensure a luxe touch. We like the cosy Garden View Rooms for their angled eaves, bay windows and private courtyards overlooking the gardens. If you're travelling in a group, we recommend the three-bedroom Vineyard Residence for its vast walk-in wardrobe, two swish bathrooms and secluded gardens with a lake. It accommodates three couples, or five if you book the adjoining Guest House, which has its own bathroom. The open-plan kitchen and dining area is ideal for a private cooking class with pals; the helipad makes for an impressive entrance.

Hotel bar Separated from the main restaurant by a roaring fireplace, the bar teams comfy sofas with serene lake views; perfect for working your way through the wine list.

Hotel restaurant Executive chef Tony Howell keeps both guests and critics raving at the lakeside Cape Lodge Restaurant, the jewel in the hotel's crown. An emphasis on fresh local produce, the daily-changing modern Australian menu and the famous 14,000-bottle, temperature-controlled wine cellar mean reservations are a must.

Top table Ask for a table on the deck, which stretches over the lake.

Room service Available 11am–10pm, with gourmet platters, sandwiches and a fuller evening menu on offer.

Dress code Country-club chic. Blazers and boaters for croquet, huge sunglasses for alfresco dining.

Local knowledge The much-vaunted Margaret River wine region beckons. Respected producers in the neighbourhood include Vasse Felix (www.vassefelix.com.au), Moss Wood (www.mosswood.com.au), Cullen (www.cullenwines.com.au) and Pierro (www.pierro.com.au), all of which offer tastings and the chance to buy fine local wines at the cellar door. The pristine beaches nearby are the perfect hangover cure, whether you fancy serious surfing or just a quick dip.

LOCAL EATING AND DRINKING

Inspired by his father's apothecary, chef Simon Beaton and his partner Flip Boreham have created the **Food Farmacy** (08 9759 1877), in Dunsborough, a quirky eatery where water is served in a conical flask and test tubes of salt, pepper, sugar and oil hang in wooden racks. With wall-to-wall bottles snaking around a minimal space, wine bar **Must Margaret River** (08 9758 8877) is a chic spot for a drink, but its bistro is also open for lunch and dinner daily.

GET A ROOM!

Use our free online booking service: check availability and make reservations through www.mrandmrssmith.com.

 SMITH CARD OFFER A gift pack of Cape Lodge Estate wine on departure.

Cape Lodge Caves Road, Yallingup, Western Australia 6282 (08 9755 6311; www.capelodge.com.au)

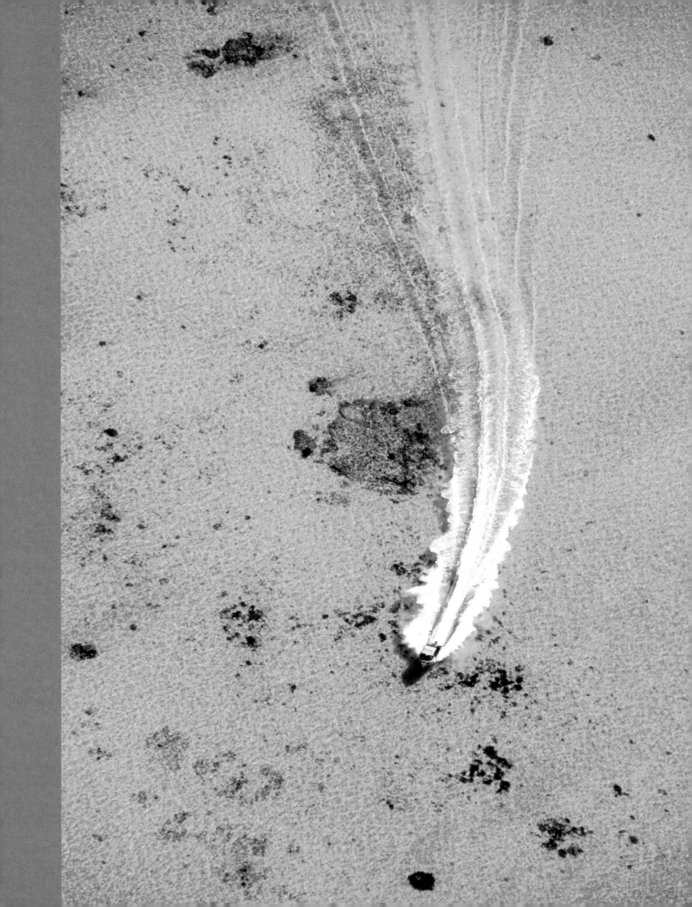

NINGALOO REEF

COASTLINE Dune-backed beaches, reef-fringed sea
COAST LIFE Weighty whale shark watching

The tourist hoards may head for Queensland's Great Barrier Reef, but those in the know are talking up Ningaloo – a remote yet ravishing reef off the coast of Western Australia where you can swim among rainbow fish and psychedelic coral just metres from shore. No boat trips or long schleps are necessary here: just swim, snorkel or kayak out, and the madly beautiful underwater world is yours for the taking. The Ningaloo Marine Park stretches for 280 kilometres south along the North-West Cape, flanked by national park and edged by white-sand beaches and a dramatic desert hinterland of classically Aussie red crags and gorges. It couldn't be more of a contrast with the vibrant aquatic life offshore. To top it all off, this is the best place on earth to see, and swim with, whale sharks, gentle giants which are the world's largest fish.

GETTING THERE

Planes Skywest Airlines (www.skywest.com.au) flies daily between Perth and Exmouth (1 hour 45 minutes) and weekly from Broome. Exmouth's Learmonth Airport is 37 kilometres south of the town of Exmouth itself; Sal Salis Ningaloo Reef is 70 kilometres south of Exmouth (an hour's drive). A regular shuttle bus runs between the airport and Exmouth, or you can arrange private transfers to meet flights.

Automobiles Driving the 1,270 kilometres from Perth to Exmouth will take about 16 hours, so most folk fly in. Hire a car at Learmonth Airport from Budget (www.budget.com.au) or Europcar (www.europcar.com.au), or in Exmouth itself from Avis (www.avis.com.au).

LOCAL KNOWLEDGE

Taxis This ain't NYC, so don't expect to hail anything other than passing fish. Transport chez Ningaloo is on a BYO basis, so hire a car or contact Exmouth Visitor Centre (www.exmouthwa.com.au) to join a tour.

Packing tips Your best bikini/trunks, mask, snorkel, goggles and an underwater camera. You'll be doing most of your socialising under water, with mainly marine life to impress.

Recommended reads *Whale Sharks: The Giants of Ningaloo Reef* by Geoff Taylor will help you bone up on this ridiculously cool creature, which is solitary, speckled and feeds on plankton through its mega-wide mouth. If Ningaloo had book clubs, this tome would be in constant rotation. Alex Garland's Thailand-set *The Beach* may be an oldie, but it's still the most gripping novel about escaping to a mythically amazing beach we know (although a paradise that turns sour).

Local specialities Feast on fresh fish and shellfish, especially locally caught prawns and rock lobster. On the drinks side, look out for Chapman Valley Wines – Western Australia's most northerly winery, mind you, it's a 10-hour drive south of Ningaloo.

Do go/don't go It's warm and sunny year-round, with slightly cooler temperatures from July to September (22–32 degrees) and things hotting up from January to March (32–38 degrees). The Indian Ocean here stays a peachy 24–26 degrees. Visit in March and

April to catch the coral spawning or between April and July to see the whale sharks.

Also... Swim smart: there are dangerous currents along this coast, so check conditions are safe before you dive in (otherwise, it's next stop, Indonesia...).

WORTH GETTING OUT OF BED FOR

Viewpoint Catch a sunset, vistas of Ningaloo Reef or glimpses of passing humpback whales from the hill beside Vlamingh Head Lighthouse, 17 kilometres north of Exmouth. The best views here though are subaquatic. Paddle a sea kayak out to the Blue Lagoon, off South Mandu Beach, a five-metre-deep natural aquarium where you can gaze down as fish and turtles frolic and coral fronds waft.

Arts and culture The world's oldest necklace was found in a cave in the Cape Range National Park, but short of stumbling upon Aboriginal relics this area is more about nature than culture. To learn about threatened turtles call into the Jurabi Turtle Centre (www.ningalooturtles. org.au), 13 kilometres from Exmouth between Hunters and clothing-optional Mauritius Beaches.

Activities Ningaloo is swimming and snorkelling heaven with pristine beaches and reefs at your flipper-tips. Expect to spy anemones, clownfish, rays, staghorn coral and sponge gardens below the waves. To snorkel with whale sharks you'll need to join a boat trip from Exmouth or Coral Bay. Try Ningaloo Blue Charters (08 9949 1119), which also offers fishing, or Ningaloo Reef Dreaming (08 9949 4777), which uses a spotter plane to locate whale sharks, and can also take you scuba diving. To view the eye-popping coral, we suggest a glass-bottom boat trip: Ningaloo Ecology Cruises (08 9949 2255) leaves from Tantabiddi Beach near Exmouth. Outside the waters of the marine park, you'll find Australia's best bonefishing: see what you can catch with Blue Horizon Fishing and Dive Charters (08 9949 1620). Scuba is also rated round here, with the Navy Pier dive a favourite: Ningaloo Whaleshark 'n' Dive (08 9949 1116) offers dives, plus swimming with manta rays and humpback whale spotting. If kayaking's more your speed, contact Capricorn Sea Kayaking (www.capricorn seakayaking.com.au) for one-day or longer reef trips where you can encounter turtles, dugongs and dolphins.

Best beach South Mandu Beach, near Mandu Mandu Gorge Road, is as pristine as you get, backed by dunes and light scrub with the reef a short swim out.

Lakeside suits kids and Oyster Stacks is good for snorkelling at high tide. For information on current-free beaches, pop into the Milyering Visitor Centre (08 9949 2808), in Cape Range National Park, which provides maps and sells and hires out snorkelling kit.

Daytripper Head down to Coral Bay, at the southern edge of the marine park, an appealingly tiny town perched on a gorgeous bay. Its Main Beach is safe for swimming as it's protected by an encircling reef, with snorkelling gear, glass-bottom canoes and body boards up for hire. From Coral Bay, you can snorkel with manta rays or swim with whale sharks from Ningaloo Experience's speedy catamaran (www.ningaloo experience.com) or with Coral Bay Adventures (www. coralbayadventures.com.au), who also offer coral-viewing trips and humpback whale watching in season.

Children When they're bored of sandcastles, distract the nippers with a guided cruise or one-and-a-half-kilometre round-trip walk to Yardie Creek, a red limestone-lined, water- and mangrove-filled gorge that draw birds, marine animals and thirsty black-footed rock wallabies. Find it at the end of the sealed Yardie Creek Road or contact Exmouth's DEC–Yardie Creek Tours (08 9947 8000) or Ningaloo Safari Tours (www.ningaloosafari.com) for cruises.

Walks Two kilometres behind luxury wilderness camp Sal Salis Ningaloo Reef, a walk up Mandu Mandu Gorge makes for an inspiring three-kilometre return ramble. When you're not cooing over ancient limestone formations and fossils, you'll be sneaking peeks at the too-blue coastline.

Perfect picnic Tough call: you've got the whole of the 510-square-kilometre Cape Range National Park, as well as the wave-lapped beaches of Ningaloo Marine Park, to choose from. For scenic views on the east coast, self-drive either along the ridge of Charles Knife Canyon or the base of Shothole Canyon, which are 23 and 16 kilometres south of Exmouth respectively.

Shopping Retail opportunities round these remote parts are mainly of the diving, surfing and camping variety (Ningaloo Reef isn't on Prada's radar yet). You'll find what little shopping there is (and ATMs) in local towns Exmouth, around Maidstone Crescent, and Coral Bay, on Robinson Street.

Something for nothing Far removed from city light pollution, Ningaloo is a star-gazer's idyll. Lie back on a dune and try and count 'em all. Wildlife sightings come for free too: any short stroll should flush out a few red kangaroos, wallaroos, wallabies, Gould's goannas, birds or even emus.

Don't go home without... snorkelling at Turquoise Bay; if you walk south along the beach and swim out about 40 metres you can drift with the current over the coral and fab fish before hopping out at a sand bar and pressing repeat (always check for rips first though).

NATURALLY NINGALOO

Whale sharks are the big attraction here; they love to chow down on the spawning coral along Ningaloo's coastline. These slow-moving beasties may seem intimidating because of their size: they can grow up to 12 metres in length and weigh about 18 tonnes, plus they have a huge mouth, around 1.5 metres wide. Like whales though, they're actually harmless filter feeders who eat plankton, algae and krill – but not humans. In fact, they're happy for you to swim alongside them. The whale sharks may be headline news here, but the coral is pretty amazing too, with over 200 species of fantastically formed hard coral which spawn in sync during March and April (hermaphroditic branches ejecting eggs and sperm into the water). You don't see that every day.

DIARY

March–April Snorkel or dive in to catch the incredible mass coral spawning, about 10 to 12 days after the full moon in both months. **Late March/April–July** Swim with whale sharks as they visit Ningaloo's waters. **May-November** Don flippers and hang out with mesmerising manta rays. **July–November** Humpback whales can be spotted offshore as they migrate first north, then back south again. **November–February** Four species of turtle, including hawksbill, loggerhead, flatback and green, lay their eggs on the beach at night, with hatchlings popping out about 40 days later.

'I'd slipped on the budgie-smugglers and we were in the warm lagoon, be-snorkelled and drifting with the tide across corals'

Cape Range
National Park

Sal Salis Ningaloo Reef

STYLE Seaside safari, barefoot luxury
SETTING Cape Range coastal dunes

You know that scene in the movie *The Adventures of Priscilla, Queen of the Desert* where the three drag queens are wheeling their designer luggage down a dirt trail in the middle of nowhere? That was us arriving at Sal Salis, Ningaloo Reef. Mercifully, our guide Mike appeared over the hill in a golf buggy and drove our bags down the long track to the campsite. We, however, opted to stroll, and a good choice too. The walk was perfect foreplay, the heavy breathing of the ocean breaking on the distant reef, the sexy panting of the kangaroos and emus that padded across our path, the teasing salty sea spray off the beach. Then, as we rounded the last dune, it was love at first sight, as flawless sand met wild bush.

Now, I'm no camper, but Mrs Smith is. I think camping is seat 2B on the plane, and had considered eco to be bleako. Until Sal Salis, that is. The rustic romance of our very large, airy tent re-educated me. Polished timber floors, soft rugs, a Depression-era set of cane drawers, an old tree trunk hung with plush bathrobes, and what turned out to be one of the best beds we'd ever slept in... anywhere. Best of all, there was a bathroom, with

a lantern-lit mirror, a solar-heated shower and a luxurious, eco-friendly composting loo.

Soon Mrs Smith was decked out in her new cossie, I'd slipped on the budgie-smugglers and we were in the warm lagoon, be-snorkelled and drifting with the tide across corals of every colour as turtles, fish, stingrays and reef sharks whizzed by. Unfortunately, we'd just missed whale shark season – those massive gentle giants only migrate through here between April and July.

The landscape at Sal Salis is a striking convergence of environments, where the rugged ancient limestone ridge of Cape Range, red earth and white desert dunes meet the beach, with a reef that starts just five metres off the shore. It's the only place in the world where coral meets mainland like this, which means you can just swim out or kayak short distances to experience more diverse marine action than a spa party at the Playboy Mansion.

We escaped to our tent for a quick read and a dribbling nap in the two-person hammock on our veranda, followed by a hot shower and an audience with a kangaroo joey (strangely exciting for a Freudian who enjoyed *Skippy* as a child). Then it was time for canapés in the 'glamping' mothership, which looked like a shearing shed with its side blown off by Cyclone Tracey. This open-air living room is also the home of the camp kitchen, and has plenty of places to hide away for a snooze, browse through the library's reference books, or challenge the unsuspecting to a hand of cards. That's the great thing about Sal Salis – it's all about space, peace, remoteness, you and what you feel like doing. You can be private one minute, social the next; sporty in the morning, comatose in the arvo.

Our chefs kept the canapés and cocktails coming. I had to remind the lobster-scoffing Mrs Smith that dinner was still to come as we enjoyed a glass of bubbly, barefoot, watching an Hawaiian shirt sunset over the water. We then walked the exhausting two metres to a table that twinkled with lanterns, coral, shells and wildflowers. There was nothing Outback about the food, with local

'We were befriended by a kangaroo with a bit of sparkling mica sand stuck to his fur'

delicacies turned into dishes that felt more gourmet restaurant than canvas café.

Mrs Smith and I took our nightcaps to the top of the highest sand dune. There, we were befriended by a kangaroo with a bit of sparkling mica sand stuck to his fur. 'The only grey in the village,' we mused. Soon, we were joined by a couple of other guests and our guide Mike, who whipped out some astronomy gizmo that humanised the million points of light above us. You simply flashed the glowing red box at any random star (well, it's worked for Madonna for decades), the machine identified it and printed out everything there was to know about it, both the technical and the mythical. Does Uranus look big in this? Actually, it did.

The camp's resident butcherbird woke us early the next morning for a sunrise walk through Mandu Mandu Gorge. The name means 'many rocks' in the local indigenous language (how do they come up with them?), and they weren't bloody kidding. But it was well worth it – serene, crammed with petite wildflowers and native mistletoe (perfect for a bush pash, I'll miss that guide Carly!), black-footed rock wallabies and, atop the gorge, a rewarding view down over the beach and reef on one side and the desert on the other.

But we didn't need the mistletoe to fall in love with Sal Salis. Apart from the obvious physical attraction, there was the staff who were just so friendly and genuinely passionate about eco-tourism, the area and its wildlife. Seriously, our guide almost cried when he narrowly missed a kamikaze emu heading for our four-wheel drive on the way back to camp. Me? I was thinking, 'Could you get a belt AND a wallet out of that? Or do we need to run over two of them?'

REVIEWED BY DAVID GRANT

NEED TO KNOW

Rooms Five tents, including one suite.

Rates AU$1,460–$1,610, including return road transfers from Exmouth or Learmonth, all meals, drinks and guided activities (snorkelling, kayaking, visits to Yardie Creek and gorge walks).

Check-out 11am, but flexible. Check-in, 2pm.

Facilities Library, snorkelling gear. In rooms: 500-threadcount organic cotton bedlinen, hand-made native-herb soap, eco-friendly toiletries, ensuite with Nature Loo (composting toilet) and hand-pumped shower, fan, hammock. All power is solar-generated and there is no WiFi access or mobile phone reception.

Children Sal Salis welcomes kids aged four and over and can provide extra beds for AU$342 a child a night, when sharing.

Also There's a minimum two-night stay. If you're planning an intimate beach wedding, hire out the whole camp and throw a romantic reception on the deck of the main lodge, lit by lanterns with ocean views.

IN THE KNOW

Our favourite rooms Set in the dunes about 30 metres from the sea, the five spacious tents are all perched on individual wooden platforms with ensuites at the back and a private deck out front (jostle with visiting kangaroos for the shade). Tents 1 to 3 are at the same level as the main camp, with 4 and 5 higher on the dunes – giving a better view of the sea but slightly further away. Our top tips are 1 or 5 for maximum privacy as they only have one neighbour. The suite tent (number 5) comes with a semi-enclosed extended deck, ideal for either families (it can fit two swag beds for children) or honeymooners who fancy a larger lounge. Although comfortable, this is 'wild bush luxury', so don't expect all mod cons.

Hotel bar Help yourself to soft drinks, wine, beer and spirits from the informal bar in the main lounge.

Hotel restaurant Guests dine together, hosted by staff, in the intimate main lodge, decked out with driftwood and shells. But just because you're camping doesn't mean you have to eat beans on toast; in fact, you're more likely to be feasting on teriyaki emu rice paper rolls, baked Exmouth ruby snapper with wild lime beurre blanc or grilled lamb with blackberry sauce. Chefs whip up bush-influenced fare using local ingredients whenever possible.

Top table Swapping stories round the communal table is all part of the fun here, but if you fancy romantic dining à deux, ask to eat out at the little lantern-lit table atop a nearby dune under the stars.

Room service There's no room service, but the main lodge dining area is just a short walk away.

Dress code Bush basics not bling – pack Steve Irwin-style shorts and fleeces, rather than fancy threads.

Local knowledge Swim, snorkel or kayak out to Ningaloo Reef, a teaming rainbow of fish, dolphins, turtles and spawning corals just metres from shore. It's the best place in the world to swim with whale sharks, huge but hippie-peaceful beasts which migrate past from April to July (the hotel can hook you up with local boat trips to see them, at extra cost). You can also swim with manta rays and spot humpback whales (July to September). On shore, stroll the pure white beaches or opt for a guided walk in the Cape Range National Park, a wild hinterland of rock, gorges and desert.

LOCAL EATING AND DRINKING

It's seriously remote here, so unless you plan to start hunting, indigenous-style, your only option is to eat in. The nearest town, Exmouth, is an hour's drive to the north.

GET A ROOM!

Use our free online booking service: check availability and make reservations through www.mrandmrssmith.com.

 SMITH CARD OFFER Complimentary one-way scenic charter flight from Exmouth Learmonth Airport to Sal Salis Ningaloo Reef (for a minimum two-night stay with two people travelling together).

Sal Salis Ningaloo Reef Yardie Creek Road, Cape Range National Park via Exmouth, Western Australia 6707
(02 9571 6399; www.salsalis.com.au)

SOUTHERN FORESTS

COUNTRYSIDE Towering trees and wildflowers
COUNTRY LIFE Trekking and truffle hunting

A small area cultivating a big reputation, WA's Southern Forests is a nature- and food-lover's paradise. Chill out, by wandering majestic woods of giant karri, jarrah and marri trees – the star attraction here, blanketed with wildflowers in spring – or go fishing in pristine rivers. To refuel, sample world-class wineries or savour fruits from the largest trufferie in the southern hemisphere. Relax in the region's small towns Pemberton and Manjimup, or head for the stunning nearby coast, where wild heath clings to rolling sand dunes and rocky cliffs drop into the ocean. Margaret River's famous vineyards further west may be more established, but this region is on the up, so get in on the ground floor. Or rather, the forest floor...

GETTING THERE

Planes Western Australia's capital, Perth, is the gateway to the Southern Forests, serviced by regular flights from all major Australian cities with Qantas (www.qantas.com.au), Virgin Blue (www.virginblue.com.au) and Jetstar (www.jetstar.com). Air Australia (www.airaustralia.net) operates charter flights from Perth's Jandakot airport to Manjimup, north of Pemberton, in the Southern Forests.

Trains TransWA (www.transwa.wa.gov.au) runs daily trains from Perth, south to coastal Bunbury, which then connects with the Westrail bus service that will take you to Pemberton.

Automobiles It takes a leisurely five hours to drive the 300 kilometres from Perth to the Southern Forests region along the South Western Highway. Local bus services are available but a car is far more flexible for exploring off-piste. Hire one at Perth Airport or in nearby Margaret River. Smith members get a discount with Hertz (www.hertz.com).

LOCAL KNOWLEDGE

Taxis You'll need to call cabs in this rural area. Try Manjimup Taxi Service (04 1894 9936).

Packing tips Boots: a pair of Hunters for wet winters and Neoprenes in summer (for when you go swimming in pebbly rivers and lakes).

Recommended reads *Those Karri Days*, by local author Phil Radomiljac, tells the history of this forest-tastic area's timber industry up to the present day. *Settlers, Fishers and All Sorts* is a collection of stories about the region's quirky community by Jane Muir.

Local specialities The black truffle rules here and when it's in season you'll find menus dominated by the expensive little fungus, including scrambled eggs, salt and pepper squid, and even pannacotta. The region loves it so much that out of season you'll discover dishes using truffle honey, truffle butter, truffle oil and more. Other players in these parts are trout and marron, a large freshwater crayfish and a delicacy only found in this corner of Australia. This is also one of Oz's premier cool-climate wine regions, producing grape varieties such as merlot, sauvignon blanc, chardonnay and shiraz.

Do go/don't go With a temperate climate year-round, any time is good to visit; temperatures rarely exceed 32°C in summer (when the cool forest canopy provides relief from the sun) and winters are mild but wet – so bring a brolly and curl up in front of a cosy log fire. To see the region's famous wildflowers and orchids come in spring (October to December), or to enjoy another Southern Forests speciality – fresh truffles – time your trip between June and August.

And... On a wildlife tip, early morning and dusk are the best times to spot the area's numerous kangaroos on the hop, while whales can be seen off the coast between June and September. Don't bring your dog, unless you intend to keep it on a lead, as there is fox bait everywhere.

WORTH GETTING OUT OF BED FOR

Viewpoint If you dare, climb to the top of an ancient karri tree (once used as look-outs for bushfires), although vertigo sufferers and the less agile might not fancy the precarious 50- to 75-metre ascents. The three most famous are the Diamond Tree between Manjimup and Pemberton, the Bicentennial Tree in Warren National Park and the Gloucester Tree in Gloucester National Park.

Arts and culture If you'd rather keep your feet firmly on the ground, wander the 1.2-kilometre Southern Forest Sculpture Walk (www.southernforests.com.au), near Northcliffe, which displays specially commissioned local and international art, sculpture, poetry and music.

Activities Check out any of the numerous national parks nearby, all of which have walking paths of varying difficulty, meandering through towering forests, past waterfalls and around lakes. If you're not an outdoorsy type, indulge in a pampering session at Mudstone Day Spa which offers a hydrotherapy bath with forest views (www.mudstone.com.au). For gourmands, the Wine and Truffle Company (www.wineandtruffle.com.au) can arrange a hunt for those tasty fungal treasures (from June to August; bookings essential).

Daytripper Drive a little way down the coast to the tranquil inlet town of Walpole, bordered by Walpole-Nornalup National Park, home to the Valley of the Giants Treetops Walk (www.valleyofthegiants.com.au). The 600-metre ramp gradually rises up from the forest floor to a 40-metre-high walkway suspended above the forest canopy, offering bird's-eye views. Also in the National Park, take the scenic drive to Mount Frankland where you can climb to the summit before cooling off in Circular Pool on the Frankland River further along the

track. WOW Wilderness Cruise (www.wowwilderness. com.au) offers boats trips through the pretty inlets, complete with entertaining commentary about Aboriginal life in the area, shipwrecked pirates and salmon fishermen.

Best beach Show off your strokes at Mandalay Beach, 12 kilometres west of Walpole, a rugged, sandy beach which is also the site of the 1911 shipwreck of Norwegian barque 'Mandalay' that gave the beach its name.

Children Take the kids fishing for trout and marron in Big Brook Dam, then cook your catch for lunch at one of the handy gas barbecues on the shore. Hire fishing gear from the general store in Pemberton (08 9776 1151). Cool off later in Fonty's Pool (www.fontyspool. com.au), a picturesque natural swimming hole set in lovely grounds between Manjimup and Pemberton.

Walks Got itchy feet? Hit the Warren National Park and the Heartbreak and Maidenbush Trails should get your juices flowing. If you're feeling really energetic, the 1,000-kilometre Bibbulmun Track (www. bibbulmuntrack.org.au) passes through here. It's one of the world's longest walking tracks, stretching between Kalamunda and Albany, and takes about eight weeks to cover in full. Don't worry, it can be tackled in stages.

Perfect picnic Pick up some dips and smoked delights from Holy Smoke (see 'Shopping') and some local wine from a cellar door, and head to any of the area's enticing national parks. Our top tip is to take the well-signposted Karri Forest Explorer Drive Trail, which starts just

outside timber town Pemberton, and wends past Big Brook Dam (an ideal picnic spot), Beedelup Falls, the 60-metre Gloucester Tree look-out and several wineries (for details see www.pembertontourist.com.au).

Shopping Buy gourmet goodies from popular local company Holy Smoke (08 9771 8822; www.holysmoke.com.au), including delicious smoky dips, duck, chicken and fish. Another gourmand's playground is the Wine & Truffle Company (08 9777 2474), which will satisfy your every truffle desire. Foodies should also look out for the regular farmers market in Manjimup (usually held on the third Saturday of each month). For floral- and fruit-infused food, soap and oils, try the Lavender & Berry Farm (www.lavenderberryfarm.com.au) on Browns Road in Pemberton.

Something for nothing Pop into the visitor centre in Nannup (www.nannupwa.com.au) and read up about the legendary Nannup tiger, a striped dog-like creature with a stiff tail. It is very rarely spotted these days but a rumoured sighting recently has allayed fears it may be extinct like its Tasmanian cousin.

Don't go home without... visiting one of the Southern Forests boutique wineries. Our favourites include Silkwood (www.silkwoodwines.com.au) and Lost Lake Wines (www.lostlake.com.au), both near Pemberton.

SUITABLY SOUTHERN FORESTS

Black truffles (also known as 'black diamonds' or 'black gold' because of their rarity and value) are grown here in the largest trufferie in the southern hemisphere. From June to August these highly regarded black fungi are sniffed out by dogs, rather than the usual pigs, so that oinkers like us can devour them at restaurants across Australia. Delicious.

DIARY

February Don your cowboy hat for the Boyup Brook Country Music Festival (www.countrymusicwa.com.au) near Bridgetown, which teams bands with less melodic ute and truck racing. **February–March** Roll up at the annual Nannup Music Festival (www.nannupmusicfestival.org) for performances spanning jazz to rock. **May** For a bit of local community action, enjoy foodie and family fun at the Pemberton Autumn Festival (www.pembertonwa.com). **December** For larks with fruit check out the quirky Manjimup Cherry Harmony Festival (www.cherryfestival.com.au), which includes gourmet food tastings, gigs and art exhibitions. You can even participate in a Cherry Pip Spitting Competition and be in the running to take out the Australasian title.

'The walk-through ends at our room, where a view of the dam, a four-poster bed and a roll-top tub greet us'

Pemberton

Stonebarn

STYLE Rustic-deluxe retreat
SETTING Truffle-touting timber town

ends at our room, where a view of the dam, a four-poster bed and a roll-top tub greet us. We have, indeed, arrived.

Both Mrs Smith and I have the same thought: we uncork a bottle of local chardonnay, head to the porch to unwind and watch the sun set over the hazelnut trees. Dinner is being served at 7pm tonight, so we enjoy the rest of the wine over a succulent meal of local fish with a pine-nut crust prepared by our host's expert hands. After devouring our food we fall into the Stonebarn stride by picking up a game of Scrabble – out of character for us, yet very natural in a remote setting that encourages rest and relaxation. Friendly fun quickly turns fiercely competitive and soon we're burning the midnight wordplay oil; we call a temporary truce and retire for the night to the neutral territory of Room 6.

The sound of cackling kookaburras reminds us that the forest wakes up at the crack of dawn and, more importantly, that we agreed to a three-course breakfast at 9am followed by a lightning round of Scrabble. Once these are out of the way, Mrs Smith and I hit the road to see what the region has to offer, since high-street shopping and cafés are out of the question.

Much to my lazy heart's delight, the forests around Pemberton are ideal for an 'indoors man' like myself. The brilliant folk of the Southern Forests have created a network of winding roads known as the Karri Forest Explorer Drive, which takes you through Beedelup, Gloucester and Warren National Parks, as well as Big Brook Forest. We stop and explore the area around Big Brook Dam, where the water's stillness and mirror-like reflection reminds Mrs Smith of a Monet masterpiece and me of Friday the 13th's Camp Crystal Lake, minus the hockey-masked villain and with more karris.

We reach the iconic Bicentennial Tree, a historic 75-metre fire look-out that doubles as a daredevil tourist destination. A teenager struck by fear a third of the way up makes us think twice about having a go at it ourselves, especially as there is no safety net and room for only one person on the iron pegs that act as a ladder. Instead we visit the

'Welcome to the Southern Forest' announces a sign as we drive at the best speed we can manage in our rented Hyundai. Mrs Smith, my co-pilot, is on full alert as she's tasked herself with kangaroo patrol. I personally cannot see how a kangaroo could navigate through the thick roadside vegetation unless it was armed with a machete – although that's not too hard to believe either in this fairytale-forest meets Australian-bush setting.

Local hub Pemberton, once a bustling logging centre, takes a back seat to the real highlight of the region: the biodiverse nature. We choose to drive straight through the town and head to Stonebarn, 20 minutes away. There, the dynamic duo who expertly run the property, a chef and his partner, are waiting with generously filled flutes of champagne; I confess we down these swiftly during our tour of this intimate contemporary lodge. The walk-through surrounding wineries, where we are pleasantly surprised by the variety and quality of the vino in a region that usually plays second fiddle to Margaret River.

Back at Stonebarn, Mrs Smith suggests soaking the day's adventures away in our room's freestanding bath, a decadent proposal considering all the hotel's water is filtered from collected rain. Afterwards we throw on a change of clothes and head downstairs where the smell of our dinner reminds us just how hungry one gets in the country. Thankfully the chef's portions are more munificent than measly, and tonight's rack of lamb is accompanied by some hearty polenta that really hits the spot. Inspired right down to our REM, that night we dream of swimming in lagoons, climbing giant trees and hiking through dense forests.

The next morning is – rather bizarrely – marred by a freak Scrabble accident. My celebratory victory leap lands on some letter tiles lying on the floor. Have you ever heard of a more middle-class accident? We reluctantly pack, say our goodbyes to our hosts and head off to a new attraction that is partly responsible for the region's revival: the Wine & Truffle Company near Manjimup.

Benefiting from being seasonally countercyclical to the more well-known truffle regions in Europe, the early stages of this venture are looking bright, with exports already in place. We taste the wines and enjoy a meal where each platter showcases the local Perigord variety of black fungi in very different ways, from tapenade-smothered tagliatelle to truffle honey and pannacotta. Don't go home without trying the truffle butter on toast. Better yet, order it while tasting the local drop.

'The next morning is – in a bizarre turn of events – marred by a freak Scrabble accident'

Truffled out, we embark on a leisurely drive to Perth, where our flight home awaits. Mrs Smith and I take one last breath of the eucalyptus-infused air in the forest that is the lung of Australia's south-west. Despite not being avid nature-lovers, we both treasured the individuality of Stonebarn. Feeling as though we'd hit the reset button, we left without a worry in our minds, our batteries fully charged and bodies naturally detoxed – all this without packing hiking boots, paying for spa treatments or taking dietary supplements. And, thankfully, not one encounter with a machete-wielding kangaroo either.

REVIEWED BY MR & MRS SMITH

NEED TO KNOW

Rooms Six suites.

Rates AU$345–AU$375, including cooked breakfast.

Check-out 10.30am, but flexible subject to availability. Check-in, 2pm.

Facilities Library, board games, painting supplies for the artistically inclined, free WiFi and gardens. In rooms: pre-loaded iPod with dock, flatscreen TV, L'Occitane toiletries, kitchenette, minibar and private balcony.

Children The hotel is an adult retreat, with no cots or highchairs available and hazards such as open fires and a lake nearby. Leave the littlies at home.

Also Enjoy a soak in the bush bath, a candlelit roll-top bath outdoors in the forest which overlooks the hotel and dam.

IN THE KNOW

Our favourite rooms All rooms come with contemporary king-size four-posters, except for Room 5, which has twin beds which can be joined into a king. If you like natural light ask for Rooms 1 or 6, which have an extra set of windows (as they're on either side of the property). Rooms 2 and 3 have bath tubs that only fit one person. Ensuites include antique claw-foot baths, separate showers and double sinks.

Hotel bar Stonebarn serves a range of alcoholic drinks in the informal dining room and public areas of the lodge, with an emphasis on fine wine. To promote local vineyards, it also sells cases for you to take home too.

Hotel restaurant French chef Xavier Poupel (who co-hosts Stonebarn with wife Janette) whips up a three-course breakfast and dinner, and can accommodate dietary requests. He specialises in French-style bistro dining and hearty portions, with top-quality local ingredients sourced from providers in Manjimup and Pemberton. Expect crayfish from Stonebarn's dam, veggies, fruit and herbs from the garden, and treats from the hotel's own trufferie. Former restaurateur Xavier used to cook for Princess Caroline of Monaco and the Jordanian royal family, so he's fairly handy in the kitchen.

Top table The vast dining room includes a long communal table at the back for dinner parties, and six more-intimate tables for two. For the best view – and light in the mornings – pick the table in the front corner with windows on both sides.

Room service None per se, but breakfast and dinner can be served in your suite if you fancy some privacy, and minibars come well stocked with snacks and drinks.

Dress code Lumberjack meets sommelier – feel free to let your hair down but bear in mind the setting is intimate so you're bound to bump into fellow guests.

Local knowledge Picnic on the property's river within a 10-minute walk of your room. Alternatively, just enjoy sunset over Stonebarn's dam from the comfort of the front porch (you can fish in it too, and ask the chef to cook your catch afterwards). Six clearly marked fire breaks act as walking trails nearby if you fancy stretching your legs, and you can take a walkie-talkie to stay in touch.

LOCAL EATING AND DRINKING

Head to a local winery to sample the fruits of this emerging epicurean area fast making a name for itself with its spoils. Try a tasting at the cellar door of the Wine & Truffle Company (08 9777 2474), south-west of Manjimup, followed by lunch at its airy café.

GET A ROOM!

Use our free online booking service: check availability and make reservations through www.mrandmrssmith.com.

 SMITH CARD OFFER A glass of quality Australian sparkling wine on arrival, a bottle of local wine and a Stonebarn memento.

Stonebarn Telephone Road, off South Western Highway, Pemberton, Western Australia 6260 (08 9773 1002; www.stonebarn.com.au)

Northern Territory
AUSTRALIA

NORTHERN TERRITORY

TOP END
Bamurru Plains

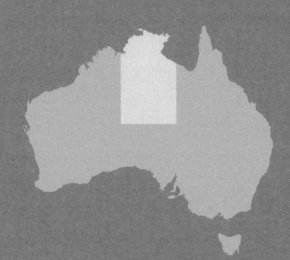

TOP END

COUNTRYSIDE Wetlands and wildlife
COUNTRY LIFE Croc watching and saltwater angling

Tropical weather, rich indigenous culture and national parks are headline acts in themselves, but add to this the territory's impressive cast of brilliant sunsets, world-class fishing and a colourful calendar of outdoor events and you have a taste of this northernmost point. Darwin's the modern and multicultural capital of this wonderfully vast region where much is remote, yet easy to access. World Heritage-listed Kakadu and Litchfield National Parks provide an exciting antidote to hectic urban lives – zebra crossings are well and truly gazumped by waterside signs warning of crocodiles. Even if you can't spy any of the snap-happy reptiles, be assured they might be eyeballing you. So, as infectious as the laid-back lifestyle is up there, let that little frisson keep you on your toes.

GETTING THERE

Planes International and domestic airlines fly into Darwin International Airport (08 8920 1811; www.darwinairport.com.au).
Trains For a grand adventure before you get to your destination, travel on the famous Ghan (132147; www.gsr.com.au). Transit from Adelaide to Darwin in a private cabin with ensuite is pretty special, but budget classes are also available. The route runs through Alice Springs and Katherine.
Automobiles Having a car enables you to really explore the area. The Automobile Association of the Northern Territory will advise on driving through the Outback (08 8981 3837; www.aant.com.au).

LOCAL KNOWLEDGE

Taxis Ring Darwin Radio Taxis (131008) for a cab.
Packing tips Make sure you bring industrial-strength insect repellent and a sun hat that means business.
Recommended reads Though books about the Northern Territory are few and far between – mainly because so few people actually live here – there are plenty of novels that evoke the Outback experience.

Louis de Bernières' *Red Dog* is a collection of stories about an itinerant canine that criss-crosses the Australian Bush; *Dirt Music* by Tim Winton is a gripping tale of passion and revenge in the country's arid interior; Xavier Herbert's epic *Poor Fellow My Country* is a state-of-the-nation novel about European and indigenous cultures meeting in 1930s and 1940s Northern Australia.
Local specialities As Indonesia and Malaysia are just a couple of hours' flying time over the horizon, and with a hugely multicultural population, it's hardly surprising that the Top End takes a lot of its culinary cues from Asia. Large market gardens produce a steady stream of mangos, pineapples, papayas and other tropical fruit, which combine deliciously with barramundi and mud crab – the spoils of world-class fishing. Crocodile is a popular delicacy as farms here breed these snappy creatures for their skins and meat. Hey, it really does taste a lot like chicken.
Do go/don't go There are two seasons in the Top End: the wet and the dry. If you want to see spectacular waterfalls, lightning storms and monsoon rains then

head to the Top End between November and April. However, many roads are closed at that time so most touring is done by boat or plane. The dry season – between May and October – is far less humid. It's the best time to visit if you want to see wildlife, as the area's animals gravitate towards a few billabongs in search of scarce water supplies.

WORTH GETTING OUT OF BED FOR

Viewpoint The only way to really see this ruggedly beautiful and largely uninhabited landscape is from the air. Kakadu Air (1800 089 113; www.kakaduair.com.au) and North Australian Helicopters (1800 621 717; www.northaustralianhelicopters.com.au) offers scenic tours.

Arts and culture The Top End's cultural centre is indisputably Darwin. There's a great collection of Aboriginal works at the Museum and Art Gallery of the Northern Territory (08 8999 8264; www.magnt.nt.gov.au), where there's also a powerful exhibition on Cyclone Tracy, which devastated the city on Christmas Eve 1974. The East Point Military Museum (08 8981 9702) provides a sobering reminder of the capital's World War II history, when Japanese bombs rained down on the city.

Activities The Mindil Beach Sunset Market in Darwin is a must if you're visiting the region during the dry season. Held on Thursday and Sunday evenings, it draws a huge crowd who come for the cosmopolitan cuisine, free entertainment and fabulous sunsets. Sample food from more than 30 nations, and pick up everything from Aboriginal art and crafts to kangaroo-skin belts. Round off your evening at the harbourside Deckchair Cinema (08 8941 4377; www.deckchaircinema.com), where you can watch stars both on the screen and in the sky.

Daytripper Take a scenic flight to the World Heritage-listed Purnululu National Park in the adjacent Kimberley region, where you'll fly over the 45,000 hectares of orange- and black-striped beehive-like mounds that make up the famous Bungle Bungle range.

Children Crocosaurus Cove (08 8981 7522; www.crocosauruscove.com) in the centre of Darwin houses some of the biggest captive saltwater crocodiles in the world. Thrillseekers will love the Cage of Death, a Perspex box that is lowered into a croc-swarming tank. It may be perfectly safe, but it still provides a serious adrenaline rush.

Walks Litchfield National Park, just 100 kilometres south of Darwin, has spectacular spring-fed waterfalls that cascade down rocky cliffs into crocodile-free swimming holes. There are plenty of clearly marked walking trails that leave from the car parks, including one that takes walkers through a series of unusual rock towers known as the Lost City.

Best beach Casuarina Beach, just minutes from Darwin's city centre, is the best of the glorious white-sand swathes close to the territory capital. Prudes beware, though; it does have a 'clothes optional' section. Swimming in the sea during the humid tropical summer can be dangerous – keep an eye out for deadly box jellyfish, and take note of any warning signs.

Perfect picnic If you're visiting the Top End during the dry season, stock up on supplies from Darwin's Mindil Beach Sunset Market, then head out to either Berry Springs or Annaburroo Billabong, both near the Mary River, for a lovely day of lazy lounging and swimming.

Shopping The Top End is the best place in Australia to pick up some affordable Aboriginal art, either directly from the artist in the markets or from one of the numerous galleries that can be found in and around Darwin city centre. The world's best South Sea pearls are farmed in the region too. Snap some up from Paspaley Pearls (08 8982 5555), on the corner of Bennett Street and the Mall in Darwin. It's also acceptable to buy a didgeridoo from here – you are in their original home, after all. Just don't go mad playing it once you get back home. It's rarely appreciated.

Something for nothing Take part in the daily fish-feeding frenzy that takes place in Doctor's Gully at the end of Darwin Esplanade. Hundreds of fish swarm into the cove at high tide to be met by adults and excitable children with armfuls of bread. You'll have them eating out of your hand – literally. Times are published in the local *Northern Territory News*.

Don't go home without... some Aboriginal art, and a handbag or belt made from crocodile skin. Make sure your croc-skin product comes with a certificate to say where it came from; you'll need it at customs.

TANTALISINGLY TOP END

At a whopping 200,000 square kilometres, World Heritage-listed Kakadu National Park is the largest in Australia. Famed for its natural and cultural wonders, it's not just home to several Aboriginal rock-art sites and plenty of saltwater crocs. No sir. Grab your lizard-skin waistcoat and doff your tooth-trimmed cowboy hat to Mick Dundee. Indeed *Crocodile Dundee* was based on a real-life hunter from the Top End.

DIARY

June Join Darwin's thriving Greek community for Greek Glenti, two days of dancing, music, food and wine down at the city's Bicentennial Park. **August** Held annually in Arnhemland, the Garma Festival (www.garma. telstra.com) is one of Australia's most significant events, showcasing the country's indigenous cultures, and it is a great opportunity to learn about the heritage and traditions of Australia's original inhabitants. The popular two-week Fringe at the Bank festival (www.darwinfringe.com.au) – originally named the Darwin Fringe Festival – celebrates the unique culture of the Top End with concerts, exhibitions and parties based at the old commonwealth bank building on the corner of Smith and Bennett Streets.

'Ever stayed at an African safari camp? Replace elephant for buffalo, and impala for wallabies, and you have the perfect replica'

Bamurru Plains

STYLE Safari glamour
SETTING Croc-flocked floodplains

Flying to Darwin isn't like flying anywhere else. You might leave from the same Sydney airport but once airborne you're on a journey to the frontier – and you can feel it. On this plane to the Top End sits actor Anthony LaPaglia, army types, German backpackers, old blokes sucking beer, a couple of Aboriginal elders and two slightly buttoned-up Smith reviewers heading to Bamurru Plains with a curious blend of excited anticipation and dread (there really have been quite a lot of croc attack stories in the NT recently).

On arrival at the frontier airport, we jump a cab around the corner to the charter flights and are away. Now, small planes landing on dirt strips in the middle of the Territory might not be for everyone but I love it and so, thankfully, does Mrs Smith. The flight (you can make the three-hour drive if you must) isn't cheap, but in less than half an hour you are in one of those African safari-style Land Cruisers with the green canopy, rattling through the bush and getting excited by the sight of a red-tailed black cockatoo.

Already I am relearning skills from previous bush safari trips. Rule one: appear interested in nature, particularly fauna. Rule two: strike up conversations with people you don't know despite your normal aversion to it – this helps to make you appear nicer. As Mrs Smith says, if I am engaging with strangers then we must really be on vacation.

Ever stayed at an African safari camp? Replace elephant for buffalo, and impala for wallabies, and you have the perfect replica. The fit-out's the same – communal area with leather lounges, library, well-stocked bar and long dinner table that leads onto a massive deck with day-beds, an infinity-edge pool and a view across wide, open space. Of course, it's all eco-friendly with solar power, artesian water and no mobile phone coverage.

Bamurru is situated at the edge of Kakadu on a private farm (some 300 square kilometres of it) called Swim Creek Station. There are just nine rooms, six identical and new (they are the best), with the three closest to the camp bigger but less exotic since you don't feel like you're sleeping under the stars as you do in the newer rooms.

The rooms are glam safari with a local feel – lots of corrugated iron, tans and khakis. The bed is literally in the open air (protected by netting wall-screens), raised up on a wooden platform. It is tops – Aussie but not kitsch. There are candles and gas lamps and, as I watch the buffalo amble past on their on their way somewhere on the station, I think to myself, 'This is good, very good indeed.'

Dinner is perfect for the surrounds: salty mussels, crisp riesling, good pork and excellent shiraz. I even manage a perfectly enjoyable conversation with a Californian republican – now that doesn't happen every day.

Dawn at Bamurru puts you in the middle of an Outback oil painting – soft grey, pink and pale blue. We are woken at 6.30am, breakfast is at 7am and by 7.30am we pile into the troop carrier and head to Sampan Creek where we putt-putt up and down the stream looking at birds. Secretly, though, we want just one thing: a monster croc. Garry tells us it's unusually quiet and my heart sinks. It needn't have – after an hour or so of relatively fruitless but quite pleasant boating, we come upon not one but dozens of crocs. And then the money shot: the five-metre

monster that waits till you are in good camera range before snapping around, rustling like fury down the bank and then somehow gliding in silence into the water. It's bloody unreal and has made my day – almost. Seriously, my entire trip is made when we return to camp to find prawns and lamb cutlets on the barbecue. How good can it get? Who needs foie gras and sauternes when you have crocs, beer, prawns and lamb cutlets? And it's not even half past 12!

I then spend two hours doing something I never do – I lie on a shady day-bed, pick up a book and relax. And somehow, as in Fiji and a few other places on earth, the body just puts on the brakes. Some advice for those who plan to come to Bamurru: two nights is enough so don't worry if you can't afford the Kakadu option. We found the all-inclusive offerings – the early-morning adventure and late-afternoon amble – ample enough.

In the afternoon we trot around the billabong with our guide Justin, looking at birds, wallabies and buffalo and talking about nature, life and climate change. It's truly revelatory for me – a couple more days here and I could have become the world's fattest hippie (hence the advice to only stay for two days – the world needs no more hippies). Another fine three-course dinner is followed by our second morning in camp, which turns out to be one of the most stunning mornings of the decade for me, fair dinkum. (By day two Mrs Smith reckons I start sounding like Hugh Jackman in *Australia*. I just wish I had his biceps.)

I have one word to explain my brilliant morning: airboat. Yep, one of those hovercrafty things with the huge fan at the rear you see on the Everglades in Florida. Soon we are gliding and sliding among thousands of magpie geese ('bamurru' in local Aboriginal dialect), resting in a field of stunning pink lotus flowers and tailing four-metre crocs through swamps shaded by thousands of paperbark trees. It is brilliant, breathtaking and awe-inspiring. I have plenty more adjectives I could throw at airboating, but suffice to say if I'd spent the morning on a Pirelli calendar shoot, I could not have been happier.

REVIEWED BY STUART GREGOR

NEED TO KNOW

Rooms Nine stand-alone bungalows.

Rates AU$1,860, including all meals, drinks and scheduled activities (air boating, river cruises, guided walks and safari drives). Check-out 11am, but flexible upon request. Check-in, 2pm.

Facilities Outdoor pool, library. In rooms: king-size beds, organic cotton bedlinen, ensuite with high-pressure shower, deck, air-conditioning (in three of the bungalows, for AU$100 extra per night; request it when you book).

Children Bamurru welcomes kids aged eight and over, and is planning special family programmes for the school holidays. Rates for a child aged 16 and under, sharing with two adults are AU$470 a night; or AU$837 a child sharing their own room.

Also There's a two-night minimum stay at Bamurru, and the camp is closed from 1 November–31 January. Pets are not allowed – unless, maybe, as crocodile bait.

IN THE KNOW

Recommended rooms We love West 4, the bungalow that's furthest from the main lodge, for its secluded position and great views of the wetlands. Set on a timber platform, it's lined with 'outlook', a mesh fabric that allows you to keep an eye on passing wildlife even though nobody on the outside can see in, and it comes with comfy beds with bush-style canvas bedspreads. Extra 'swag' beds can be provided for a third adult or kids sharing your room (a fun update on traditional bushmen's bedding rolls). If you must have air-conditioning, then bungalows West 1 and 2 or East 1 are the ones to book.

Hotel bar Guests can help themselves to drinks at any time in the central timber-and-iron lodge, where couches abound, but the early starts tend to keep a lid on late-night revelry.

Hotel restaurant Dining at Bamurru is a relaxed and convivial communal affair, and guests bump elbows around three solid-timber tables in front of an open kitchen that dishes up robust country-style dishes such as wild barramundi with home-made tomato relish or warm emu salad with a pepper-and-strawberry dressing. Lunch is from 12.30pm; dinner after sundowner drinks and canapés at about 7pm.

Top table It's all very egalitarian around the shared tables at Bamurru, but you could have a private meal in your bungalow if you wish. You'd miss out on all those 'who saw the biggest crocodile?' conversations, though.

Room service While it doesn't really exist at Bamurru, staff will do their best to deal with guests' requests between breakfast and dinner.

Dress code Sun-smart safari threads: perhaps omitting any crocodile-skin accessories.

Local knowledge Bamurru is set on the edge of the Mary River wetlands, east of Darwin and west of Kakadu National Park. Head out in an open-topped 4WD for some pre-sunset wildlife spotting. This is when the animals are most active and are moving off the open floodplains to spend the night in the safety of the savanna woodland. You'll see hundreds of agile wallabies, water buffalo and birds, and there's a good chance you'll spot brumbies, wild boar and crocodiles too. Touring extends to water-skimming airboats which dart across the floodplains and grass, dodging buffalo and giant saltwater crocs. There's also a boat for evening river trips, ideal for croc-spotting. For venturing further afield, highly recommended Lords Kakadu & Arnhemland Safaris (08 8948 2200; www.lords-safaris.com) offers specialised private safaris to difficult-to-access areas, at extra cost. Its owner, Sab, was born in Kakadu before it was granted World Heritage status.

LOCAL EATING AND DRINKING

All meals are included in the rates, so you wouldn't want to eat out – besides, the lodge is on a working buffalo station in the middle of the wetlands; the nearest civilisation is a roadhouse selling petrol and burgers about an hour and a half away.

GET A ROOM!

Use our free online booking service: check availability and make reservations through www.mrandmrssmith.com.

 SMITH CARD OFFER A gift-wrapped book on Australian birds.

Bamurru Plains Swim Creek Station, Harold Knowles Road, Northern Territory 0836 (02 9571 6399; www.bamurruplains.com)

Queensland
AUSTRALIA

QUEENSLAND

BRISBANE
Limes Hotel
GREAT BARRIER REEF
Lizard Island
Qualia

BRISBANE

CITYSCAPE Ritzy riverside metropolis
CITY LIFE Tropical fun in the sun

Australia's third largest city has long lived in the shadow of
Sydney and Melbourne, but in recent years Queensland's capital
has come into its own, shaking off its small town mentality. The
BrisVegas tag may sum up this city's love of glitzy good times,
but it's also got great galleries, hot bars, restaurants and clubs,
and a happening music scene. The hilly waterside location's no
slouch: flanking the winding Brisbane River, it is within easy
reach of beaches, islands and national parks. If it's major sights
you're after, make for the CBD and South Bank arts complex
across the river, but base yourself in edgier inner north district
Fortitude Valley for maximum buzz. Residents of rival cities may
mock, but folk are moving here in droves, drawn by a winning
combination of no-nonsense attitude with fast-paced fun.

GETTING THERE

Planes Regular flights wing their way to Brisbane
Airport (www.bne.com.au), 16 kilometres north-east
of town, from all major Australian cities with Qantas
(www.qantas.com.au), Virgin Blue (www.virginblue.
com.au) and Jetstar (www.jetstar.com). Numerous
international carriers also service the airport.
Trains The best way to reach Brisbane's CBD from the
airport's international and domestic terminals, two
kilometres apart, is by Airtrain (www.airtrain.com.au),
which departs every 15 minutes during peak times
for the 20-minute journey (single, AU$14.50; return,
AU$27). Regional trains come into the main Roma
Street Transit Centre (see www.qr.com.au);
CountryLink (www.countrylink.info) operates daily
express trains between Sydney and Brisbane.
Automobiles Walking is an option in the city centre,
but Brisbane is hilly and gets hot in summer, so you
may prefer to drive. All major car hire companies can
be found at Brisbane Airport or at downtown locations,
including Hertz (www.hertz.com.au), Avis (www.avis.
com.au) and Europcar (www.europcar.com.au).
Boats CityCat catamarans and CityFerries are a great
way to get around, with stop-offs all along the river

at major destinations. Translink tickets can be used
across the transport network (www.translink.com.au).

LOCAL KNOWLEDGE

Taxis Plentiful in Brisbane's city centre, with ranks in
the CBD and at the train station. To call one, try Yellow
Cab Co (131924) or Black & White Cabs (131 008).
Packing tips A pair of designer thongs (flip-flops)
and big shades to look the part; glam gear for
BrisVegas by night.
Recommended reads For a creepy take on the ghosts
beneath Brisbane's sun-kissed surface, Stephen M
Irwin's horror novel *The Dead Path* tells the tale of a
man's return to the city after 20 years, a missing child
and a friend's murder. Brisbane writer Nick Earls' latest
novel, *The True Story of Butterfish*, will appeal to
musos: it's about a drummer from a once-successful
band drawn into a neighbour's family.
Local specialities Make the most of all that fresh
coastal fish and seafood: try Moreton Bay bugs
(a local species of lobster), prawns, mud crabs and
barramundi. The Castlemaine-Perkins XXXX Brewery
(www.xxxx.com.au) is based in Milton, west of

Brisbane's main train station, if you fancy a tour before sampling the world-famous beers.

Do go/don't go Brisbane basks in year-round sun, with temperatures rarely dipping below 20°C. The peak of summer can be super-hot and wetter, with many locals escaping the sweltering city, which can make it quiet; winter is sunny and mild with little rain.

Also... Time your visit between June and November for a chance to spot humpback whales flocking through Moreton Bay off the coast of Brisbane.

WORTH GETTING OUT OF BED FOR

Viewpoint Drive up to the look-out on top of Mount Coot-tha for gasp-inducing views over Brisbane, Moreton Bay and the volcanic Glass House Mountains. Seven kilometres south-west of the city, it's a reserve of bush and parkland named after the Aboriginal word for 'honey', once gathered here, and the trails and picnic spots are still sweet.

Arts and culture Despite the tinseltown jibes, there's serious culture here, with key galleries holding court in the South Bank arts zone. Start at the Gallery of Modern Art (GoMA; www.qag.qld.gov.au), Australia's largest modern art gallery, focusing on works from the 20th-century onwards including indigenous, Pacific Island and international collections. Its Asia-Pacific Triennial of Contemporary Art is a must-see show. Sister space, the Queensland

Art Gallery (QAG; same website) features Australian and global work prior to 1970, including pieces by Queensland talent, Ian Fairweather. For cutting-edge theatre, music and arts, our tip is the riverside Brisbane Powerhouse (www.brisbanepowerhouse.org) in gentrifying district New Farm. The adjacent park also hosts the Moonlight Cinema (www.moonlight.com.au) in summer.

Activities Near Fortitude Valley, the Story Bridge Adventure Climb (www.storybridgeadventureclimb.com.au) is one of only three bridges in the world you can climb without getting arrested, and the views are breathtaking. From AU$89 for adults. If you'd prefer something more sedate, barefoot lawn bowls is gathering cult status, with a younger crowd; they head for the greens for barbecue-and-beer-fuelled Sunday-afternoon sessions. Try your silky skills out at Merthyr Bowls Club (www.merthyrbowlsclub.com.au), New Farm. It's AU$5 a person, including bowls hire and coaching for two hours.

Best beach In South Bank Parklands, fringing the river across from the CBD, you'll find Australia's only man-made inner-city beach, Streets Beach, a subtropical oasis linked to a lagoon. Ideal for a dip without even leaving town.

Daytripper Head to the Moreton Bay islands (www.moretonbayislands.com.au), a short ferry or catamaran ride off the coast east of Brisbane, which is a haven for marine life including dolphins, rare dugongs, turtles and sea birds. Moreton Island itself combines beaches with lagoons and National Park land. Sandboard on the dunes or snorkel among the spooky boat wrecks at Tangalooma. At North Stradbroke Island (aka 'Straddie'), take a freshwater dip in tea tree-stained Brown Lake, stroll to pretty Blue Lake, or hit the alabaster beaches: there is safe swimming at Cylinder Beach and Amity Point, and wilder surf at Main Beach.

Children This is koala central, so introduce the kids to some of the sleepy fur-balls at Lone Pine Koala Sanctuary (www.koala.net), 11 kilometres south-west of town. Arrive in style by river cruise (www.mirimar.com). Brisbane's Alma Park Zoo (www.almaparkzoo.com.au), 28 kilometres to the north, is also home to koalas and native dingoes, kangaroos and possums. Both cost AU$19 a child, AU$28 an adult, with deals for families. In town, the free Queensland Museum

(www.southbank.qm.qld.gov.au) offers exhibits on dinosaurs, dung beetles and endangered species – which just about covers all the kids' favourites.

Walks For a slice of Brissie life, kick off at the pretty City Botanic Gardens, south of the CBD, and follow the river north past the skyscrapers and buzzing eateries to the floating RiverWalk, which connects over 20 kilometres of foot and bike trails along parks and the riverside.

Perfect picnic Once a race track, New Farm Park is now a big green space on the edge of the Brisbane River with views of the city skyline. Not to be missed when the jacaranda trees are flowering.

Shopping Fortitude Valley is the city's boutique shopping hub, with one-of-a-kind fashion pieces up for grabs. Browse Ann, Brunswick, James and Wickham Streets. The massive Queen Street Shopping Mall (www.queenstreetmall.com) in the CBD is home to over 700 outlets, dominated by Myers and David Jones department stores, or head west to Paddington's La Trobe and Given Terraces for antiques, curios and collectables.

Something for nothing Watch rock climbers scale the pink cliffs at Kangaroo Point, on the south of the illuminated-by-night riverbank, or contact the Riverlife Adventure Centre (www.riverlife.com.au) if you fancy a go yourself.

Don't go home without... trying a Moreton Bay bug, a tasty local type of lobster.

BRILLIANTLY BRISBANE

Queensland is known as the Sunshine State with over 300 days of golden rays a year. For Brissie, this mood-boosting mellow weather means constant access to the outdoors, with a seductive, subtropical climate begging you to come out and play, dine or dance alfresco.

DIARY

January The kooky Cockroach Races (www.cockroachraces.com.au) have been going for 26 years at the Stony Bridge Hotel on Australia Day. **April–July** Queensland Winter Racing Carnival (www.queenslandracing.com.au) sees horse racing every weekend, including the Brisbane Cup in May. **September–October** Brisbane River Festival (www.riverfestival.com.au) offers 10 days of arts and performance fun around the water. **October** Valley Fiesta (www.valleyfiesta.com.au) is a free three-day music and arts party in Fortitude Valley.

'Mrs Smith is particularly fond of the welcoming gift of locally made Dello Mano brownies (they don't stand a chance of lasting through the entire weekend)'

Brisbane

Limes Hotel

STYLE Hip design hang-out
SETTING Edgy, urban Fortitude Valley

'Welcome to Limes,' says an attentive young man as he negotiates our luggage. 'I know you're going to enjoy your stay here.' Mrs Smith and I have just arrived in Brisbane and are already enjoying it – the weather particularly. We've driven from the airport with the windows in the taxi wound right down, the warm air welcoming us like an old friend.

We're shown to our room. Like all rooms on the ground floor, this one has a private courtyard complete with a hammock. It's just the spot to enjoy these tropical climes, and at this point we're very glad not to have been allocated one of the higher levels.

Limes Hotel has been wowing people with its thoroughly modern design since it opened a few years back, and although the room is quite compact, everything in it is carefully considered: elegant, moody lighting; dark grey and white bed coverings; there's even a kitchen area – which doubles as a workspace with free WiFi if needed – with its own espresso machine. The whole effect is pared back but still feels warm and comfortable. While slightly Lilliputian in its dimensions, the bathroom is slick, and its

L'Occitane products are a nice touch. Mrs Smith is particularly fond of the welcoming gift of locally made Dello Mano brownies (they don't stand a chance of lasting through the entire weekend), and the well-edited minibar, with Voss water from Norway and a tempting selection of soft drinks.

Located just outside the CBD in an area called Fortitude Valley (just 'the Valley' to the locals), Limes is perfectly positioned for exploring the edgier side of town. Taking advantage of the sunshine, and a tip from the knowledgeable girl on reception, we stroll to nearby James Street. Mrs Smith loves the district's hip mix of fashion boutiques: Bettina Liano, Sass & Bide and Little Joe by Gail Elliot. We also peruse the James Street Market, where local produce is beautifully displayed, and there's an outdoor café. It's funny that on a sunny day in Melbourne everyone jostles for a table kissed by rays, but here in Brisbane they all sit in the shade under umbrellas. I guess that's what happens when you live in a city that is warm and bright all year round.

Back at the hotel as the sun's setting, we decide to check out the rooftop bar. It's not at all crowded yet, and has quite a loungey mood. There's a group of women – the kind most of us would label as 'ladies who lunch' – who are having champagne and plates of tapas from the bar menu, and there are also a few couples enjoying a pre-prandial tipple. It really is a magnificent spot to enjoy a cocktail or cold beer, with a 360-degree view of the city. (During the week, it's also often used as a venue for movie screenings, and I can't imagine there are too many cinemas in the world that can boast this sort of non-celluloid vista.) As the night wears on, however, it becomes a focal point for the young and hip, and the music gets louder and more dance-oriented. Not that Mrs Smith and myself are exactly old and unfashionable, but when an 18th birthday party gets underway, we decide that it's time to head out for some dinner. A friend of mine, Paolo Biscaro, owns a pizzeria called Beccofino in the nearby neighbourhood of Teneriffe, just a short cab ride away, so we decide to drop by. It's a great find – the wood-fired pizza is among the best I've had anywhere.

Appetites suitably sated, Mrs Smith and I forego the lure of the many bars and clubs around Fortitude Valley and decide to head back to our room. On the website, Limes warns that it's not a quiet hotel – and you can tell why. You can hear the music from the bar until it closes around midnight, but well after that chattering clusters of people come and go from the lobby. On the upper floors that might not be a problem, but unless you're a night owl with a penchant for eavesdropping, I'd suggest packing some earplugs if you're on the ground floor.

Sunday arrives fresh and sunny (it is Queensland, after all), and we set out to see what Brisbane has to offer. First, it's off to Harveys in James Street to stock up on some perfectly poached eggs, French toast and first-class café lattes. Mrs Smith is an architect, so we venture to the other side of the city to stroll along South Bank with its impressive array of galleries, boutique shops, tempting cafés and a designer market. We love the Queensland Art Gallery's Australian and international collections, but aren't quite so keen on the newer Gallery of Modern Art, although the building is stunning. We continue walking back towards the city and are impressed by the beautiful former Treasury Building that is now home to the city's casino.

Late into the afternoon, we head to a Brisbane institution that I've always wanted to visit: the Breakfast Creek Hotel, on Kingsford Smith Drive in this part of town – now nicknamed the Brekky Creek. Located right on the river, it is a massive establishment that is famous for its steaks. And rightly so. With so many people ordering, it does take a little while for your piece of beef to come off the chargrill, but it's definitely worth the wait – tasty, juicy and big enough to overcome a man-size hunger.

Some of us from the south of Australia have considered Brisbane the poorer cousin – small and a little bit behind the times – but this visit has opened my and Mrs Smith's eyes. The weather is rather spectacular, and the city appears to be progressive and fashionable. Much like Limes Hotel, which is a unique place to spend the weekend. Mrs Smith and I only wish we were 20 again, so that we could have enjoyed the rooftop bar as much as the kids at that birthday party.

REVIEWED BY ANDREW CHIODO

NEED TO KNOW

Rooms 21.

Rates AU$209–$289. Breakfast is extra at AU$5.50–$17.50.

Check-out 11am but flexible (after 12pm you'll be charged a half-day rate; after 2pm, for a full extra night). Check-in, 2pm.

Facilities Free WiFi and broadband throughout, Mac computer for guest use, gym pass for Fitness First. In rooms: flatscreen TV, Foxtel cable, CD player, iPod dock, Nespresso coffee maker, T2 tea, minibar, kitchenette, Dello Mano brownies on arrival, L'Occitane amenities.

Children This is an adult playground – leave the nippers at home.

Also For just AU$12, you can watch a film alfresco under the stars at Limes' open-air rooftop cinema, perched on comfy contemporary poufs, with illuminated city skyline views. There are usually two nightly screenings, several times a week; buy a ticket from the bar, where you can also order drinks or tapas.

IN THE KNOW

Our favourite rooms We love the larger, lower level Courtyard rooms, which have a private grey slate-walled courtyard with a hammock. Smaller rooms on the upper level offer a balcony instead. All are light, clean-lined and contemporary, with king-size beds, black-tiled showers and a dinky white Corian kitchenette. A sleek palette of white, grey and chocolate brown adds to the modern understated yet feel, with timber bedheads, black sheepskins and bespoke furniture.

Hotel bar Limes' rooftop champagne and cocktail bar is open to guests and locals, and is a hot destination for the city's bright young things. Warm weather year-round means it's perfect for Balearic-style partying, with colour-morphing LED lights, all-white tables and chairs and net-covered cabanas for lounging. Pop up for a sunset fruit martini, or snack from the extensive bar menu, and socialise with BrisVegas's pretty people. The bar sees action from 5pm until midnight Monday to Thursday, and from 3pm Friday to Sunday, with house, soul and chill-out tunes, and live DJs on Sundays.

Hotel restaurant There's no restaurant at Limes, but it's in the Valley (Fortitude Valley), an inner-city neighbourhood packed with cool cafés, bars and restaurants.

Room service Available 5pm–10pm, including light meals such as butternut pumpkin soup and asparagus, grilled haloumi and rocket salad, or heartier fare such as the Limes beef burger and chips. In-room breakfasts (ordered in from local café Cirque) are available until 10.30am.

Dress code Smart, stylish and sexy. No thongs (flip-flops), singlets or sneakers if you want to get into the rooftop bar.

Local knowledge Pick up creations by young designers at the weekend Brunswick Street markets, at Brunswick Street mall. Nearby clubs include the cavernous, four-level Family (07 3852 5000) at 8 McLachlan Street, with top international DJs and lots of bars to get lost in. The more boutique, mature Alhambra Lounge (07 3216 0226) next door, is a cool mini-club with great music, a chill-out area and friendly, efficient bar staff. Its red, Hispanic-themed interiors include private booths.

LOCAL EATING AND DRINKING

Cirque Café (07 3254 0479) at 618 Brunswick Street, New Farm, is a good bet for all-day breakfasts, with vegetarian offerings. If you have a sweet tooth, don't miss award-winning E'cco (07 3831 8344) at 100 Boundary Street, where chef Philip Johnson's desserts are legendary. Watt Modern Dining (07 3358 5464) at Brisbane Powerhouse, 119 Lamington Street, is popular for alfresco lunches on its big, riverside decks. Bowery (07 3252 0202) at 676 Ann Street is a seductive little cocktail bar with low lighting, gorgeous staff and a tasty bar menu.

GET A ROOM!

Use our free online booking service: check availability and make reservations through www.mrandmrssmith.com.

 SMITH CARD OFFER AU$20 bar tab voucher.

Limes Hotel 142 Constance Street, Fortitude Valley, Queensland 4006 (07 3852 9000; www.limeshotel.com.au)

GREAT BARRIER REEF

COASTLINE Coral islands and castaway shores
COAST LIFE Snorkelling, sailing and sun worshipping

With azure waters, powder-white sandy bays and spectacular snorkelling and diving, the sun-kissed tropical islands of the Great Barrier Reef are the kind of escape you dream about, but wake up here and they're blissfully real. Stretching 2,300-kilometres up the length of Queensland, the reef can be seen from space, but you don't have to work for NASA to suss why its unique geography has been declared a World Heritage Area. With over 90 islands, you're sure to find your own pocket of paradise, with a boho mix of backpackers and millionaires for company, or many uninhabited coral cays if you want 'quality time' solo. Even if donning a scuba suit isn't your bag, you'll encounter awesome nature, exciting aquatic activities and some mouth-watering restaurants and luxe bars for après-sun lounging.

GETTING THERE

Planes Regular flights are up for grabs from all major Australian cities to the Great Barrier Reef, with Qantas (www.qantas.com.au), Virgin Blue (www.virginblue.com.au) and Jetstar (www.jetstar.com). Rex (www.rex.com.au), Tiger Airways (www.tigerairways.com) and Alliance Airlines (www.allianceairlines.com.au) also service the area. Cairns Airport (www.cairnsairport.com) is the jumping-off point for the northern part of the reef, including charter flights to Lizard Island (www.lizardisland.com.au) and Dunk Island (for Bedarra) with Hinterland Aviation (www.hinterlandaviation.com.au); central Hamilton Island Airport serves the Whitsunday Islands. Sunlover Helicopters (www.sunloverheli.com.au) offers transfers from Cairns Airport to most resort islands.
Trains The high-speed Tilt Train and the Sunlander run between Brisbane and Cairns, hugging the scenic coast, but you're looking at around 25 hours in the saddle. Book via Queensland Rail (www.traveltrain.com.au).
Automobiles The usual car hire firms can be found at Queensland's airports, including Hertz (www.hertz.com.au) at Cairns, but chances are if you're island-hopping you won't need wheels, you'll want wings or sails. Cars can be left in secure parking at main ferry hubs.
Boat Fantasea (www.fantasea.com.au) operates daily 30-minute catamaran trips between Shute Harbour at mainland Airlie Beach and Hamilton Island, as well as other Whitsunday islands.

LOCAL KNOWLEDGE

Taxis Outside the larger towns, you've more chance of hitching a ride on a dolphin than finding a cab, especially on the islands themselves where transport is often restricted to buggies or hotel transfers. In Cairns, book ahead with Black & White Taxis (131 008).
Packing tips A capsule wardrobe to take you from boat deck to beach to below the waves in style.
Recommended reads Castaway by British adventurer Lucy Irvine, which inspired the Tom Hanks film, tells of her self-imposed exile on Tuin Island in Queensland's Torres Strait, and captures the tropical life to a tee. David Colfelt's 100 Magic Miles of the Great Barrier Reef – the Whitsunday Islands, is

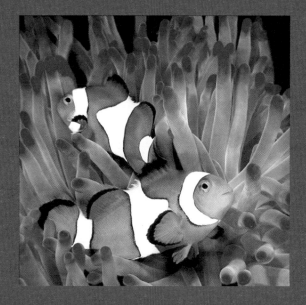

Arts and culture Many of the reef's islands are of totemic significance in local Aboriginal mythology. Lizard Island, for example, is believed to represent the body of a stingray while the neighbouring islets make up the tail, and has been a place of pilgrimage for the Dingaal Warra people for millennia.

Activities Snorkelling and diving the reef are life-changing experiences, and there's no better place to learn to scuba than at one of the many dive schools on the islands or in Cairns. Diving Cairns (www.divingcairns.com) offers beginners courses; Calypso Dive (www.calypsodive.com) arranges diving and snorkelling excursions from Mission Beach and Dunk Island, and jet-ski trips from the latter too. For one of Australia's best dives check out Cod Hole, at the north end of Ribbon Reef off Lizard Island, famous for its enormous but friendly potato cod. If you'd rather avoid full immersion, Sea Kayaking Whitsundays (www.kayakwhitsunday.com) offers paddling trips from Hamilton Island, or for inspiring aerial views, the Great Barrier Reef Helicopter Group (www.gbrhelicopters.com.au) operates scenic flights over the reef.

Best beach Beautiful Whitehaven Beach on the south-east coast of Whitsunday Island is the most-photographed beach in Australia and the largest in the 74-island Whitsunday archipelago, with seven kilometres of snow-white sand and crystal-clear waters. Reach it from Airlie Beach on the mainland with Cruise Whitsundays (www.cruisewhitsundays.com), or from Hamilton Island nearby. Lizard Island has more than 20 beaches to choose from – sheltered Pebbly Beach is great for swimming.

Daytripper Get high on Cairns' eco-friendly Skyrail (www.skyrail.com.au), a breath-stealing seven-kilometre cable-car trip gliding over the rainforest canopy to the tiny artsy village of Kuranda (around 90 minutes one-way). Browse the craft markets and Aboriginal art galleries, then head back to town on the century-old Kuranda Scenic Railway (www.ksr.com.au), through the beautiful Barron Gorge National Park.

Children If the kids are beached out, distract them with some creature features: www.wildlifetnq.com has details of Cairns Tropical Zoo, Cairns Night Zoo, which specialises in nocturnal beasties, and the too-cute Kuranda Koala Gardens.

considered 'the bible' for this popular sailing area, with maps, anchorages and beach details.

Local specialities Lipsmacking fish and seafood-snacking opportunities abound, freshly hauled from the reef's waters. Coral trout is a menu staple, as is wild saltwater barramundi. Shellfish is also a highlight, including the tricky-to-tackle (but worth-the-effort) mud crabs, and barbecued Moreton Bay bugs – an ancient flat-headed lobster creature found only in Queensland. Expect exotic tropical fruit too.

Do go/don't go With average temperatures of 27°C, it's warm year-round. Reef visibility is better in winter when the seas are calmer, and days are clear and sunny, but the water temperature is cooler than in summer. The hotter but rainier part of the year spans November to December and April to May, peaking in the wet from January to March, when storms can threaten.

Also... Tropical cyclones and poisonous jellyfish can be unwelcome guests between December and April.

WORTH GETTING OUT OF BED FOR

Viewpoint On northernmost reef resort Lizard Island, take a dawn bushwalk up to Cook's Look, the highest point (368 m), where Captain Cook once surveyed the area. It's a three- to four-hour return hike. On Hamilton Island, One Tree Hill is a good spot for sunset cocktails.

Walks Not content with palm-fringed seaside strolls? Hamilton Island has more than 20 kilometres of bushwalks, and on Lizard Island, you can arrange guided Watson's Bay Discovery Walks across Chinaman's Ridge, past a colony of flying foxes to the historic site of local heroine Mary Watson's cottage (a fisherman's wife who died in the 1880s fleeing hostile locals).

Perfect Picnic Tiki Beach, on Bedarra Island, is perfect for romantic picnics as it can only be reached by boat. Off Lizard Island, the aptly named Picnic Beach on Palfrey Island allows you to access the stunning Blue Lagoon.

Shopping Retail round these parts is mostly of the upscale beach kit variety. Lizard Island's bijou resort boutique sells stylish sun hats by Sydney designer Helen Kaminski, sarongs by Firefly, swimwear by 2 Chillies and semi-precious jewellery by Riley Burnett. At Hamilton Island's marina, stores include Driza-Bone for all-weather Aussie outerwear, swish sailing-wear labels Slam and Henri Lloyd, as well as flowers and gifts at Floral Collections.

Something for nothing There's a fistful of free stuff to enjoy in Cairns: tour the tropical Flecker Botanic Gardens north-west of the centre, then cool off in the saltwater swimming lagoon at the Cairns Foreshore Promenade. Kids can horse around at Muddy's Playground, where slides and swings compete with climbing nets and water play zones.

Don't go home without... spending a day sailing, an elegant way to explore the islands. For divers or snorkellers try the luxurious and eco-friendly *Aristocat* (www.aristocat.com.au), which sallies forth from coastal Port Douglas to the Agincourt Ribbon Reefs, and has hot showers on board, espresso coffee and offers 'passive dives' with minke whales. Lots of sailing trips operate in the Whitsundays too.

GLORIOUSLY GREAT BARRIER REEF

The world's biggest reef system meanders 30–300 kilometres offshore, supporting a kaleidoscopic marine world of dazzlingly diverse tropical fish, coral, seaweeds and sponges as well as awesome sea-life sights such as whales, dolphins, turtles, manta rays, reef sharks and sea birds. It's bigger than the Great Wall of China, one of the seven wonders of the natural world, and has been declared a marine park and World Heritage Area.

DIARY

June The Hamilton Island Outrigger Cup is Australia's oldest outrigger canoe event (www.hamiltoncup.com). **July–September** Keep your eyes peeled during the annual humpback whale migration past the Barrier Reef islands. **August** Hamilton Island Race Week (www.hamiltonislandraceweek.com.au) brings offshore racing buzz as well as off-water wining and dining. **October–March** Look out for green and loggerhead turtles as they visit the waters around Wilson and Heron Islands.

'The resort sounds like a love shack built by God and Godzilla, yet it's a short bus trip from the airstrip, reminding us of its Marine National Park status'

● Lizard Island

Lizard Island

STYLE Reef encounter
SETTING Rugged island Eden

Pigs can fly. And when they jet to Lizard Island they can swim, snorkel, sail and scuba dive, too. They can even charter private dinghies to secluded beaches and frolic on the sand. For this little piggy, Lizard Island promised one long trough (for two) – a rare opportunity to swine and dine and snuffle out truffles in paradise. 'Take my trotter,' I told my love. 'We'll live high on the hog 24/7 until they drag us squealing wee-wee-wee all the way home.'

Mrs Smith and I fly to Lizard Island from Cairns at the northern tip of Queensland. It's a 240-kilometre, hour-long flight and our four-seat plane is soon dwarfed by the duelling big blues of ocean and sky. Below is the only patch of the planet where two World Heritage-listed locations – the Great Barrier Reef and ancient Daintree Rainforest – kiss. It's here Lizard Island looms into view. From a distance, its thousand-hectare sprawl is as Captain Cook discovered it in 1770, but closer inspection reveals the jewels that make it so exotic and exclusive a getaway.

Lizard Island resort sounds like a love shack built by God and Godzilla, yet a short bus trip from the airstrip reminds us of its Marine National Park status. There are no manicured gardens or sprinkler-strewn golf courses here. Instead wild scrub and rocky mountain ranges dominate an interior hemmed from a turquoise sea by powdery white sand and a nexus of 40 private villas, rooms and suites overlooking Sunset Beach and Anchor Bay. Our TV-free timber Anchor Bay Room is nestled amid a forest of trees with a day-bed and balcony bang on Watsons Beach. One quirk: it's a share suite. Tiny cute geckos dot the walls and, in the days to come, we strike a deal: they keep the insects down; we let them share our digs and drink our wine.

The resort's nucleus is the Lodge, home to a grand bar and restaurant whose decadent contents are totally free for the duration of our stay. And what marvellous liberties it affords us. Crude reminders of the real world – wallets, cash, credit cards, watches and mobiles – are stowed. Hell, there aren't even keys to the suites or price lists for the minibar. On Lizard, you come, go and do exactly as you please. And what pleases us immediately after arrival is toasting our new home from the Osprey's Restaurant by swilling several

mojitos, pigging out on cuttlefish salad and rabbit ragu, and soaking up a panoramic view of the wide blue yonder that, like the food and booze, is absolutely priceless.

Alas, while gluttony is encouraged on Lizard, our plans to render inactivity an art form are diverted by the Beach Club. Here we're kitted out with snorkelling gear and given our own motorised dinghy and a picnic basket laden with delicious treasures of the sea and soil. Soon we're puttering across the Blue Lagoon to deserted Mermaid Beach. Donning masks and flippers, we gorge on the glories of the Great Barrier Reef: swarms of neon-bright fish grazing hectares of spectacular coral gardens and underwater canyons filled to the gills with enchantments like starfish, stingrays, squid, sea cucumbers and giant clams older than us and lit from within by flickers of electricity and mystery. It ignites

our own passions and we clamber back to land and roll blissfully in the sand. Afterglow accompaniment? Fat prawns, fresh fruit and chilled champagne. Happy daze.

In the days that follow we're tempted to explore Lizard Island's other delights – the various walks, dives, fishing trips and yachting available to guests, the tour of the research station on the island's south side and the ruins of a stone cottage of an ill-fated early settler – but the truth is we simply can't be bothered, and here that's respected. Instead, we while away mornings in a haze of lobster omelettes, breakfast beers and reef snorkelling. Afternoons are spent beachside with books, cocktails and covert dips between rocks and hard places. When tropical night falls, we wander to Osprey's and mercilessly assail the bar while running riot through chef Vanessa Grace's ever-changing menu of gastronomic triumphs. Finally, with cheese platter and posh bottle of plonk in tow, we weave back to base and wink out on the day-bed, our soundtrack the trill of the birds and bugs in the trees and the lapping ocean beyond, and our cinema the reef of stars above.

Our final morn dawns with my finding a gecko in a glass of grenache. He's dyed pink and pissed as, er, a newt. It's a sign: the party is over. As he staggers into the bush, front desk rings to grant our request for a late check-out. ('How late?' they ask. 'Christmas?' Mrs Smith replies.) We can't complain. Aside from an elbow-heavy masseuse and a siesta chainsawed by a ride-on mower, they've met our every whim and wish. Now, sipping one last cocktail, we try to tattoo on our mind's eye the magic of a sacred place the Dingaal Aborigines know as Jiigurru. To them, this land mass is a stingray with Lizard Island as the body and adjoining rocky outcrops as the tail. Here, at the bar, it's easy to believe it. To them and to us, Lizard Island will always be Dreamtime.

REVIEW BY ANGUS FONTAINE

'Swarms of neon-bright fish graze coral gardens and underwater canyons lit from within by flickers of electricity'

NEED TO KNOW

Rooms 40, including 18 suites and 15 villas.

Rates AU$1,700–AU$3,750, including all meals, alcoholic and soft drinks, plus watersports activities.

Check-out 11am, but flexible subject to availability. Check-in, 2pm.

Facilities Pool, spa, gym, tennis court, library with books and games, TV lounge with free internet. In rooms: Bose sound system with CD player and iPod dock, free minibar.

Children This resort is better suited to romantic couples in search of desert-island relaxation, and it doesn't cater to children 12 years or under.

Also There's a two-night minimum stay – no hardship given there are 24 ivory-white beaches to bask on and spectacular diving, fishing and snorkelling on your doorstep. For a full-on pamper, Lizard Island's Elemis-stocked Azure Spa specialises in hot-stone massage, steam rituals, and lime and ginger salt treatments. There's no mobile phone coverage on the island so just switch off and chill out.

IN THE KNOW

Our favourite rooms For privacy, book into one of the Anchor Bay Suites at the far end of the bay (numbers 23 to 26). These have expansive balconies offering glimpses through the trees to the tranquil turquoise waters of Anchor Bay and Sunset Beach, and a path straight from balcony to beach. Suites 17 and 18 have the best views and are suitable for families. In summer, stay in one of the Sunset Point Villas – numbers 5 to 8 look out onto Sunset Beach, where the sun sinks spectacularly below the horizon in the summer months. Honeymooners and celebrities usually opt for the Pavilion – secluded, luxurious and boasting sweeping beach views, a wraparound sun-deck and a private plunge pool.

Hotel bar Guests sip champagne and swap stories at the L-shaped marble bar in the restaurant. Cocktail nights are held every Thursday in the gazebo beside the main building.

Hotel restaurant Osprey's – named in honour of the birds nesting on the tiny island that are visible from the restaurant – serves French-accented Modern Australian dishes with a seafood bias and a barbecue every Thursday. It's set in an open semi-circular building, with lacquered hardwood flooring, comfy wicker chairs, chunky granite tables and gasp-inducing views.

Top table Tables 9 and 10 are the top spots for admiring the view at breakfast and lunch, but by dinner time there's no view to speak of once the sun's gone down, so any table will do. Although the resort doesn't do reservations, staff may make an exception if you've a proposal in mind.

Room service Not available as the resort is so spread out, but request a free picnic hamper if you fancy a beach outing.

Dress code Gucci sandals (the boardwalks eat heels), flowy sarongs, big sunglasses and even bigger hats.

Local knowledge You're at the northernmost tip of the Great Barrier Reef, so there are a plethora of water-based diversions on offer – wetsuits and snorkelling gear, catamarans, glass-bottom paddle boats and motorised dinghies are all provided free. You can also book half- or full-day dive trips on the resort's boat around dozens of top scuba sites, including the famed Cod Hole, where you can hand-feed colossal potato cod. Back on land, while away an afternoon on the tennis court or arrange a private beach picnic.

LOCAL EATING AND DRINKING

Osprey's is the island's only restaurant, serving breakfast, lunch and dinner.

GET A ROOM!

Use our free online booking service: check availability and make reservations through www.mrandmrssmith.com.

 SMITH CARD OFFER A Lizard Island oil burner.

Lizard Island Great Barrier Reef, Queensland 4870 (07 4043 1999; www.lizardisland.com.au)

'It feels a lot like a lavishly
appointed treehouse, perched amid
rainforest and oriented seaward –
nothing has been overlooked'

Hamilton Island

Qualia

STYLE High-end luxury
SETTING Tropical Hamilton Island idyll

I'm pleased I nabbed the window seat. As we descend, the spectacular Whitsundays bulge out of the depths like a great bunch of potbellied sea creatures lolling about in the midday sun.

A gracious envoy welcomes us on arrival with cool drinks, before a picturesque 10-minute drive to Qualia. This seems the ideal time to ask the obvious question: 'Why the choice of hotel name?' Mr Smith and I, having imagined myriad definitions of an indigenous term, couldn't have got it more wrong. It's ancient Greek, meaning a deep multi-sensory experience. Just what the doctor ordered.

'Welcome to Qualia' is the gentle greeting on our arrival at the Long Pavilion, the heart of the resort. It would be a cynical traveller who didn't find themselves in awe of the breathtaking view from this space – it's here that we begin to fully appreciate our good fortune. Standing in the middle of the world's largest marine park is in itself a rare gift, never mind that we're on the tip of an island peninsula taking in a 250-degree view of pristine nature and countless islands as far as the eye can see. The space itself sets an architectural tenor consistent throughout the resort – natural materials, mostly wood and stone, meticulously detailed and finished, furnished with muted organic tones. The pervasive atmosphere is luxurious calm. Honestly, you could just sit here all day – looking over the step-straight-in infinity pool – without ever making it to your room.

'Glass of French? Don't mind if I do. It's my usual tipple.' What am I saying? Well, in a place like this I can even believe it myself. Lounging on couches, we're taken through a tantalising orientation of the premises. No standard check-ins here; just a cosy poolside chat, followed by a golf-buggy ride through the grounds for a spot of lunch.

The resort is revealed as a 'community' of pavilions enveloped by lush tropical gardens and forest. At the base of the hill, nestled on a pebbly beach is – you guessed it – Pebble Beach, another of Qualia's network of retreats. There's a second gorgeous infinity pool and an open-air café, should you need refreshment while you swim.

Following a scrumptious meal of Moreton Bay bugs – also known as the bay lobster – we might well be tempted to grab a towel and rest by the pool, or perhaps opt to use the catamarans or kayaks calling out to us from the beach. Nah. In truth, we're dying to take a look at our room.

'Swiss Family Robinson circa 2010,' says Mr Smith. It does, indeed, feel a lot like a lavishly appointed treehouse, perched amid rainforest and oriented seaward. It's totally private and nothing has been overlooked. Really, it's an open-plan apartment, with a subtle dividing off of exterior, sitting, sleeping and bathing spaces. We plunge into our personal infinity pool and emerge, re-energised enough to appreciate the giant day-bed.

Time for some serious relaxation. I'm determined not to go any longer without testing Spa Qualia. Given the extensive possibilities – everything from hot-stone therapy to detoxifying wraps – I'm concerned my choice of a bespoke massage might seem tame. I needn't have worried. From the delicious signature herbal tea on arrival to the fabulous rub-down and Vichy shower that follows, this is pure pampering Great Barrier Reef style. My post-ritual meditation, however, is halted by a demanding Mr Smith wanting to explore the entire five square kilometres of this Queensland island, before the sun hits the watery horizon.

There are virtually no cars on Hamilton, so most holidaymakers explore in golf buggies. The residual effect is that the place is wonderfully quiet. We stop for a cocktail atop a hill, where a sunset bar is set up each evening so people can enjoy the extraordinary vista, drink in hand, or spy on distant islands through a coin-operated telescope. On the island's main street, a group of shops, cafés and restaurants are upstaged by the pretty harbour. White weatherboard buildings and sparkling yachts remind us of Californian fishing villages. Every Sunday evening there's a laid-back acoustic performance here on the grassy banks, so we settle in with ice-creams to listen for a while.

The romance of the Long Pavilion, and chef Jane-Therese Mulry's tropical delicacies, beckon. Mr Smith and I, seated on the deck under a brilliant sky, give the seven-course degustation menu a thorough sampling. Mod Oz dishes such as foie gras pithivier, crab and coriander tians and desiree-wrapped blue-eye cod give our tastebuds, and our mental dictionaries, a satisfying workout. We retire for armchair coffee in the bar, and we are sufficiently caffeinated to visit the library for some post-prandial cerebration. Mr Smith takes up an archaeological tome, while I opt for a limited-edition photographic compilation. So many gorgeous books, so little time. Back in our room I head for the pod-shaped tub to soak up the Aesop products. Mr Smith instead flexes his technological muscles with the audio/video choices. As a couple who often choose to relax in different ways, Qualia allows us to rev up or wind down in perfect synchronicity.

On our final morning we consider our brief indulgence. Mr Smith reminds me of the legend of Marc Antony transporting a beach of sand to the island of Sedir, off the Turkish coast, so that Cleopatra could meet him in an exotic location and still claim Egyptian soil between her toes. This unique hideaway evokes such fantasies. Indeed, Qualia lives up to its etymology: all five senses have been stimulated and also sated. A sixth one tells me this affair will be long remembered. And if you think that sounds sexy, it is intended to.

REVIEWED BY SIGRID THORNTON

NEED TO KNOW

Rooms 60 pavilions, including 33 north-facing Windward Pavilions, 26 south-west-facing Leeward Pavilions and one secluded Beach House.

Rates AU$950–$3,500, with a choice of either breakfast (Qualia Classic) or breakfast and dinner at the Long Pavilion or Pebble Beach (Qualia Gourmet).

Check-out 11am, but flexible subject to availability. Check-in, 2pm.

Facilities Two infinity pools, gym, spa, library, free WiFi, two-seater buggies for every suite. In rooms: flatscreen TVs, DVD/CD players available on request, iPod dock, minibar, Aesop toiletries, private plunge pool (Windward Pavilions only).

Children This serene hotel is better suited to couples, and doesn't cater for children under the age of 16.

Also The resort has 12 hectares of immaculately landscaped grounds to explore, and the spa promises ocean views and a soothing mix of treatments using Sodashi and LI'TYA products.

IN THE KNOW

Our favourite rooms The Beach House, a super-private, self-contained pavilion, is our dream stay. It comes with a master bedroom and ensuite, a spacious living area with a dining table for 10, a separate guesthouse and its own 12-metre infinity pool. We also love Windward Pavilions 5, 6 and 7 (which have uninterrupted views over the Great Barrier Reef), and Leeward Pavilion 23, which has an extra deck.

Hotel bar Drinks can be taken in the sunken lounge of the Long Pavilion, where you can sip tropical fruit-inspired cocktails on low-slung couches, or in a raised area that overlooks the resort's lap pool.

Hotel restaurant The Long Pavilion is the resort's fine-dining eatery, where you'll find Modern Australian cuisine – Barossa Valley chicken terrine, kangaroo tail consommé – served up at candlelit tables swathed in white linen. Pebble Beach comprises a balcony set over the water and it is a more informal affair.

Top table If it's a hot night, ask for any of tables 60 to 65 so you can dine beneath the stars.

Room service Available 24 hours a day if you'd prefer to order a food platter in the privacy of your own pavilion.

Dress code Little black dress and jewellery for her; open-necked shirt and trousers for him.

Local knowledge Take a short boat trip to Whitehaven Beach, often rated as one of the most beautiful in the world. With seven kilometres of pure-white sand, it's the largest in the archipelago, stretched along the south-east coast of nearby Whitsunday Island.

LOCAL EATING AND DRINKING

As Qualia features two top-notch restaurants you probably won't want to stray further afield, but if you fancy a change of scene head for the marina. Home to most of the bars and restaurants which aren't part of a hotel, it's a good spot to score an ice-cream, fish and chips or deli treats. For a fuller meal, lively **Romano's Italian Restaurant** is set waterside on this aquatic hub, serving up classic dishes and a fresh daily-changing seafood menu. **Manta Ray Pizza** offers wood-fired pizzas and a little bar with marina views. **Beach House Restaurant** at the end of Catseye Beach specialises in Mod Oz dishes and its seductive vistas of distant islands make it ideal for a relaxed lunch or romantic dinner. For an alfresco drink head to **Marina Daze**, an open-air bar under the canopy of a mock ship's mast and sails, 'moored' on a grassy area by the waterfront. There's a central number for all reservations on the island (07 4946 9999).

GET A ROOM!

Use our free online booking service: check availability and make reservations through www.mrandmrssmith.com.

 SMITH CARD OFFER A bottle of champagne.

Qualia Hamilton Island, the Whitsundays, Great Barrier Reef, Queensland 4803 (02 9433 3349; www.qualia.com.au)

+61

+64

North Island
NEW ZEALAND

NORTH ISLAND

AUCKLAND

CITYSCAPE Handsome high-rise harbour
CITY LIFE Boats, beaches, boutiques and bands

If New Zealand's not shy at flaunting her natural beauty, her largest city is a positive show-off. Not just a buzzy place, this volcano- and ocean-flanked North Island hub is one of the world's best appointed, its come-hither harbours and beguiling beaches also blessed with a clement climate. Scratch beneath the shimmering surface and expose a vibrant young culture fast gaining international credibility for design and the arts, with its rich Maori heritage fuelling a uniquely Polynesian 21st-century allure. Sleepier parts of the country may accuse Aucklanders of an air of arrogance – but there's no denying they've reason to be proud. Stylish shopping, rewarding vineyard-hopping and world-class galleries are only a few feathers in their hometown's colourful cap. Indeed, the City of Sails has all the cool confidence of a capital, even if Wellington wears that crown.

GETTING THERE

Planes Auckland Airport (www.aucklandairport.co.nz) is located 21 kilometres south of the city.

Boats Ferries (www.fullers.co.nz) connect with the North Shore, Hauraki Gulf islands and Half Moon Bay near Howick. The trip to Waiheke Island's Matiatia Wharf takes 35 minutes, or catch a SeaLink car ferry (www.sealink.co.nz), a 45-minute ride to Kennedy Point.

Trains Only one train, the Overlander, operates out of Auckland, running daily to Wellington via Hamilton and Palmerston North (www.tranzscenic.co.nz).

Automobiles If you're just visiting as a stopover, you won't need a car, but if you intend to do some exploring, wheels are a must. Beach Road's car hire firms include Avis (www.avis.co.nz) and Budget (www.budget.co.nz). If you fancy something more boy-racer, try NZ Motorcycle Rentals (www.nzbike.com).

LOCAL KNOWLEDGE

Taxis Pick up a taxi from one of the ranks in the CBD or around town, or hail one in popular areas. Auckland Co-Op Taxis (09 300 3000) is a good bet, or on Waiheke Island, try Waiheke Taxis (09 372 8038).

Packing tips Kiwis will tell you Neil Finn wrote the Crowded House hit 'Four Seasons in One Day' about Auckland (actually, it's about Melbourne) and that should give you a hint: take something warm, something for a hot day, something for a glam night out and something for a day on a yacht.

Recommended reads Witi Ihimaera, one of NZ's greatest living writers, reimagines the country's colonial history through Maori eyes in *The Matriarch*. *Hibiscus Coast* by Paula Morris is a fast-paced, fictional view of the world of art forgery in Auckland and Shanghai.

Local specialities Auckland is fiercely proud of its food and wine, and with reason. Best described as Pacific Rim fusion, its signature cuisine brings together elements from South-East Asia and the surrounding Pacific nations with Mediterranean and European traditions. In addition, the produce is first rate, much of it sourced locally using sustainable methods.

Do go/don't go The warmer months (November to April) are perfect for enjoying life outdoors, though you should avoid the weeks after Christmas when NZ kids are on school holiday. June to August is the winter high season for skiing further afield on both the North and South Islands, so factor in a few days in Auckland first.

WORTH GETTING OUT OF BED FOR

Viewpoint Auckland's iconic Sky Tower is the southern hemisphere's tallest structure at 328 metres. Enjoy the scary but unmissable views through the observation deck's glass floor – it's NZ$28 to visit the top, or NZ$11 for kids (www.skycityauckland.co.nz). If you haven't got a head for heights, the North Shore's Takapuna Beach Café (www.takapunabeachcafe.co.nz) has views of Rangitoto Island and serves a mean all-day breakfast.

Arts and culture This cosmopolitan city's 800-year Maori history is celebrated at the Auckland Museum (www.aucklandmuseum.com). If time is on your side, join Potiki Adventures (www.potikiadventures.com) for a memorable trip through contemporary Maori life. Art fans should make for the Auckland Art Gallery (www.aucklandartgallery.govt.nz), which houses the most impressive collection of national and international works in New Zealand. If you're more of the nautical persuasion, the National Maritime Museum (www.maritimemuseum.co.nz) should float your boat.

Activities New Zealand is the place for adventurers, but even if adrenalin coursing through your veins isn't quite your thing, the outdoors have much to offer. Sailing is massive here, with loads of Aucklanders owning boats, and it's a chilled-out way to get active. Take to the harbour in style with Sail NZ (www.sailnewzealand.co.nz). For two hours, you can either help to crew or just sit back and enjoy the ride.

Best beach For moody atmospherics it's hard to beat Karekare, 35 kilometres west of Auckland. Black sand leads down to the surf at this star of the big screen (it featured in *The Piano*). There's no public transport, which keeps visitor numbers down, and the surf can be wild, so only swim when lifeguards are on duty.

Daytripper Worth a day exploring, and even an overnight stay, is the boho but increasingly upmarket Waiheke Island (www.waihekenz.com). Just a half-hour ferry ride from Auckland city, it offers boutique wineries, an extensive community of artists, sheltered beaches and plenty of activities, including kayaking and

windsurfing. Take a walk around the Connells Bay Sculpture Park (bookings essential; www.connellsbay.co.nz), before heading to Cable Bay Vineyards (www.cablebayvineyards.co.nz) for lunch and a wine tasting. To truly spoil yourself, plan a day's sailing on Flying Carpet (www.flyingcarpet.co.nz), an 11.5-metre yacht, designed by the captain, Bernard Rhodes.

Children It's not only the kids who'll love Goat Island Marine Reserve, 90 kilometres to the north of the city. Knee-deep in the water, you'll come up close to sea creatures such as blue maomao and snapper fish. Snorkelling is safe, and gear (including wetsuits) is available to hire from Seafriends (www.seafriends.org.nz). Within Auckland, Devonport's quaint beaches on the North Shore are also child-friendly.

Walks Take a stroll through the serene Auckland Domain, a 75-hectare park within the crater of the Pukekawa volcano. There's a sculpture walk, playing fields, duck ponds and the Wintergarden, where tropical plants grow in two gorgeous glasshouses.

Perfect picnic Waiheke Island's Palm Beach is a perfect stretch of white sand in a sheltered bay. If you're coming from the mainland, pack your basket before you leave – there's a barbecue area, so stock up on Euro-style sausages at Frankies Wurstbude, Shop 4, Elliott Stables at 41 Elliott Street (09 365 2700). If

you're not that organised, try Island Thyme, a delicatessen in nearby Surfdale, or, on Saturday morning, the Ostend Market (www.ostendmarket.co.nz), both on Waiheke.

Shopping Edgy Ponsonby Road plays host to labels you may know, and some you may not. Storm (www.stormnz.com), Carlson (www.tanyacarlson.com) and Marvel Menswear (www.marvelmenswear.co.nz) are all worth tapping. For cool Kiwiana, try the Garden Party (www.thegardenparty.co.nz). Running off Ponsonby is the famous K Road (short for Karangahape). It's a grungier destination for lovers of vintage fashion, and fans of comic books should also check out For Sale (www.heroes4sale.co.nz). The suburb of Newmarket is home to two major NZ fashion talents, Karen Walker at 6 Balm Street (www.karenwalker.com) and Kate Sylvester at 1 Teed Street (www.katesylvester.com), who also have stores around hip High Street in the CBD. For alternative underwear, pop to Thunderpants (www.thunderpants.co.nz).

Something for nothing If you can handle the smell, check out the daily early-morning auction at Auckland Fish Market (www.aucklandfishmarket.co.nz), where the google-eyed fish make a fascinating sight.

Don't go home without... visiting Otara Market. The world's biggest Polynesian bazaar, held every Saturday from 6am till noon, is hidden in the city's south, on Newbury Street, off East Tamaki Road. Buy exotic fruit and veg, woven baskets, paua shell jewellery and tuck into cheap eats galore – but it's the crowd which is just as entertaining.

ABSOLUTELY AUCKLAND

Many cities grow up in close proximity to volcanoes, but 50 of them? That's how many make up the Auckland Volcanic Field, and not all of them are extinct. Rangitoto (www.rangitoto.org), on an island off the city's North Shore, was the last to erupt about 600 years ago, and you can walk to the summit in about an hour.

DIARY

March Pasifika Festival (see events at www.aucklandcity.govt.nz) celebrates the South Pacific's diverse cultures with trad and contemporary music and performances in Auckland's Western Springs Park. Auckland Festival (on odd years) (www.aucklandfestival.co.nz), the country's biggest arts festival, takes over the city, showcasing global theatre, dance, music and visual arts. **May** The NZ International Comedy Festival (www.comedyfestival.co.nz) sees comedians from all over the world infiltrate the city's clubs and pubs. **July** The New Zealand International Film Festival (www.nzff.co.nz) features local productions as well as retrospectives, world cinema and animation. **September** Air New Zealand Fashion Week (www.nzfashionweek.com) promotes NZ's top designers, with sales, shows and seminars on the weekend. Heritage Week (www.aucklandcity.govt.nz) explores unique aspects of the city's history.

'Shutters open out towards the bay; the common areas in the main house are strewn with travel books and magazines'

Waiheke Island

The Boatshed

STYLE Nautical chic
SETTING Bayside bliss

Things had not got off to an auspicious start. Flights to Auckland were full and we'd been put on stand-by, only to leave 24 hours later. Mr Smith's luggage was lost somewhere in Abu Dhabi (it did finally arrive... three days later) and, as we travel across the Hauraki Gulf of New Zealand on the passenger ferry to Waiheke Island, the weather is dark and stormy.

Mercifully, the managers at the Boatshed had organised for a taxi to collect us from the jetty. The driver also randomly collected another older man, who lived locally and needed a lift. 'The weather's a bit crook,' he says from the front seat, turning around to give us a wink.

Thankfully, things start to improve almost as soon as we arrive at the Boatshed, five minutes away. The sun peeks through the clouds, and Jonathan, the owner of this small, unique hotel, greets us warmly. As he's showing us around, he tells us that the house, which is just what this feels like, started life as the beachside getaway for his designer father, David Scott. Shutters open out towards the bay, the common areas in the main house are strewn with travel books and magazines, and everything feels very homely and beachy. We finally begin to relax.

The attention to detail extends to the accommodation. There are just seven rooms and Jonathan shows us to our Boathouse Suite (there's no official check-in, forms to fill out or talk of money – how chic and discreet). Even Mr Smith, who's still feeling put out about his bags, raises a smile. The pale tones, nautical touches (a large model yacht reminds us of what this part of the world is famous for), comfy sitting area and huge bed made up with super-soft linens and piles of pillows are completely gorgeous. There's also an entertainment system with a selection of CDs. 'Look,' says Mr Smith, holding up discs by V V Brown and Sebastien Tellier, 'there are even ones we like.' Things are definitely on the up. Then we notice our private deck. There's a view of the ocean, a pair of deckchairs and it's undercover, so we can retreat there for book-reading and snoozing if the rain makes a reappearance.

Our international flight means we've arrived early, so Jonathan has organised breakfast for us. Fruit, yoghurt, toast and freshly brewed coffee certainly are a welcome change after more than 24 hours of aeroplane food. We even make a new friend; Jonathan's sweet pooch, Rupert, nuzzles up to Mr Smith and makes him finally forget that he's supposed to be grumpy.

With jet-lag taking hold, we could easily come over all supine on the deck and watch the day disappear, but Waiheke Island is waiting to be explored. The closest village, Oneroa, is just a 10-minute walk away along a beachfront path. It's a peaceful village, with a few shops, cafés and galleries. We stop at the i-SITE (for the uninitiated, that's the tourist information office) and are told that while there's no shortage of activities on offer – Connells Bay Sculpture Park, sea kayaking, horse riding and scuba diving – we shouldn't miss the wineries.

We jump on the local bus and tell the driver we're heading to Stonyridge Vineyard. He drops us at the end of a dirt track with just a sign pointing us in the right direction. Fortune favours the brave, so we traipse off and soon feel as though we've been transported into the heart of Tuscany. The afternoon has turned

on the sunshine, before us are rolling fields of vines, olives and lavender, and there's a spectacular building housing a café and cellar door. There's also a tour of the winery, but we decide instead to grab a table on the veranda and sample the tapas menu and merlot.

Eventually we call a taxi and take our tipsy selves to the east side of the island and the village of Onetangi. There's not a whole lot to do but take a long stroll along the beach, admiring the houses that overlook the bay. We loved the wine at Stonyridge so much that we decide to stop at Charlie Farley's, the local bar, for some more but instead put away a couple of shandies.

With the sun setting, we head back to our love nest at the Boatshed. Mr Smith, sent to fetch a DVD, comes back with – well, it's a chick flick if you must know. But let's pretend it was something arthousey. What more could you want? To stay awake for it, for a start. I nap through most of the second half of the film before Mr Smith rouses me for dinner at the main house. Jonathan is playing chef tonight and serves up some beautiful canapés, glasses of wine and a three-course meal. We love the entrée of ravioli with crispy pancetta, king prawns and burnt butter sauce. Back at our boudoir, the turndown fairies have been: the candles are lit, music is playing softly and we slip between the crisp sheets. I know, I know, call the cliché police – there's just no other way to put it – it's the perfect end to a perfect day.

REVIEWED BY MR & MRS SMITH

'Fortune favours the brave, so we traipse off and soon feel as though we've been transported into the heart of Tuscany'

NEED TO KNOW

Rooms Seven suites.

Rates Low season, NZ$630–$790; high season, NZ$745–$910, including breakfast and on-island transfers.

Check-out 12pm, but flexible subject to availability. Check-in, 2pm.

Facilities DVD, CD and book library. In rooms: TV, DVD/CD players, iPod dock, free WiFi, minibar, Living Nature toiletries, beach kit (including parasol, sun hats, beach bag, sand mat and sunblock).

Children The hotel isn't suitable for kids under 12, so make this a romantic break.

Also For stylish beach-hopping, hire one of the Boatshed's speedy Mini Moke Togs – Jeep-style buggies replete with an iPod loaded with jazzy, summery tunes (NZ$150 a day; book one when you reserve your room). Beauty and spa treatments can be arranged in your room if you'd prefer to be pampered.

IN THE KNOW

Our favourite rooms We adore the three Boatshed Suites for a nostalgic beach hut look; open up the pale louvred shutters and enjoy sea breezes from your sunlounger on the secluded teak decks. Most romantic, though, is the three-storey retreat the Lighthouse, a whitewashed wooden hideaway with a separate bedroom and dayroom; vast glass doors lead onto private decks. Keep an eye on passing boats with the handy telescope like a lighthouse keeper surveying your domain. Evocative seaside accessories throughout include ships' bells and toy sailing boats.

Hotel bar Open all day, the bar sports an impressive list of local wines. The speciality cocktail is a Moscow Mule with organic ginger beer; the soundtrack spans jazz and Café del Mar tunes. There's also free port in-room for sunset lounging.

Hotel restaurant Join other guests in the light, airy dining room, or opt for private dining on your balcony, by the fire or alfresco. There is a daily-changing lunch menu (NZ$20–$35) and a four-course dinner (NZ$110). Enjoy fresh Mediterranean-style fare, gourmet meat cuts or seafood platters (grilled scampi or barbecued snapper are our top tips). The free breakfast teams roasted Waiheke coffee with heavenly hot dishes such as ricotta hotcakes with maple-poached figs.

Top table For breathtaking ocean views, ask to be seated out on the deck.

Room service Available 24 hours a day with a changing menu, or request a picnic. If you're dining privately at the Lighthouse Suite you can have dishes delivered via a trad dumb waiter.

Dress code White linen separates and a striped Breton top for relaxed seaside chic.

Local knowledge Pristine Little Oneroa Beach, and adjacent Oneroa Beach, are just five minutes' walk away, or stroll to nearby Oneroa village, where you can trawl antique and thrift stores, arts and crafts studios and galleries.

LOCAL EATING AND DRINKING

With views of vineyards and olive groves, **Cable Bay Winery** (09 372 5889) is ideal for courtyard lunches or dinners washed down with its acclaimed wine. For a mellow atmosphere, Oneroa's **Mudbrick Vineyard & Restaurant** (09 372 9050) offers award-winning cuisine, including fish and lamb, and **Stonyridge Vineyard** (09 372 8822) on Onetangi Road is renowned for organic reds (think cabernet blends), with a romantic veranda café. To dine on tapas on a pretty patio amid olive trees, go Spanish at **Casita Miro** (09 372 7854) at Miro Vineyard in Onetangi, or hit cheery local beachside bar/restaurant **Charlie Farley's** (09 372 4106) on the Strand at Onetangi Bay.

GET A ROOM!

Use our free online booking service: check availability and make reservations through www.mrandmrssmith.com.

 SMITH CARD OFFER A tasting plate of local Waiheke delicacies on arrival.

The Boatshed corner Tawa and Huia Streets, Little Oneroa, Waiheke Island 1081 (09 372 3242; www.boatshed.co.nz)

'The classical-music theme
pervades the hotel, starting with
a grand piano in the salon — for
those celebrated nightly recitals'

Mollies

STYLE A fine romance
SETTING Pretty Ponsonby port

Amid a forest of candles and lavish floral arrangements, Mollies' proprietor Frances Wilson sits at the Steinway piano, as she does every evening, providing the accompaniment to the hotel's famous pre-dinner drinks soirée. A student from Wilson's own Auckland Opera School (which Frances runs from the hotel) sings an aria, and the music embraces the room and everyone in it. It's an indication, if we hadn't already realised it, that a stay here will be something we won't soon forget.

Ah yes, there is romance in the air at Mollies, despite the fact that on this particular visit Mr Smith and I are accompanied by our eight-year-old Junior Smith. Luckily, unlike some luxury boutique hotels, this one welcomes small folk, providing them with the same lavish experience as its more mature guests.

Located in Ponsonby, a few streets back from Auckland Harbour, Mollies is all about stylish luxury. Wilson and her partner, Stephen Fitzgerald, share a love of design and are responsible for the hotel's glam interiors. Combining French provincial elegance with rich layers of fine fabrics, oil paintings and excellent glassware, the decor is luscious and eclectic, without being confused. The classical-music theme pervades the hotel, starting with a grand piano in the salon – for those celebrated nightly recitals – and amplified by the artworks and musical instruments scattered throughout, including a show-stopping harp.

As a middle-aged visual artist prone to bouts of grumpiness I can be hard to please, but as much as my inner curmudgeon tried to be critical, only one verdict was possible: Mollies is spot on. Colour is used sparingly, highlighting the exquisite choice of textures expressed in the artworks, textiles, marble and plaster walls. Whether it's sumptuous red-velvet bolsters against snow-white bedlinen or differing hues in the layered curtains in the downstairs salon, the result is a visual feast.

And to our room. A two-storey Premium Villa Suite, it has a generous downstairs lounge and private dining area that opens onto a balcony overlooking the charming courtyard garden and the highly acclaimed day spa (Auckland kept us too busy to use it, sadly – hopefully next time we'll fit it in). With heated travertine marble floors throughout and a gas fire with marble mantel, even winters in Auckland feel deliciously warm. A small kitchenette, tucked discreetly away behind bi-folds, houses everything you could desire, from fine starched-linen napkins to beautiful antique porcelain teacup sets. Just the ticket for any tea snobs who think it too vulgar to take their tipple from a mug.

The king-size bed in the master bedroom is the definition of dreamy: I counted six pillows on the bed, each a different enticing feel. The large marble bathroom has twin sinks, heated towel rails (surely an invention of the Romans), a spa bath, an oversize shower and armfuls of big squishy white towels. It is refreshing,

too, that Mollies encourages guests to consider their own environmental accountability, with fine toiletries available from stylish dispensers rather than an array of unnecessary landfill-feeding disposable bottles. Eco luxe – we like.

By the time we go downstairs to dinner, Junior Smith, who quickly assumed the role of HRH Princess Smith, is ensconced upstairs in her own spacious mezzanine room, with antique wooden bed, large television and private balcony with wonderful views. The mezzanine, with a clear glass balustrade, allows Her Royal Highness to deliver instructions from above, 'Please run my spa bath now' and 'I'm ready for my pre-dinner mocktail' among them. With the phone and concierge's number at her side, this was also a fine place for Princess Smith to enjoy a DVD of *Grease* from the hotel's library, while her parents dined peacefully downstairs.

Mollies is justifiably famous for its superb dining; the food and setting are sublime. The speciality is a five-course tasting menu (six if you count the canapés), each with matching New Zealand wines from Marlborough, Hawke's Bay and Waiheke Island. The attentive waiter explained each course in detail while spotlighting our culinary sculptures with the mini torches provided at each table (so the candlelit atmosphere doesn't trick you into eating something you shouldn't). Multiple under-plating further dramatises the parade of delights that includes smoked cauliflower soup, duck liver parfait, fresh local salmon and other kaleidoscopic miniature towers of tempting treats.

The next morning, as the three of us pack, we agreed that Mollies had every base covered. The staff had thought of everything that might make our stay fabulous. The service is exemplary – attentive but never stifling – and we never felt we needed to be anyone we were not. As we were preparing to leave, Princess Smith had found a gift left behind by the room fairies (possibly the same ones who came in to tidy twice a day): a small, velvet-lined box covered in mosaic disco-ball mirrors. She's not the only one who thinks we should sell our home in Australia and move permanently to Mollies.

REVIEWED BY HELEN BODYCOMB

NEED TO KNOW

Rooms 13 suites.

Rates NZ$613–$979. Breakfast is extra, at NZ$39.

Check-out 11am, but can be extended for a night's tariff. Check-in, 3pm.

Facilities CD, DVD and book library, free WiFi throughout, spa, gym, gardens. In rooms: flatscreen satellite TV, DVD/CD players, iPod dock, minibar, Molton Brown toiletries, balcony.

Children The hotel can supply baby cots for NZ$65 a night and arrange babysitting with a nanny for NZ$35 an hour. The restaurant offers a children's menu.

Also Mollies has a musical bent, with a magnificent piano in the lounge area and a penchant for sophisticated soirées. Be sure to catch one of the regular, 20-minute evening opera recitals held most nights around 7.30pm to get you in the mood for dinner.

IN THE KNOW

Our favourite rooms If you're musically inclined, ask for one of the Premier Villa Suites with a grand piano (some overlook the verdant garden terrace with its outdoor fireplace, others come with views of Auckland Harbour). At the front of the hotel with vistas of distant water, ground-floor room 1 offers contemporary white decor, and room 8, above it, is more of a New York-style loft. All Mollies' spacious suites are individually decorated with a boho blend of antiques and vintage finds, and evocative distressed walls.

Hotel bar Pre-dinner drinks are popular at pretty, white Mollies Bar. Order a classic cocktail or port, cognac and liqueurs.

Hotel restaurant Food is a major event at Mollies, with chef Lance Tripp whipping up contemporary New Zealand cuisine in the Dining Room (here's a taster: tempura quail with cauliflower purée, wasabi, aïoli, radish and rhubarb, for dinner), accompanied by fine wine. Decor is a maverick mix-and-match of Victorian and modern, with oversized blue vases, ornate glass serving vessels and quirky figurines for place settings, all bathed in romantic candlelight.

Top table Ask for a spot in the glass atrium at the front of the dining area, where tables overlook the water.

Room service A selection of hot and cold food is available 24 hours a day.

Dress code With its operatic leanings and swelligant interiors, Mollies is a place to dress up, not down.

Local knowledge Mollies is located in chic district St Marys Bay, within a 10-minute stroll of Auckland's city centre. It's about five minutes to Ponsonby Road, a top tip for designer shopping (www.ponsonbyroad.co.nz).

LOCAL EATING AND DRINKING

If you can tear yourself away from Mollies' tasting menu, you'll find tempting restaurants, bars and cafés on happening nearby Ponsonby Road. **SPQR** (09 360 1710), at number 150, is a good bet for thin-crust Roman-style pizzas, drawing a cool crowd with its spartan interiors and low-level lighting. At 226, Italian eaterie **Prego** (09 376 3095) also serves up pizza alongside more experimental dishes. For fine dining, head for iconic **Vinnies Restaurant** (09 376 5597), at 166 Jervois Road, where you can choose between a seasonal or tasting menu, washed down with award-winning wines in glam surrounds (there's even a tiny art gallery showcasing area talent). For waterfront dining at Viaduct Harbour and Princes Wharf, check out buzzy contemporary restaurant **Soul** (09 356 7249), which offers alfresco seafood with views of yachts and sails. Also in the area, **Euro** (09 309 9866) teams harbour views with tasty Pacific Rim cuisine.

GET A ROOM!

Use our free online booking service: check availability and make reservations through www.mrandmrssmith.com.

 SMITH CARD OFFER Home-baked cookies and fruit on arrival.

Mollies 6 Tweed Street, St Marys Bay, Auckland 1011 (09 376 3489; www.mollies.co.nz)

BAY OF ISLANDS

COASTLINE Cliffs, coves and clear blue sea
COAST LIFE Maori culture, maritime nature

'Easy does it' is the mantra in this subtropical sanctuary where you can frolic amid 144 islands, craggy coves and crystalline waters on the breathtaking north-east coast of NZ's North Island. Animal lovers can spot dolphins, whales and penguins, while culture-vultures can soak up the area's fascinating early history and rich Maori heritage. It's the best of both worlds: plenty of buzzy surf-and-turf activities with loads of slacker alternatives for just kicking back and recharging. Do the rounds of pretty tourist hub Paihia, sleepy, historic Russell and mellow Kerikeri (known for its orchards and cafés) – as well as the famous Waitangi National Reserve. Or just tap into the laid-back pace of small-town seaside life by banking some beach time (Mother Nature has pulled out all the stops in this idyllic bay-bedecked wilderness). Captain Cook visited for a week in 1769; we suggest you do the same.

GETTING THERE

Planes Auckland (www.aucklandairport.co.nz) is the main international gateway for travel to Northland. Air New Zealand (www.airnewzealand.com) operates daily flights from there into Kerikeri Airport (www.bayofislandsairport.co.nz). There are also a number of charter operators offering helicopter and fixed-wing transport into the region (see www.saltair.co.nz; www.mountainair.co.nz; www.skylink.co.nz; www.skywork.co.nz; and www.airnational.co.nz).
Automobiles The drive from Auckland to the Bay of Islands is just over 200 kilometres and takes about three and a half hours. State Highway 1 goes to Paihia, where you can continue on to Kerikeri or hop to Russell on the ferry, which departs every 20 minutes.

LOCAL KNOWLEDGE

Taxis Local hubs Kerikeri and Paihia have taxis but they are usually run by tour operators and can be expensive. Dial-A-Ride offers a taxi and shuttle service between Kerikeri Airport and the Bay of Islands (www.dial-a-ride.co.nz). Water taxis are also available, but again are used mostly for private tours and start from NZ$130 for up to six people (www.islandshuttle.co.nz).
Packing tips Stock up on sunblock – and space on your camera's memory card.

Recommended reads *The Tales of the Angler's Eldorado*, by US Western writer Zane Grey, evokes an angling addict's passion for this marlin-fishing paradise.
Local specialities It doesn't get fresher than this; local produce, from vegetables to seafood, is plentiful. Test-drive it in the region's clutch of top restaurants, or in its many cafés serving tasty meals and mighty fine coffee.

Do go/don't go The warmer months from September to April are the best time to visit as it can get chilly in winter, when many tour companies close down.

Also... At the Russell Museum catch mementoes of the whaling trade, which had its heyday here in the 19th century, when the number of brothels and booze shops catering to the international whalers saw the region dubbed 'the hellhole of the Pacific' (www.russellmuseum.org.nz). Don't worry, the town has upped its game since.

WORTH GETTING OUT OF BED FOR

Viewpoint For a high-impact hit of the Bay of Islands head up to Flagstaff Hill (Maiki) in Russell. It was here that the Maori Hone Heke chopped down the flagstaff as a protest against British rule in the 1840s and this picturesque spot boasts panoramic views over town, across the islands and out to Waitangi.

Arts and culture Hone your Maori history with a pilgrimage to Waitangi Treaty Grounds, near Paihia, known as the birthplace of New Zealand, where the Maori and the British Crown signed the country's founding agreement in 1840. Check out the Treaty House, carved Maori Meeting House and ceremonial war canoe (www.waitangi.net.nz). For the inside track on the region's history, head for Russell Museum, and if you're interested in publishing, don't miss a tour of fascinating Pompallier (09 403 9015), an 1842 French Catholic mission and printing press famous for producing over 40,000 early religious texts in Maori.

Activities Scratch that watersports itch with fishing, sailing, sea kayaking, diving, snorkelling or parasailing (Paihia is the main hub for operators). The warm waters mean you can spot marine life year-round, including bottlenose dolphins and killer whales. For some of NZ's best diving, head for the Poor Knight Islands, a marine reserve off the coast near Tutukaka. Local dive firms include Dive! Tutukaka (www.diving.co.nz) and Knight Diver Tours (www.poorknights.co.nz).

Daytripper For an alternative day trip, swim with beautiful-and-brainy dolphins in their natural habitat. The Dolphin Eco Encounter departs from both Paihia and Russell for NZ$86 a person for adults and NZ$43 for kids (www.awesomenz.com).

Best beach There's candidates aplenty, but Roberton Island (Motuarohia) is a wildlife refuge with sweeping beaches, lagoons and great snorkelling, making it one of the most beautiful spots in the region. Reach it from Paihia for NZ$48 return, including snorkelling gear (www.islandshuttle.co.nz).

Children Actionworld, run by two former trapeze artists, has lots of high-wire action, tarzan swings, water slides and trapeze time to tire out your young charges (www.actionworld.co.nz). If your kids prefer creature comforts, they can get hands-on with farm animals at Lily Pond Farm Park in Paihia (09 402 6099).

Walks The Cape Brett Track is a challenging day's walking, but hey, you'll be saving on gym membership. The route goes through conservation areas and Deep Water Cove is a top spot for a snorkel. If you make it to the track's end, at the Cape's lighthouse, spectacular views of the outer Bay of Islands await (see www.doc.govt.nz). For an easier ramble, walk to Haruru Falls, a heavenly horseshoe-shaped waterfall three kilometres from Paihia. Haruru means 'big noise' and according to Maori legend a tanihwa, or water monster, lives in the lagoon below, so watch your step.

Perfect picnic Make like a millionaire and hang out on a yacht. Trips on the speedy 15-metre Phantom ocean racer include a picnic lunch (www.yachtphantom.com), at NZ$99 a person for adults and NZ$50 for kids, with a maximum of 10 guests.

Shopping Kerikeri is our tip for retail therapy and gallery hopping. There's an arts and crafts trail that takes in the local stores, with maps available from visitor centres. Russell's highlights include the Just Imagine Art Gallery (www.justimagine.co.nz) and Mudflats Pottery (09 403 8892).

Something for nothing If you're an architecture buff, get your kicks for free by taking a gander at some of the area's old missionary-founded buildings, such as musket fire-scarred Christ Church in Russell, which dates from 1836 and is the country's oldest church (www.oldchurch.org.nz). We wouldn't normally advocate hanging out in public toilets, but the one in Kawakawa, at 60 Gillies Street, should be on your to-do list. It was built by famous radical Austrian architect Friedensreich Hundertwasser, who spent the last 25 years of his life in the town from 1975 until 2000.

Don't go home without... getting a gannet's-eye view of the region by taking a scenic flight. Heliops offers a number of helicopter flight routes, from NZ$135 a person for a 20-minute bay-view whirl (with three on board), as well as heli-fishing trips to remote islands and rocks (www.heliops.co.nz).

BEAUTIFULLY BAY OF ISLANDS
The last resting place of the famous Greenpeace vessel *Rainbow Warrior* is here, at the Cavalli Islands, and is an evocative spot for diving. The ship was sunk by French saboteurs in 1985 in Auckland Harbour, but its skeletal remains were later transported to the Bay of Islands, where it now serves as an artificial reef that is home to a huge variety of aquatic life. Dive HQ operates trips out of Paihia (www.divenz.com). To find out more see www.rainbow-warrior.org.nz.

DIARY
6 February On Waitangi Day, commemorations are held at the Treaty Grounds. **May** A country music festival takes place in Paihia, Russell and Waitangi (www.country-rock.co.nz). The Maori new year, Matariki, is celebrated in Paihia at the end of May. **August** Catch the popular jazz festival in Paihia, Haruru Falls and Russell (www.jazz-blues.co.nz).

'The sun is beating down and beyond the deck is a view you could stare at for days: I'm reminded of scenes of Jamaica in *Live and Let Die*'

Russell

Eagles Nest

STYLE Modern, minimal, magical
SETTING Private peninsula paradise

'The name's Smith... Mr Smith.' We've just been shown to our villa at Eagles Nest and memories of the three hours of travel from Auckland have magically dissipated. It's not hard to imagine why Mr Smith has gone all 007 on me. For the next few days, the two of us are staying in the Eyrie, a super-luxe, ultra-contemporary three-bedroom bolthole. There's a home theatre, magnificent all-white bathroom, paintings by New Zealand artists and, best of all, an enormous deck with private infinity pool and Jacuzzi. Up to six people could stay here, but having this sort of space and privacy – we can't hear any other noise or see evidence of other guests – feels pretty rock star.

Already Kelly has given us a tour of our digs, including the fully equipped kitchen and, most importantly, the fridge stocked with all types of delectables. She's barely out the door when I crack open the bottle of complimentary champagne and tuck into the chocolate treats from the larder. She's also recommended a spot in nearby Russell where we might find ourselves some dinner before having an early night. An hour or so later, we've plonked ourselves in front of the television and are unwrapping the spoils of our food run: piles of hot fish and chips. The catch of the day, according to the man in the chippie. I don't recall – did James Bond ever kickback with a takeaway?

Jet-lag has Mr Smith up the next morning way too early for my liking, but my disappointment doesn't last long. He's opened the shutters and within seconds I am literally drooling. The sun is beating down and beyond the deck is a view that you could stare at for days: boats zip across the bay that is itself dotted with islands. I'm reminded of scenes of Jamaica in *Live and Let Die*. Palm trees line the sides of the deck, stopping anyone from seeing into our pool. We dive in but it's a little chillier than anticipated, so Mr Smith and I quickly duck into the steaming Jacuzzi and stare out at that water. We've heard you can spot dolphins out there, so, on a whim, Mr Smith pops inside to call the Eagles Nest office and see if they can organise for us to go on a tour of the Bay of Islands. Not only is it possible, they say, but we can go this morning.

Having already collected passengers at Pahia, the boat stops at Russell to get us. The crew is extremely knowledgeable about the sea life in the area, but after 40 minutes we've yet to see a dolphin. Then a call comes in from another vessel: there's a big pod of the mammals having their morning feed not far away. Within minutes we've spotted them and they put on a show, swimming alongside the boat and leaping acrobatically into the air. Everyone on the boat is beside themselves with excitement.

Heading out to our next spot, the Hole in the Rock, the weather turns and the boat starts to bob. 'I think I'd rather be having breakfast in bed right about now,' says Mr Smith, as we both start to feel decidedly green around the gills. The seas soon calm and we keep the contents of our stomachs where they belong, our nausea eclipsed by the scenes we're being treated to.

Back on shore, we head to one of Russell's waterfront cafés and indulge in some real comfort food: nachos for Mr Smith and a bacon and cheese toastie for me. Back at the villa, we decide to make the most of our five-star surrounds. I send Mr Smith up to the office to collect a

copy of *The Spy Who Loved Me* from the DVD library – it seems strangely appropriate, perhaps minus the Russian submarines and nuclear warheads.

Unlike many of New Zealand's luxury accommodation options, Eagles Nest doesn't have a central lodge where guests can gather or have meals. It can, however, organise for a chef to whip you up a fine spread to enjoy in your villa. To make sure we didn't miss out, Mr Smith organised all of this before we arrived. At 7.45pm, our personal chef Michael knocks on the door – we've already opened a bottle of bubbly – and he starts preparing our feast. We sup on starters of tiger prawns with citrus and rocket salad, and lamb and feta with roasted capsicum on crostini, followed by filet mignon served with portobello mushrooms, pommes Anna, roasted garlic and red wine jus (for Mr), and duck breast wrapped in prosciutto with roasted vegetables, baby potatoes and anise demi-glaze (for Mrs). Not only is he a great cook, but Michael is an amazing host, too. If only we could eat like this every night.

Having not made use of the amazing gadget-packed kitchen ourselves, the next morning Mr Smith and I decide to prepare an enormous departure breakfast (anything to delay leaving). Big servings of bacon and eggs, toast and juice are the perfect prelude to our upcoming drive. We grudgingly wave goodbye to our beautiful villa and its stunning subtropical setting. From behind the wheel of our tiny hire car, Mr Smith stares back with regret on his face and starts humming 'Nobody Does It Better'. He's right; we've never before experienced anything like Eagles Nest, and for a few days at least we got to live out enough Bond fantasies to last a lifetime.

REVIEWED BY MR & MRS SMITH

'I don't recall – did James Bond ever kickback
with a takeaway?'

NEED TO KNOW

Rooms Five villas, ranging from one to four bedrooms.
Rates NZ$1,295–$19,995 a villa (depending on size), including breakfast, fruit, champagne and some minibar drinks.
Check-out 11am. Check-in, 2pm. Earlier arrivals can be arranged for 50 per cent of your nightly tariff.
Facilities In rooms: flatscreen TV, DVD/CD player, home cinema including Sky satellite, free WiFi, kitchen, minibar, deck with barbecue, Jacuzzi, heated infinity lap pool (except First Light Villa).
Children All ages welcome. Infant cots and highchairs are free if booked.
Also Rahimoana Villa bookings require a three-night minimum stay.

IN THE KNOW

Our favourite rooms One-bedroom villa First Light is most intimate for couples, but for wow factor we love panoramic Rahimoana Villa, which has four spacious ensuite bedrooms, a fireplace, home cinema, bar and a 25-metre heated lap pool, as well as a Jacuzzi, sauna, gym and private beach. Rates include a dedicated concierge, well-stocked fridge and loan of a Porsche Cayenne Turbo. The crisply contemporary blue and white interiors and modern art are gorgeous too.
Hotel bar Rahimoana has its own bar – otherwise just dial the EN crew and drinks will be delivered; there's no main bar.
Hotel restaurant Each villa has a kitchen which is restocked daily with breakfast delights. However, most guests forego DIY and make use of the resort's private chefs (even Jamie Oliver likes a day off occasionally), who will prepare anything you'd like. Local venison, lamb and freshly caught crayfish and lobster are all on offer. You can also bring in your own chef if you prefer. The wine cellar at Eagles Nest boasts several thousand bottles from around the globe.
Top table It's hard to beat eating outdoors on your own private deck, but Rahimoana's sleek glass eight-seater dining table is our favourite indoors.
Room service Anything, any time. Chefs, butlers and shoppers are also on call.
Dress code You're surrounded by sleek style, so why not look the part? We suggest an Audrey Hepburn-style scarf to keep your hair tamed while you zoom around in the Porsche and a huge pair of sunglasses.
Local knowledge For a break from your sunlounger, you can book Eagles Nest's personal trainer, then relax with a beauty or massage treatment. There are also free mountain bikes at every villa if you want to explore the hotel's 30 hectares of subtropical bush and secluded beaches. Further afield, sail to one of the area's 144 islands, enjoy a gull's-eye view from the retreat's chopper or play a round of golf at Kauri Cliffs. Make the most of your seaside setting with a spot of waterskiing, scuba diving, snorkelling, sea kayaking or fishing.

LOCAL EATING AND DRINKING

If you fancy a change from private dining in your villa, venture out to **Omata Estate** (09 403 8007) at Aucks Road in Russell. This winery restaurant has incredible views and offers rustic dining indoors and outside in a sheltered courtyard, including barbecue food. Alternatively, waterfront **Kamakura Restaurant** (09 403 7771) at 29 The Strand in Russell is a seductive spot to watch the sunset and enjoy modern Kiwi dishes with Asian influences, such as market fish with papaya and lime salsa.

GET A ROOM!

Use our free online booking service: check availability and make reservations through www.mrandmrssmith.com.

 SMITH CARD OFFER A one-hour massage treatment.

Eagles Nest 60 Tapeka Road, Russell, Bay of Islands 0252 (09 403 8333; www.eaglesnest.co.nz)

'It has the ambience of an American billionaire's plantation lodge in the Deep South, with the most remarkable view of the Bay of Islands'

Kerikeri

The Lodge at Kauri Cliffs

STYLE Upscale country manor
SETTING Coastal cliffs, Pacific panoramas

They're not my usual Smith escape accessories, but my golf shoes and gloves are packed at the top of my luggage. I'm also carrying with me an air of expectation: Kauri Cliffs is a luxury golf resort comparable to few others in New Zealand. Large wooden gates open slowly to reveal a lengthy gravel drive, and we pass sheep and cattle grazing in paddocks dotted with pines. Finally, we come to a clearing where the lodge sits atop the cliffs of the North Island's Matauri Bay. Across a perfectly manicured lawn, Mr Smith and I spy the first indication that this is no ordinary golf resort: two flagpoles bear the US and New Zealand flags, waving in the breeze. With huge smiles and warm handshakes, a member of staff opens the lobby doors, inviting us into what will be our home for the next few days.

The aura is of understated elegance: the dining rooms have roaring fireplaces, the sitting room has enormous, squishy couches, and collections of art and antiques on display give the whole space that personal touch. It has the ambience of an American billionaire's plantation

lodge somewhere in the Deep South, except that when you walk outside on to the veranda there's the most remarkable vista of the Bay of Islands.

When we're taken to our room, I think I've died and gone to heaven. This is a room you want to steal back home in your hand luggage so nothing gets broken. Every detail is considered: caramel-colour soft furnishings sit against natural timber walls, rattan armchairs with wool throws are arranged before an open fireplace in the sitting room, and the sunken bath looks over a lush, private garden. I'm crazy about the his-and-hers wardrobes, the minibar complete with home-made biscuits for that early morning cuppa, and there's a terrace with attention-demanding views to the ocean.

The next morning, the sun rises on a picture-perfect day and we gear up for the 18 holes that lie ahead. Greg, the resort pro, talks us through the course. Six holes follow the cliff's edge, dropping off into the Pacific Ocean. Away from the sea, fairways wind their way through farmland and remnants of rainforest. It's not hard to see why aficionados from all over the world travel to play here. (Should you tire of the game, there's a beautiful diversion a 15-minute stroll from the seventh hole: a private beach that's an exquisite shade of soft pink, the result of pounding waves crushing shells into the tiniest flakes.)

After the ninth, Mr Smith and I are feeling a little peckish, so we drop into the clubhouse. Browsing the menu, we decide on coffees and toasted brie, pesto and roasted vegetable paninis. How special do we feel when it's suggested we keep playing and someone will deliver our order to us when it's ready? Sure enough, while I'm putting the tricky 10th, I spot a golf cart loaded up with lunch heading our way. Does holidaying get any better?

Following a tough day on the greens, I decide it's imperative to treat ourselves. It's not just the golfing that's world-class here; the spa is as good as it

'Do I have a body massage or indulge in a facial and
foot reflexology alfresco by the outdoor fireplace'

gets. Walking through a tranquil subtropical garden at
the edge of a totara forest, we notice quails skipping
over the pathways that lead to the spa. The verdant
views even extend to the inside. The treatment rooms
have floor-to-ceiling windows looking into a grove
of ferns and over a trickling stream. Spa manager
Nadia explains the treatment menu, putting me in a
spin. Do I have a body massage or indulge in a facial
and foot reflexology alfresco by the outdoor fireplace?
In the end, our busy golfing schedule makes the
decision for us. Mr Smith and I only have time for
a sauna and soak in the Jacuzzi. Regardless, it still
feels quite decadent.

Earlier, wandering through the main lodge, I'd noticed a
room decked out like an African-themed den. 'Wouldn't
that be a nice spot to have a private dinner,' I'd thought
as I took in the fireplace and sumptuous couches. That

evening, after cocktails and canapés with the other
guests, Mr Smith and I are escorted into this very
enclave – the Tiger Room. The perfect table for two has
been laid in front of that flickering fire. Taking a peek at
the five-course menu, I become quietly excited: Peking
duck consommé; Japanese tempura quail with wasabi,
avocado and ponzu; Hawke's Bay rack of lamb with
potato gratin, spinach and rosemary.

On our final morning, as the first rays of sunlight touch
my shoulder through the bamboo blinds, I listen to
the morning calls of the native birds and make a promise
to myself: I'll be back to conquer the 18th hole. As I
cast my eyes around the pure luxury of our gorgeous
suite, I give Mr Smith a warm cuddle and secretly plan
our next date at Kauri Cliffs.

REVIEWED BY DEBORAH HUTTON

NEED TO KNOW

Rooms 22 suites (six standard, 16 deluxe), and the two-bedroom Owner's Cottage.

Rates NZ$1,160–$2,380, including breakfast, apéritifs and dinner; two-bedroom Owner's Cottage, NZ$5,500–$8,750 a night. (Excludes 12.5 per cent tax.)

Check-out 11am, but flexible subject to availability. Check-in, 2pm.

Facilities Free WiFi throughout, spa, swimming pools, sauna, Jacuzzi, gym, 18-hole golf course, practice range, putting and chipping greens, golf shop, Callaway clubs for hire. Tennis courts, clay-pigeon shooting and mountain bikes. In rooms: TV, DVD/CD players, minibar (soft drinks free), Evolu toiletries and private porch.

Children Under-fives can share for free. Baby cots available for no charge; extra beds possible for deluxe suites only (from NZ$320–$735 a night, depending on the season).

Also The hotel is closed in June. Don't miss the uplifting spa, surrounded by verdant totara forest; treatments make use of local mud, minerals, crystals, stones and shells.

IN THE KNOW

Our favourite rooms We're partial to the six spacious standard suites paired in pretty cottages flanked by forest. All are neutral-toned with comfy armchairs by the fire, walk-in wardrobes, luxurious bathrooms and private porches overlooking the ocean. But if you fancy more space and your own infinity pool, book into the two-suite Owner's Cottage.

Hotel bar Kauri Cliffs' inviting cocktail hour from 6.30pm is an ideal time to hobnob with fellow guests. There's no bar as such, but free wine, beers, spirits and canapés are served on the veranda to tinkling piano and jazz music.

Hotel restaurant The Lodge's dining room has a warm, relaxed farmhouse feel and a great open veranda. Executive chef Barry Frith oversees the daily-changing à la carte menu, which specialises in modern, seasonal, local dishes including New Zealand lamb, beef and seafood; pastry chef Quentin Sere whips up dreamy desserts. Take advice from the sommelier, as his knowledge and top tips can make your meal.

Top table A balcony table for island-studded ocean views – they're all-weather-friendly thanks to heaters and wind shields. In winter, romantics should set up camp by the indoor fireplace.

Room service Available 7am–10pm, with a daily-changing menu.

Dress code Glam golfing threads. If you don't have your own golf gear, there's a shop at the hotel where you can pick up the latest NZ and global labels, from Fairway & Greene to Polo. Jackets are required for gents for cocktails and dinner.

Local knowledge Aquatic activities include sailing around the Bay of Islands, world-famous game fishing, scuba diving, snorkelling and swimming with dolphins; the general manager even takes guests out sea kayaking or canoeing himself. For landlubbers, staff can arrange riding, sand dune surfing, romantic picnics and suggest walks around the hotel's vast grounds, taking in waterfalls, kauri trees and three secluded beaches (one with pink shells).

LOCAL EATING AND DRINKING

Right on the waterfront at pretty nearby Paihia, **Island Life** (09 402 6199) at 78–94 Marsden Road is worth a visit for its tasty Pacific Rim dishes with European and Asian influences. Overlooking Motumaire Island, it has an adjoining deli for freshly baked treats, great coffee and picnic goods. Sample top local wines at award-winning **Marsden Estate** (09 407 9398) at Wiroa Road in Kerikeri. Relax afterwards over lunch in the vineyard restaurant, where estate-grown wines are matched with everything from Thai curry to chargrilled lamb.

GET A ROOM!

Use our free online booking service: check availability and make reservations through www.mrandmrssmith.com.

 SMITH CARD OFFER NZ$50 spa voucher on arrival.

The Lodge at Kauri Cliffs Matauri Bay Road, Matauri Bay, Kerikeri 0245, Northland (09 407 0010; www.kauricliffs.com)

HAWKE'S BAY

COASTLINE Forests, fertile plains and wild coasts
COAST LIFE Golfers, gourmands and wine toasts

Does a cab sauv in hand, sea lapping at your toes sound a tempting scene? Then make tracks for the floodplains and foothills of one of NZ's fêted grape-growing regions. This east-coast swathe of the North Island has got it all: a head-turning ocean setting, nostalgic 1920s architecture and a Mediterranean-style microclimate. Add nation-high sunshine levels to the allure and you're probably packing your bags. Once your palate is pickled from all that wine sampling, uplift your soul with swimming and sailing in these South Pacific waters, or treat your eyes to a gulp of art deco towns Napier and Hastings. Chuck in golf, gastronomy or plain R&R and you should be assured that Hawke's Bay brags it all.

GETTING THERE

Planes Air New Zealand (www.airnewzealand.com) operates domestic flights between Hawke's Bay (Napier–Hastings) Airport (06 835 1130) and Auckland, Wellington and Christchurch, as well as flights to and from Oz. The airport is eight kilometres north of Napier, within easy reach of Hastings and Cape Kidnappers.
Automobiles This part of the North Island isn't serviced by the Overlander train, so driving really is the only way to get around. The usual car hire suspects are based at Napier Airport, but driving from Auckland – about 450 kilometres away – is definitely the scenic option.

LOCAL KNOWLEDGE

Taxis You'll want to book cabs in either of the two larger towns: try Napier Taxis (06 835 7777) and Hastings Taxis (06 878 5055). The Hawke's Bay region is large, though, so this isn't really an economical way of getting around, unless you're simply travelling back to your hotel after dinner.
Packing tips Oversize sunnies, a Callaway golf outfit and a designated driver (of the human variety, as well as the golf club kind).
Recommended reads Delve into the area's strong Maori roots, with Witi Ihimaera's The Whale Rider, about a young Maori girl's struggle to assume leadership of her tribe (Niki Caro's moving film of the book was shot here). Alternatively, try distinguished Maori poet Hone Tuwhare's collection Deep River Talk or David Fingleton's Kiri Te Kanawa: A Biography – the opera star was born in nearby Gisborne, with Maori and European ancestry.
Local specialities If the buzzwords in the food world right now are fresh, local and seasonal, Hawke's Bay is well ahead of the times. With fertile land and the perfect climate, just about everything is grown or gathered here: meat, seafood, cheese, honey, olive oil, fruit and vegetables, and even coffee. Sample the end result in the area's inviting cafés and restaurants, where top-class chefs are blending Asian and European tastes to create appetising Pacific Rim cuisine. Order a local glass of wine to match: names to watch out for near Havelock North and Cape Kidnappers include Craggy Range Winery (www.craggyrange.com) and Te Mata Estate Winery (www.temata.co.nz).
Do go/don't go Summers (November to February) are bright, warm and mellow, ideal for Hawke's Bay's outdoorsy way of life, and winters are temperate here too. Besides, even if it does rain, you can still go wine tasting.

Also... The amazing clifftop-meets-ocean greens at the Tom Doak-designed golf course at Cape Kidnappers (www.capekidnappers.com) are enough to convert even the most uncertain swinger.

WORTH GETTING OUT OF BED FOR

Viewpoint There are no skyscrapers with viewing decks to take advantage of in this part of the world, and many of the natural peaks take more than a little energy to reach. So what better way to get a bird's-eye view of the area than from a chopper? Helicopters Hawke's Bay (www.helicoptershawkesbay.co.nz) offers a range of trips starting with 20-minute scenic flights over the craggy coastline and the inland region's lush forests.

Arts and culture The Maori village of Whangara, just north of the Hawke's Bay region, was so overwhelmed by the influx of tourists when the film *Whale Rider* was released that there are now signs outside the town asking visitors to stay away. The only way you can see the town, *marae* (Maori meeting house) and beach, and hear about the legends that inspired the book and film, are to join Hone Taumaunu, an elder and consultant on the movie, on one of his two-hour Whale Rider Tours (06 862 6118).

Activities Rugged Te Mata Peak, south of Hastings, has both staggering landscapes – sheer cliff faces and an eerie atmosphere – and views across the mountains, vineyards, forests and distant ski fields. Get your heart pounding by tandem-paragliding off this rugged peak with Airplay (www.airplay.co.nz).

You'll swoop over awe-inspiring, otherworldly landscapes with views across the region.

Best beach Go gaga over gannets at Black Reef Beach. The serene ocean-side cliffs here, and nearby sites at Cape Kidnappers, are home to the world's largest mainland colony of the seabirds, which come here to nest from late September until early May, with chicks hatching December and January. It's a two-hour walk from Clifton; or take an organised tour by tractor, 4WD or helicopter. Try Gannet Safaris (www.gannetsafaris.com) or Gannet Beach Adventures (www.gannets.com).

Daytripper If you're a history buff head for Gisborne, a cute coastal town at NZ's most easterly point which claims to be the first city in the world to see the sun each day. It was also the first part of the country to feel the imprint of a European foot, when Captain Cook arrived on the *Endeavour* in 1769 and his crew promptly killed six Maoris who greeted them with the traditional welcome (admittedly the *wero* looks aggressive, but Cook's guys obviously had a 'shoot first, ask questions later' directive). Throughout town, you can see monuments to this moment, and the Tairawhiti Museum (www.tairawhitimuseum.org.nz) covers both colonial history as well as that of the local Maori groups. Enough learning for one day? Waikanae Beach is great for swimming or for beginners to try their luck hanging ten.

Children City kids in particular will get a kick out of Wool World at Clifton Station (www.cliftonstation.co.nz), a working farm at Cape Kidnappers. There are shearing shows, sheep dog demos, wood-chopping displays, a museum and the chance to interact with sheep, a milking cow and the station's pet pig.

Walks Picturesque Lake Waikaremoana is hidden in the massive Te Urewera National Park, north of Hawke's Bay. A 46-kilometre track runs around the lake, but it can be attacked in short sections. Some of the walking, particularly going uphill to Panekiri Bluff, can be pretty strenuous, so you'll need to have proper boots and plenty of water. The Department of Conservation (www.doc.govt.nz) has downloadable publications of lake walking trails and other hikes in the national park.

Perfect picnic You won't need to pack a bottle of wine when you prepare lunch for an alfresco spread at Ngatarawa, a vineyard 10 kilometres west of Hastings. It's a beautiful place, with vines (of course), gardens, an historic stable yard and an ace view of Te Mata Peak.

Shopping Meet the growers, taste their produce and ask them all about it at the Hawke's Bay Farmers Market on Saturday in Napier and Sunday in Hastings (www.foodhawkesbay.co.nz). Having stocked the picnic basket, regular viewers of guilty pleasure *Antiques Roadshow* should explore Napier's vintage shops (www.villageinfo.co.nz/shopping).

Something for nothing Plenty of cellar doors in the area offer complimentary tastings, and if you're a fan of red you'll want to spend at least a few hours sipping slowly. At last count there were 71 wineries, with 4,700 hectares under grape. Download a list from Wine Region Tours (www.wine-region-tours.com).

Don't go home without... snapping a photograph of yourself in front of the hill known as one of the longest named in the world: Taumatawhakatangihangakoauauotamateaturipukakapikimaungahoronukupokaiwhenuakitanatahu. As attested by the *Guinness Book of Records*. It's a Maori moniker that translates roughly as 'The summit where Tamatea, the man with the big knees, the climber of mountains, the land-swallower who travelled about, played his nose flute to his loved one'. Your next challenge? Pronouncing it.

HISTORICALLY HAWKE'S BAY

In 1931, an earthquake devastated the region's two biggest cities, Napier and Hastings, pushing earth from below a lagoon to the surface, adding an extra 40 square kilometres to Napier's dimensions. Optimistic rebuilding started straight away in the depths of the Depression, leaving behind a charming art deco legacy. Don a rakish trilby and enjoy a guided walking tour or drive yourself around the jauntily coloured architectural highlights (for details and maps see www.artdeconapier.com).

DIARY

February At Harvest Hawke's Bay (www.harvesthawkesbay.co.nz) buses shuttle merry punters between vineyards over a weekend, with tastings of fine food and wine. For the oenophile, there are also tutored tastings and workshops. For one weekend during the Geon Art Deco Festival (www.artdeconapier.com) Napier goes back to the Thirties, with displays of vintage cars and costumes, a soap-box derby, dinners, concerts and dancing.

February/March Lionel Richie may have been washed out in 2009 for the Mission Estate Winery Concert (www.missionconcert.co.nz), but past performers at the popular outdoor gig include Tom Jones, Eric Clapton, Rod Stewart and Cliff Richard. **September** Celebrate spring at Hastings Blossom Festival (www.blossomfestival.co.nz) with a week of hijinks including the Blossom Parade, the Blossom Dance and the Proms. **October** The Kelt Capital Stakes, New Zealand's richest open-age horse race, is run at the Hastings Racecourse (www.hastingsracecourse.com).

'Plump oversized couches before the fire invite you to snuggle up with a glass of fine New Zealand pinot and your favourite person'

Hawke's Bay

The Farm at Cape Kidnappers

STYLE Spa-studded lodge
SETTING Ocean-view farmland

There's no mistaking it: we are smack-bang in the middle of the countryside. Bob, a charming local, has picked us up from Napier Airport and whisked us away in his Mercedes. Now, as we pass through the art deco township, he begins telling Mr Smith and I about the evolution of Cape Kidnappers from a working sheep farm to a luxury travel destination. The road follows a riverbed and cuts through pine forests, while we spot plump, happy lambs grazing in the valleys. My anticipation is rising. Soon, we glimpse the ocean, and then the broader panorama of Hawke's Bay reveals the majestic lodge that appears, from here, to be perching on top of the world.

Lisa warmly greets us in the courtyard, but I can't wait to get into the main lodge to absorb it all in full. I'm not disappointed. The styling is reminiscent of a French country house. The common areas feature exposed wooden beams above rough grey stone walls, natural wood panelling and stone floors scattered with cowhide rugs. Plump oversized couches before the fire invite you to snuggle up with a glass of fine New Zealand pinot and your favourite person. I smile at Mr Smith, who already has a twinkle in his eye.

First things first though. I might not be a fine golfer, but I do love the game, and Cape Kidnappers' course has been voted one of the world's best. It's easy to see why. For the experienced golfer, the par 71, Tom Doak design presents a challenge of accuracy as the distant greens seem to disappear into the ocean. For an experienced (yet unpolished) hack like myself, it offers the forgiveness of open fairways that allow you to enjoy your game and take in the gob-smacking scenery as you find your ball.

Appetite duly stimulated, Mr Smith and I head back to the lodge for dinner. There's a multitude of venues to choose from here, but being a hopeless romantic, I've organised for the two of us to dine privately in the snug. With its pale wooden walls, it's a little like being seated in an oversized wine barrel, albeit one with a roaring open fire. After a delicious five-course meal – the menu changes daily but there's always local lamb, beef and seafood on offer – we curl up on the leather day-bed and let the immense satisfaction wash over us. Our Lodge Suite, a blend of country charm, state-of-the-art finishes and heavenly Italian bed linen, is part of

the main building and we're grateful for the short stagger to bed.

Surrounded by the luxury of the lodge, it's easy to forget you're on a 2,400-hectare working farm. You could sit back and take it in from a distance, but there's also the opportunity to get your hands dirty. Mr Smith and I have decided to take the quad bike tour of the property. It's led by Carolyn, a local with as much charm and character as the Cape itself. Not having driven one of these four-wheelers before, I'm relieved to discover it's easy to establish who's boss. As we splash our way through puddles in stony riverbeds, climb steep sheep paths, spot newborn lambs, pass through cattle paddocks and work our way through the hills, I have a smile pasted on my face. This much fun is normally hard to find.

Carolyn also runs the skeet shooting on the property. In no time at all, she has us hitting targets like we are sharpshooters on the way to the next Olympics. After half an hour of precision shooting, Mr Smith's ego is as plump as the neighbouring sheep.

Following a laid-back lunch in the sun-drenched loggia, we pull on our trainers to stroll along the lavender walk, one of the easier yet most picturesque walks on the property. Passing through a field of scented lavender, we follow a canopy of pine trees to a look-out on the cliffs. Here, the earth drops away to a beach. The view is absolutely breathtaking and as I sit on the pebbles, cosied up to Mr Smith, I realise it's a moment I'll never forget.

Back at the suite, even though the sun is still high in the sky, I fill the tub and light the scented travel candle I always carry with me. Relaxing in the warm water is the perfect antidote to the exhilaration of the past few days' activities. After I've extracted myself, Mr Smith and I prepare for one final sunset on the suite's veranda. The sky blazes in shades of pink and lilac as we gaze out towards the ocean. When dusk fades, we go inside; the lamps glow warmly, the fire is lit and my iPod is playing Van Morrison. If this scene were a food, it would be a delicious just-baked apple pie – indeed, it is as inviting as hotel settings get.

REVIEWED BY DEBORAH HUTTON

'Passing through a field of scented lavender, we follow a canopy of pine trees to a look-out on the cliffs'

NEED TO KNOW

Rooms 22 cottage suites and the Owner's Cottage.

Rates NZ$1,160–$2,380, including breakfast, apéritifs and dinner. Owner's Cottage, NZ$3,500–$12,500 (rented as a two- or four-bedroom house). Excludes 12.5 per cent tax.

Check-out 11am, but flexible subject to availability. Check-in, 2pm.

Facilities CD, DVD and book library, free WiFi throughout, gym, spa, outdoor Jacuzzi and heated swimming pool, golf course. In rooms: flatscreen TV, CD/DVD players, iPod dock, minibar (soft drinks free), Evolu toiletries, private balcony.

Children Baby cots free up to age two; extra beds for older kids NZ$320–$500 a night, depending on the season. Babysitting with a local nanny NZ$35 an hour; 24 hours' notice required.

Also Wine tastings are held regularly – the hotel even has its own vineyard. If you need to detox afterwards, the hillside spa has three treatment rooms offering serenity-boosting views.

IN THE KNOW

Our favourite rooms We love the secluded Ridge Suites as they're a little further away from the main lodge and feel more private. If you're feeling flush, the standalone Owner's Cottage is a great pad for a family or friends travelling in a group.

Hotel bar There isn't an official watering hole, but there's a fabulous cocktail hour each night from 6.30pm in the lounge.

Hotel restaurant Chef Dale Gartland presides over the main dining room where decor is modern rustic and the à la carte dinner menu of classical French and English dishes, influenced by fine seasonal New Zealand produce, changes nightly. Local ingredients, such as lamb and beef, get star billing, as well as fresh seafood from the area. By day, enjoy breathtaking ocean views; by night, it's candlelit. Lunch is more casual, ranging from sandwiches to three-coursers. Informal dining at the Pro Shop is also an option after hotel restaurant hours.

Top table Bag a table on the covered balcony for ocean views – especially desirable at sunset. Or opt for James Bond-glam with drinks or private dining in the circular lounge snug, or in the wine cellar.

Room service A daily-changing room service menu is available 7am–10pm.

Dress code Chaps should don a jacket for cocktails and supper, but there are some to borrow from reception. Ladies, imagine you're weekending at Sandringham.

Local knowledge You'd be mad to pass up a round of golf, as the hotel's beautiful course offers 18 holes set over dramatic rolling green hills and ravines which cascade down to the crashing waves below (fees are extra; rent gear on-site). Animal life is also abundant. Take a tour of this 2,400-hectare working sheep and cattle farm on foot or by 4WD, or head out on safari – Kiwi Discovery Walks helps you track down New Zealand's famously rare and endangered kiwi bird as part of a local conservation project.

LOCAL EATING AND DRINKING

For mouthwatering French and NZ food, make a trip to **Terrôir** restaurant at the Craggy Range Winery (06 873 0143) at 253 Waimarama Road in Havelock North. Team its own-label wines with local seafood. **Elephant Hill Estate & Winery** (06 872 6060) at 86 Clifton Road in Te Awanga, serves up Mediterranean-influenced cuisine, such as duck risotto or fresh ocean fish, in its architecturally arresting modern restaurant and bar. Soak up striking vistas of Cape Kidnappers through floor-to-ceiling glass windows or from outdoors on the poolside terrace. For Italian food with a side serving of watery views, head for **Milk & Honey Restaurant** (06 833 6099) on Hardinge Road, Ahuriri, Napier.

GET A ROOM!

Use our free online booking service: check availability and make reservations through www.mrandmrssmith.com.

 SMITH CARD OFFER NZ$50 spa credit.

The Farm at Cape Kidnappers 446 Clifton Road, Te Awanga, Hawke's Bay 4102 (06 875 1900; www.capekidnappers.com)

LAKE TAUPO

COUNTRYSIDE Raw and rugged lakeside
COUNTRY LIFE Active – like the surrounding volcanoes

You won't be able to stop staring. This is some of the most eye-popping, jaw-dropping landscape in NZ. On the North Island's Central Plateau, extending south-west of the town of Taupo, you'll see the country's largest lake and the source of its longest river, backed by rugged mountains. Like nearby Rotorua to the north, the land surrounding Lake Taupo is still volcanically active, with steaming thermal hot-spots another big attraction. If you're looking for outdoor pursuits against a ravishing backdrop, this is the place to come, with legendary trout-fishing, adrenalin-rush rafting and all manner of scenic watersports up for grabs. In winter, you'll be tempted by the ski fields, but come summer the surrounding national park becomes a haven for trekking. Or, for a real high, get airborne – Taupo is also the world's skydiving capital.

GETTING THERE

Planes Air New Zealand (www.airnewzealand.com) offers regular flights to Taupo Airport (www.taupoairport.co.nz) from international hubs Auckland and Wellington. Alternatively, Rotorua Regional Airport (www.rotorua-airport.co.nz), just an hour's drive away, also operates flights from Auckland, Wellington and Christchurch.
Trains The Tranz Scenic Overlander (www.tranzscenic. co.nz) runs between Auckland and Wellington and stops twice in the region: at National Park and Okahune.
Automobiles If you intend exploring the area, the easiest way by far is by car. Avis (www.avis.co.nz) has a counter at Taupo Airport, eight kilometres south of town. Otherwise, numerous shuttle bus services run year-round between Taupo, Turangi and the Tongariro National Park, and up to the Whakapapa ski fields (about 90 minutes away) during winter.

LOCAL KNOWLEDGE

Taxis There are three cab companies operating in Taupo, but you're best to book one. Try Taupo Taxis (07 378 5100).

Packing tips Hiking boots, binoculars, ski gear, a handful of dry flies (the ones you catch trout with).
Recommended reads The Lord of the Rings by JRR Tolkien (mountainous park Tongariro, near Taupo, makes a cameo appearance in Peter Jackson's film of the books as Mordor's Mount Doom). Read Hamish Campbell and Geoff Hicks' Awesome Forces: The Natural Hazards that Threaten New Zealand if you want to scare yourself silly about how volcanoes, tsunamis and earthquakes could impact on this environment.
Local specialities The Kiwis are proud of their tasty, wholesome produce and you'll find it all – excellent trout, lamb and beef, especially – on offer around the Taupo region. As it gets colder, most of the restaurants, particularly those around the ski fields, will bump up the big winter-warmer flavours.
Do go/don't go The elevation means things can get mighty cool. If you crave walking, mountain biking or throwing yourself into other outdoorsy adventures, stick to the warmer months (December to February). Prefer to ski and indulge in all its après fun? July to October

is the time for you. Fan of fishing? February and March are best for brown trout, and June to September for rainbow trout, but the Tongariro River has fantastic year-round offerings.

And... Here's something for the 13-year-old boy in everyone. When it comes to Maori names, the letters 'wh' are pronounced like an 'f'. The ski region on Mount Ruapehu is called Whakapapa. Go on, you're allowed to giggle.

WORTH GETTING OUT OF BED FOR

Viewpoint This is not an area short on great vantage points, but climbing to the summit of Mount Tauhura on Lake Taupo's north-eastern shore is an especially easy-access look-out with just as much aesthetic reward. It should take about two hours to get to the top, 1,088 metres above sea level. From there, you can see over the lake and Taupo town and, on a clear day, over most of the plateau. The weather changes quickly around here, so take a warm, waterproof jacket.

Arts and culture There's a strong Maori culture here, the home of the Tuwharetoa *iwi* (tribe). At Wairakei Terraces, about five kilometres north-east of Taupo, take part in the evening Maori Cultural Experience (www.wairakei terraces.co.nz). Displays of traditional greetings, stories and dance culminate in a *hangi* (a meal cooked in coals below ground) and the awe-inspiring *haka*, a war dance familiar to anyone who's ever seen the All Blacks play.

Activities Calling all would-be daredevils. This is one big drop zone, with more skydivers taking the plunge here than anywhere else in the world. To book in for a tandem jump contact Skydive Taupo (www. skydivetaupo.co.nz), Taupo Tandem Skydiving (www. taupotandemskydiving.com) or Freefall (www.freefall. net.nz). For white-water rafting head for the Tongariro River (www.raftingnewzealand.com). If you prefer something more sedate, catch dinner on the lake or river. Guides can be hired to take you fishing for brown and rainbow trout. Try the guys at Taupo Fly Fishing (www.taupoflyfishing.com).

Best beach Walk along Taupo's Lake Terrace and only about five minutes out of town you'll come across Hot Water Beach. Even on the coldest days hot water seeps to the sand's surface at low tide. Take care though: it can be really hot.

Daytripper If the local geothermal activity has you wide-eyed, then a drive to Rotorua, about 75 minutes to the north, could be in order. Once you get used to the unusual smell, there's plenty to explore. At Te Puia (www.tepuia.com) you can see the Maori Arts and Crafts Institute, attend a *hangi*, watch concerts or wait for Pohutu (Big Splash) to erupt. The local people still live at Whakarewarewa Thermal Village (www.whakarewarewa.com) and show visitors around. Also worth checking out is the Rotorua Museum of Art & History (www.rotoruamuseum.co.nz) in the Government Gardens by the lake.

Children A lot of what goes on around Taupo might be a bit rough and tumble for little kids, but big ones will love the adrenalin-surge activities on tap. Mountain biking around the lake or in the forests just outside of Taupo should use up some excess energy. Hire a bike from Life Cycles (07 378 6117) and take off. The tourist office has a map of bike trails around the lake, and Bike Taupo (www.biketaupo.org.nz) also has area maps.

Walks This is a tramper's paradise. People hail the Tongariro Alpine Crossing as one of the best single-day hikes in New Zealand. It's not easy though, so you have to be in good condition and an experienced rambler. The weather can change rapidly, so make sure you're fully equipped and always tell someone where you're going and when you intend to be back. The DOC (Department of Conservation) office in Whakapapa Village has maps and displays current weather conditions. For the less-serious stroller, there are some good, short walks from Whakapapa, including a two-hour ramble to Taranaki Falls.

Perfect picnic On a schedule, but not a budget? A flight with Helistar Helicopters (www.helistar.co.nz) will take you out of town, over snow-capped mountains, buzzing past Huka Falls, over the Maori rock carvings on the lake shore (otherwise only accessible by water) and inside the crater of Mount Tuahara. Some of the journeys include a landing, so take a sandwich with you, or speak to the operators about tailoring a special heli-picnic journey.

Shopping Taupo isn't really a destination for spending hours splashing cash, but worth a look is Kura Gallery at 47a Heu Heu Street (07 377 4068), which showcases contemporary ethnic art from paintings and sculpture to jewellery. Also try Zea You Contemporary NZ Art, on the corner of Heu Heu and Ruapehu Streets (07 378 1361). On Saturday morning, the Riverside Park Market (off Tongariro and Redoubt Streets) sells local produce, art and craft, clothes, collectables and more.

Something for nothing Actually this is two free things rolled into one. An easy trot from Taupo along the Waikato River is the impressive Huka Falls, an absolute must-do. Many people scoot to the bottom in a jet boat, but if you do the walk, don your swimwear: there's a hot swimming hole just off the walkway fed by a thermal creek.

Don't go home without... hurling yourself from a platform 47 metres above Waikato River at New Zealand's highest water-touch bungy (www.taupobungy.com).

LAVA-LY LAKE TAUPO

Mount Ruapehu, the home of the Whakapapa and smaller Turoa ski fields (Lake Taupo's twin resorts, considered the North Island's premier ski area), last erupted in 2007. It's one of the world's most active volcanoes and has gone off about 60 times since the mid-1940s. Thankfully, it's all closely monitored and any rumblings are of the minor variety. Still, if the idea of skiing volcanic cones gets your vote, head for this hot winter destination (www.mtruapehu.com). Lift passes are valid at both resorts and you can either drive to the slopes or grab a shuttle mini-bus from nearby Taupo, Turangi, Whakapapa Village, National Park township or Ohakune (the buzziest après-ski scene in the north).

DIARY

March Some of the world's fittest athletes head to Taupo to take part in Ironman New Zealand (www.ironman.co.nz). Don't worry, you can join the rest of us watching from the footpath. Also in March, the tiny town of Taihape – which claims to be the galoshes-throwing capital of New Zealand – holds an annual Gumboot Day festival (www.taihape.co.nz). **September** Taupo Day–Night Thriller (www.daynightthriller.co.nz) is the biggest mountain bike event in New Zealand, with about 3,000 riders pouring into town to take part in a 12-hour race near the Spa Park. **October** During Ohakune Carrot Carnival (www.carrotcarnival.org.nz), held on one Saturday a year, this mountain community goes carrot crazy. There's a parade, stalls, entertainment and, naturally, a cake competition.

'In New Zealand you can channel Brad Pitt in *A River Runs Through It* by going fly-fishing. At Huka Lodge, you might just run into him'

Taupo

Huka Lodge

STYLE Trad Twenties hunting lodge
SETTING Banks of the Waikato

In New Zealand you can channel Brad Pitt in *A River Runs Through It* by going fly-fishing. At Huka Lodge, though, you might just run into him – and his mates. This is a playground for celebrities. Mr Smith and I had done our research so – excuse us for name-dropping – we knew Barbra Streisand, Bill Gates and Kate Winslet had all holidayed here.

Determined to fit in, I had a pre-arrival blow-dry. I might not be rich and famous, but if I happened to find myself standing near George Clooney at least I'd have fabulous hair. As soon as Mr Smith and I drove into the manicured estate, our host appeared with a warm greeting. When you're staying at a place this luxurious there is no checking in; there's simply a welcoming champagne by the fire and a tour with the convivial Louis, who could have been showing off his home rather than pointing out facilities.

When he showed us to our Double Lodge Suite I came over all Julia Roberts in *Pretty Woman*. This place is breathtaking. An entrance hall divided off to two rooms. The first housed a chaise longue, two armchairs and a king-size bed, complete with mosquito net (even in winter it adds a touch of romance; I'm not going to mention getting trapped in it when I went to the loo in the middle of the night – it ruins the image). Through the walk-in wardrobe and minibar area was the magnificent bathroom. The carpet was so thick you didn't walk on it so much as pad across it. 'We're not in Kansas any more, Toto,' I whispered to Mr Smith before even laying eyes on room two. It was the same size as the bedroom with couches, armchairs, a dining table, fireplace and a mirror-image walk-in robe and bathroom. Every chair had a cashmere throw draped over it, complementing the soft green and cream decor. A veranda ran the length of the suite. Its reclining chairs looked over the perfect grass to the mesmerising, fast-flowing river. Mr Smith and I had planned to explore the grounds, but I'm not sure if it was the ultimate luxury, the complimentary bottle of wine or if they hide kryptonite around the room – somehow we didn't have the power to leave.

We dressed for dinner and gathered with the other guests around the fire for cocktails and canapés. There were only 12 others in attendance, none of them famous. Oh, but there were tales of them. Director Peter Jackson was there just the week before; not to mention the Queen of freaking England having stayed three times. Apparently she loves the place. We, however, think that snipers in the woods, SAS troops in zodiacs upstream and helicopters hovering above might kind of spoil the serenity.

Mr Smith and I are pondering this as we're taken to our private table in the wine cellar for a five-course meal. Flatteringly lit by candles and surrounded by wine worth more than our car, we felt like the VIPs in residence.

The next day we decided to try fly-fishing. Our guide, David, was a Kiwi version of Steve Irwin: knowledgeable and passionate. Decked out in waders, we instantly felt the part. Now, my dad taught me to fish off the beach when I was just a fingerling, so I was excited and confident. Mr Smith, on the other hand, had never fished in his life. Within an hour he'd landed a handsome two-kilo rainbow jack. After the compulsory photo, he

released his prize back into the wild. Four hours later I still had nothing. I was happy for Mr Smith though. So damned happy, and determined not to be out-fished, I immediately booked David for the next day.

There are plenty of other activities on offer at Huka if you're made of money: hunting, helicopter tours and bungy jumping just a one-hour hike away, for example. Or you could follow Mr Smith and my lead and opt for delicious afternoon naps – the sound of the water approaching nearby Huka Falls was a lullaby all of its own.

That night, Mr Smith regaled other guests with fishy tales. The more wine he had, the bigger the fish got. This time dinner was on the terrace outside, with a raging fire and Burberry blankets over our knees keeping the chill at bay. When Mr Smith couldn't decide between two options for his main course, the kitchen simply presented him with both. But the winning dish was an Oreo cheesecake for dessert. 'That's just plain rude to all other cheesecakes in the world,' said Mr Smith. 'They can't compare and it knows it.'

The next morning I woke early for revenge fly-fishing. This time things were serious: we plunged through rivers in a four-wheel drive with water washing over the bonnet. But as soon as I was in my waders, calmness swept over me. Fly-fishing is like meditating – deadlines, office politics and pressures all fade away as you focus on landing the fly in exactly the right spot to tempt a trout. It was this Zen approach that rewarded me with my own rainbow jack. As I posed for the photo, I beamed: 'That's going straight to Facebook.' After all, I'm sure that's exactly what Brad would do.

Back at the room, I went to show my pic to Mr Smith but found him in his own meditative state, staring at the moss-covered trees, turquoise river and glossy ducks feeding on the manicured lawn. 'It seems a tad *Truman Show*,' I joked. 'I half expect to spot a stagehand spray-painting the bushes the exact right shade of Huka Lodge green.' Mr Smith rolled his eyes: 'Really, Mrs Smith, should you doubt perfection or just enjoy it?' He had a point.

REVIEWED BY SHELLY HORTON

NEED TO KNOW

Rooms 18 Lodge Rooms, one suite; the exclusive-use four-bedroom Owner's Cottage and two-bedroom Alan Pye Cottage.
Rates NZ$1,460–$2,750, including breakfast, apéritifs, dinner and local airport transfers. The Owner's Cottage and Alan
Pye Cottage are NZ$3,060–$8,400 a room. (All excluding 12.5 per cent tax.)
Check-out 11am, flexible subject to availability. Check-in, 2pm.
Facilities DVD, CD and book library, free WiFi throughout, swimming pools, gardens. In rooms: flatscreen TV, CD/DVD
player, iPod dock, minibar, own-label toiletries.
Children Baby cots are free; extra beds for older children in triple rooms possible for a fee. Babysitting with a local nanny
NZ$20 an hour; 24 hours' notice required.
Also The Lodge also has four single rooms, ideal for older children or nannies.

IN THE KNOW

Our favourite rooms If you want privacy, the Owner's Cottage sits on a sunny promontory above the river with stunning vistas
downstream to the falls. The new Alan Pye Cottage, named after Huka's founder, has an Arts and Crafts look, as well as your
own infinity and spa pools, a stone pavilion with outdoor dining table and fireplace, and a private chef and butler on tap.
Hotel bar The cosy, comfy main Lodge lounge has a luxurious gents-club feel. The fab views and soothing sound of the
river add to the mellow mood.
Hotel restaurant The executive chef tailors contemporary New Zealand cuisine with French influences to your desires,
harnessing the finest fresh, flavoursome local ingredients, including fruit from the orchard. Menus change daily according
to produce available, but the Lodge's own cookbook includes dishes such as freshwater lobster butter-poached with
lemon-infused gnocchi and watercress, and chocolate fondant with espresso ice-cream.
Top table In the main lodge, ask for a table on the terrace. We also love the vaulted, wine-rack-lined cellar room or
riverside under the stars (you can dine outdoors in a host of romantic spots).
Room service A variety of meals on offer 6.30am–11pm; hampers for picnics also available.
Dress code A dash of fashionable tartan to channel the hunting lodge look; a Belstaff jacket (motorcycle details are great
for rocking a modern country style).
Local knowledge With seven hectares of gorgeous grounds, walking off those meals will be a treat. If you fancy a stroll,
the landscaped, park-like garden is filled with stunning flower borders, and a short walk beyond the gates brings you to
the spectacular Huka Falls. Founded as a fishing lodge, Huka also offers world-famous trout fly-fishing in nearby rivers,
as well as fishing on Lake Taupo. Angling heaven.

LOCAL EATING AND DRINKING

At relaxed restaurant and bar **Plateau** (07 377 2425) at 64 Tuwharetoa Road, the food is Mod Kiwi, there are seven
Monteith's beers on tap and even the music is recorded by NZ artists. On sunny days, dine in the courtyard. **Bond
Lounge Bar** (07 377 2434), just down the way at number 40, is by far the swankiest spot for a cocktail in Taupo. The
weekends see events such as A Night at the Playboy Mansion or the Opshop Ball take over, so if you're after a quieter
atmosphere do the early shift. Set in a Fifties' townhouse, the **Brantry** (07 378 0484), at 45 Rifle Range Road, serves
contemporary cuisine fuelled by local produce including venison, lamb and seafood and the curious feijoa fruit.

GET A ROOM!

Use our free online booking service: check availability and make reservations through www.mrandmrssmith.com.

 SMITH CARD OFFER Lunch for two including a bottle of NZ house wine, either within the lodge or as a picnic.

Huka Lodge 271 Huka Falls Road, Taupo 3377 (07 378 5791; www.hukalodge.co.nz)

WAIRARAPA

COASTLINE Hillside villages, vine-lined plains
COAST LIFE Fine wine, farm charm, fierce surf

Wind through the jaggedy, treeless Rimutaka Range and the two-hour drive from Wellington may feel like more of an adventure than you bargained for; but grip the steering wheel and descend into benevolent villages and vineyards which provide weekend-away gold. Named after its lake and translating from Maori as Glistening Waters, it's in the grape department that the Wairarapa really shines. Pinot noir and a postcard-inspiring village green draw you to Martinborough's eateries and pubs, while beautifully restored Victorian buildings make boutiquey Greytown beguiling. Featherston and Carterton exude country charm and hardware shops and farm supplies in bustling Masterton exemplify the region's agricultural heritage. Surrender to the laid-back pace of this south-eastern stretch of the North Island and explore world-class wineries and history-steeped towns as unhurriedly as you like.

GETTING THERE

Planes The closest international airport to the Wairarapa is Wellington Airport (www.wellingtonairport.co.nz), about two hours drive away. Air New Zealand (www.airnewzealand.com) flies daily between Auckland and Masterton in the Wairarapa (return from NZ$210).
Trains Tranz Metro (www.tranzmetro.co.nz) trains run daily between Wellington and Masterton (NZ$14), stopping at Featherston, Greytown and Carterton.
Automobiles The best way to explore the Wairarapa is with your own wheels. Pick up a hire car in Wellington: all the international big-name companies have offices at Wellington Airport, or at the ferry terminal if you're arriving by sea from the South Island.

LOCAL KNOWLEDGE

Taxis Masterton Taxis (06 378 2555) services the region's main towns.
Packing tips Leave some room in your luggage for a few bottles of peppery Wairarapa pinot noir; maybe take your cycling shorts – cruising the wineries on two wheels is a low-stress way to go.
Recommended reads For a virtual journey through the Wairarapa landscape, thumb through the gorgeous photography book *Wairarapa – A Place Apart* by Pete Nikolaison and Michael Wall. For some background on white settlement in the area, check out *Early History of the Wairarapa* by Charles Bannister. *The Wine Atlas of New Zealand* by Michael Cooper has the lowdown on the best Wairarapa vintages.
Local specialities The cool-climate Wairarapa, with its gravelly soil, hot summers and dry autumns, has made a name for itself producing pinot noir – but you can also pick up some fab bottles of sauvignon blanc, pinot gris, chardonnay and riesling and, if you hunt around, the odd merlot and rosé. With all that wine-swilling, you'll want something to line your stomach: the region has plenty of pubs serving trad farmer-style roasts and fry-ups, plus a new breed of gourmet cafés and

restaurants offering city-quality epicurean delights. Local cheese, chocolate and olive oil are also a worthy culinary diversion.

Do go/don't go Summer in the Wairarapa (December to February) is a beautiful time, with hot, clear days and long, still evenings – but this is also when New Zealanders are on holidays, so things can get a bit hectic. A better bet is to visit during autumn (March to April) when the grapes are being harvested, the kids are back at school and days resonate with post-summer nostalgia.

WORTH GETTING OUT OF BED FOR

Viewpoint If you can drag your eyes away from the rather treacherous road across the Rimutaka Range between Wellington and the Wairarapa, the rocky heights offer some amazing views down onto the farmland and vineyard country below. Alternatively, the long 250-step climb up the Cape Palliser Lighthouse will reward you with breathtaking views of the South Island.

Arts and culture The Aratoi Wairarapa Museum of Art & History (www.aratoi.org.nz) in Masterton chronicles the Wairarapa's multicultural and artistic heritage. In nearby Greytown, the Cobblestones Village Museum (www. cobblestonesmuseum.org.nz) takes a quaint-meets-kitsch approach to recreating the early settler days.

Activities With around 50 producers in the Wairarapa, wine tasting is the name of the local game. Many companies offer tours through the grape-heavy landscape, departing from either Wellington or the region's main towns. Try Martinborough Wine Tours (www.martinboroughwinetours.co.nz) for a boutique wine experience, Zest Food Tours (www. zestfoodtours.co.nz) for a gourmet take on the area or Hammond's Scenic Tours (www.wellington sightseeingtours.com) for a day tour visiting Cape Palliser and Martinborough. If you'd rather minimise the legwork, you can sample a huge range of local varieties with free tastings at the Martinborough Wine Centre (www.martinboroughwinecentre.co.nz), which also has a great café out the back.

Best beach The beaches along Palliser Bay to the south-west of the Wairarapa have the most reliable breaks in the region (most of the dudes out in the waves are Wellington city-slickers). And even if the surf's not happening, you'll have kilometres of empty black-sand coast to yourself.

Daytripper Take a drive out to the fabulously remote Castlepoint, around 70 kilometres east of Masterton on the coast. It's a long-lost-and-lonesome kinda place, with some decent swimming spots, walking trails, caves, a wind-battered lighthouse and the craggy 162-metre-high Castle Rock looming over the coastline. Look out for fossil shells in the rocks.

Children All that wine tasting can be a bit of a snooze for the kids. If they need to blow off steam, take them to Queen Elizabeth Park in Masterton, which has playgrounds, aviaries, a duck pond and plenty of lawn to muck about on. Further afield, Cape Palliser's stinky seal colony, the North Island's largest breeding site, will also be a hit with children.

Walks Take in the dramatic eroded-rock Putangirua Pinnacles on the Wairarapa coast, with a choice of two- to three-hour walks and views of streams, hills and sea. The Pinnacles Track is in the Aorangi Forest Park, 13 kilometres along Cape Palliser Road from the Lake Ferry turn-off (for track details see www.doc. govt.nz/parks-and-recreation).

Perfect picnic Head for the shores of Lake Wairarapa (Glistening Waters in Maori), which gave the area its name. Pick up something delicious to drink at one of Martinborough's many vineyards and try the French Baker (06 304 8873) in Greytown for breads, pastries and treats.

Shopping The bigger Wairarapa wineries can arrange shipping, so you can enjoy a case of pinots when you get home. Got that I-need-chocolate itch? Scratch it

inside a 1920s cottage in Greytown, where creative Schoc Chocolate (www.chocolatetherapy.com) turns out trays of glorious cocoa creations with mind-boggling flavours.

Something for nothing Not far from Masterton, the Tararua Forest Park (www.doc.govt.nz) offers a change of pace from the area's more urban trappings. Take a hike through the trees, consider a dip in a chilly sub-alpine creek and track down a ranger for some free insider advice on spotting bird, animal and insect life.

Don't go home without... trying to spot an elusive kiwi at the Pukaha Mount Bruce National Wildlife Centre (www.mtbruce.org.nz), 30 kilometres north of Masterton, a sanctuary for native wildlife and birds.

WONDERFULLY WAIRARAPA

Until recent years, Wairarapa life revolved around a woolly triad of sheep, farming and sheep farming, but grape growing has now put the region squarely on the gourmet map – a must for anyone with a taste for cool-climate vino and foodie culture. Wine production volumes are low (many vineyards here are small, family-run operations), but quality is sky-high – a testament to handcrafted produce and a personal approach to oenology. Unlike NZ's better known wine regions (Marlborough, Hawke's Bay), the cellar doors here are boutique and personable, sans global hype and in-your-face marketing. See www.winesfrommartinborough.com for more info.

DIARY

March The Balloons Over Wairarapa festival (www.nzballoons.co.nz) lures dozens of balloonists from across the planet for five days of autumnal hot-air heights. The Wairarapa Wines Harvest Festival (www.wairarapawines.co.nz) is a boutique mid-March happening, showcasing the region's best food and wine. Also in March, the legendary Golden Shears competition (www.goldenshears.co.nz) plays host to three days of competitive sheep-shearing mayhem in Masterton. **September** The Carterton Daffodil Carnival (www.cartertondc.co.nz/daffodil-carnival.html) is a bloomin' marvellous event, filling the streets of springtime Carterton with yellow. **November** On the third Sunday in November, Toast Martinborough (www.toastmartinborough.co.nz) is this historic town's big-ticket wine, music and food fiesta. Around 11,000 amateur sommeliers roll into town – so book tickets well in advance.

'When I say private, I'm not counting the countless sheep in the neighbouring meadows, who have a disconcerting tendency to stare'

Palliser Bay

Wharekauhau Lodge and Country Estate

STYLE Edwardian country grandeur
SETTING Palliser Bay-side pastures

Blue lake on one side, rolling green farmland on the other – this was all the proof Mr Smith and I needed that we weren't in the city any more... 'We're in the Wopwops,' exclaimed Mr Smith (rural suburbs, for all you non-Kiwis). His boyish enthusiasm suggested that he too could feel the stresses of urban life ebbing away: fast work indeed for two die-hard townies from Auckland, who hadn't breathed so much as a lungful of country air in six months. But our drive over the Rimutaka Ranges was to prove only the start of our rustic detox.

Arriving at Wharekauhau Lodge and Country Estate (pronounced 'forry-coe-hoe' – whodathunkit?), we were greeted by the friendly staff all too keen to show us around the property. For us – fresh off the plane at Wellington – its lakeside lawns and surrounding forested foothills were the city-addict equivalent of going cold turkey. Too overwhelmed to fully appreciate the wine-label-worthy countryside just yet, we retreated to our cottage. The Palliser Bay views would wait.

Away from the grandeur of the main lodge, our stand-alone cabin was pure modern farmhouse in style: high ceilings with exposed beams, a canopied bed and a romantic gas open fire. There was nothing for it but to run a hot bath for two. I'll spare you the details of our ablutions, but the private view from the bathroom window cannot go undescribed. (Well, when I say private, I'm not counting the countless sheep in the neighbouring meadows, who have a disconcerting tendency to stare.) From my soapy look-out point, I could see over the pea-green pastures down to the mirror-calm Lake Ferry. The only thing that could improve the vista would have been a glass of champagne – cue Mr Smith's arrival with cups of peppermint tea. OK, it's not quite Krug, but it still hit the spot.

Before we could say 'More tea, vicar?', it was time to dress for dinner in the lodge. The idea of communal dining can seem strange to the uninitiated, including Mr Smith and me. We felt glad rags would help (in my case, any excuse to go glam is a welcome treat), as did the fireside cocktails and canapés. Introductions made and our trepidation overcome (at one point Mr Smith had to slap my hand away from the moreish salmon with a stern reminder that other guests might also like to sample the hors d'oeuvres), the mood lightened considerably as we adjourned to the dining room and conversation turned to more important matters: such as when, exactly, we were going to be able to sample the pinot noir.

The estate at Wharekauhau is also a working farm – raising sheep and beef cattle – and, beyond its boundaries, the wineries of Martinborough await. As a result, the set menu at the lodge is a food-mile-friendly fantasy of farm-sourced produce and equally local vintages. For me, the eye fillet of the estate's own Texel lamb was the standout – its flavourful tenderness rendering the proffered steak knife redundant. I had to remind myself to leave room for dessert – a tangily divine citrus tart that had as much bite as the banter now in full flow around the table. Mr Smith and I smiled in mute agreement across our espressos, two evangelical converts to communal dining.

It wasn't until 10am the following day that we finally managed to drag ourselves from the super king-size bed, after an indulgent lie-in, the views out of the window once more transfixing us. We struggled to make breakfast on time, but a welcoming waft of the smell of baking bread from the lodge kitchen reassured us we weren't too late. There was no need to leave this 2,200-hectare playground, where we could have taken a tour of the farm, ridden horses or borrowed quad bikes, but Mr Smith and I had viticulture on our minds – it was time to head out to sample the grapes of Martinborough.

We'd been told that many of the 29 boutique vintners in the area were within walking distance of each other, but it wasn't until we rolled up to Martinborough town square that we understood how close they really were – some actually side by side. The area is known for its cracking pinot noirs, and we found a couple of favourites at Palliser Estate and Ata Rangi (Wharekauhau Lodge staff had kindly offered to pick us up later if we were enjoying ourselves a little too much to drive back). On the return journey, we decided the perfect tonic, post wine tasting, would be a windswept stroll beside the sea, so we continued past Wharekauhau to shack-scattered Ocean Beach. The weather was wild – windy and wet – but we emerged from the car anyway to stare at the rugged beauty of the black-sand shoreline.

Our dinner à deux was booked for a romantically lit, private room in the main lodge, before an open fire. Scallops served in a delicate coconut broth, followed by tender pork fillet, were both perfection to our palates. Before our medley of pannacotta, sorbet and crumble arrived, I had no idea something as humble as rhubarb could be worked into such a tremendous tasting plate of a dessert. Relaxed, sated and pleasingly Buddha-bellied, we ambled back to our cottage, gumboots on and takeaway cheese selection in hand. Too happy for sleep just yet, we settled upon the idea of an after-dinner soak in the alfresco hot tub. Wharekauhau: in our case pronounced 'pure heaven'.

REVIEWED BY MR & MRS SMITH

'The estate is a working farm raising sheep and beef cattle – and, beyond its boundaries, wineries await'

NEED TO KNOW

Rooms 12, including 10 single-suite Guest Cottages, the three-suite Château Wellington and the three-suite Wharepapa Cottage.

Rates NZ$1,220–$1,930, including breakfast, pre-dinner drinks and canapés, and a four-course dinner (without wine). Tax is extra at 12.5 per cent. Meals are not included at Wharepapa Cottage.

Check-out 11am, but flexible subject to availability. Check-in, 12 noon.

Facilities CD, DVD and book library, free WiFi in the main lodge, gym, spa, tennis court, gardens. In rooms: flatscreen satellite TV, iPod dock, minibar.

Children The hotel can supply free baby cots and extra beds for older children for NZ$300, plus tax, a night. Babysitting with staff can be arranged for NZ$25 an hour and the restaurant offers a kid-friendly menu.

Also Borrow a guest pushbike to explore the hotel's rugged 2,200-hectare grounds, which include gorgeous forests, lakes, rivers, rolling pasture and striking coastline.

IN THE KNOW

Our favourite rooms Set a little way from the lodge with views out over sheep-dotted pastures and sea, the 10 Guest Cottages are all similar (give or take minor size and layout tweaks), although we were partial to numbers 6 and 8. All sport sitting areas (inside and out on verandas), gas fireplaces, walk-in wardrobes and ensuite bathrooms with marble floors and double spa baths. If you like squashy sofas and huge beds (screened off four-poster-style), you'll be in heaven. If you're in a posse, opt for the three-suite Chateau Wellington, a kilometre away, which includes a horizon pool and the choice of your own chef.

Hotel bar The hotel bar is open all day offering spirits and fine local wines, including rare vintages.

Hotel restaurant Evenings kick off with drinks and canapés in the lounge or courtyard, when you can hobnob with fellow guests, followed by fine feasting in the dining room, where grand shared tables create a dinner-party mood. Inspired by Pacific Rim cuisine and local produce, chef Amit Laud's Kiwi-with-a-twist dishes include Texel lamb with Mediterranean vegetables, polenta, peas, lamb jus and yoghurt. Breakfast is served in the rustic Country Kitchen, and lunch either there or outdoors (request a picnic, or barbecue, with a private chef if you prefer).

Top table For romantic private dining, ask for a table in the elegant lounge (there's a roaring fire in winter).

Room service Available from 6am to 8pm, with a full menu service. In-room minibars are also well-stocked.

Dress code Sturdy jacket and boots for farm strolls by day; smarter get-up for evenings, when communal dining sees guests go glam.

Local knowledge Take a 4WD tour of the hotel's working farm, home to one of New Zealand's oldest stocks of Romney sheep. With a mind-boggling 16,000 lambs born in spring and shearing in autumn, it's a hive of activity.

LOCAL EATING AND DRINKING

For a vineyard, cellar door, tasting room and restaurant in one, make for Tirohana Estate (www.tirohanaestate.com), a boutique winery in Martinborough. Tirohana Cellars serves up casual and fine dining, with a cosy indoor space and outdoor terraces overlooking the vines. It's open on Saturdays only in winter, when the set menu includes comfort food such as salmon fishcakes and apple strudel. At Martinborough's Alana Estate (www.alana.co.nz) choose to eat in the dining room, courtyard or barrel room, where you can team its four wine varietals with tasty matching dishes. Two other rated local wineries in town are **Palliser Estate** (06 306 9019) and **Ata Rangi** (06 306 9570).

GET A ROOM!

Use our free online booking service: check availability and make reservations through www.mrandmrssmith.com.

 SMITH CARD OFFER A three-hour guided farm tour.

Wharekauhau Lodge & Country Estate Western Lake Road, Palliser Bay, RD3 Featherston, Wairarapa 5773 (06 307 7581; www.wharekauhau.co.nz)

SOUTH ISLAND

QUEENSTOWN
Azur Lodge
The Spire
KAIKOURA
Hapuku Lodge & Tree Houses

Snowcapped alpine lakeside
Extreme sports paradise

Set on the banks of Lake Wakatipu, Queenstown is a picture-perfect town with a rich menu of restaurants and bars, amid a searingly beautiful mountain range setting. While other South Island destinations exude a sleepy Kiwi charm, alpine Queenstown operates at turbo speed with more adventure activities on offer than you could shake a snowboard or bungy cord at. Indeed, there are endless opportunities to scare yourself silly as this hub buzzes with an infectious adrenalin-fuelled energy. Welcome to New Zealand's year-round high-octane holiday hub – and buckle up – it's going to be quite a ride.

Catch a direct flight to Queenstown Airport (www.queenstownairport.co.nz), eight kilometres east of town, from Auckland, Wellington or Christchurch with Air New Zealand (www.airnewzealand.co.nz), or from Sydney, Melbourne or Brisbane, Australia. Qantas (www.qantas.co.nz) also flies to Queenstown from Kiwi cities Auckland, Christchurch and Rotorua and major Oz cities; and Jetstar routes in from Auckland and Christchurch (www.jetstar.com). Mainland Air (www.mainlandair.com) offers charter flights across the South Island. From the airport, a taxi into town costs around NZ$25.

NZ's limited, geographically challenged rail service doesn't extend to Queenstown, but you can hop aboard the Kingston Flyer (www.kingstonflyer.co.nz) for a 14-kilometre heritage steam train ride between Kingston and Fairlight, on the southern edge of Lake Wakatipu.

Cruise across Lake Wakatipu on the evocative, steam-powered TSS *Earnslaw* (www.zqn.co.nz/earnslaw), with the option of a barbecue and farmyard tour at Walter Peak High Country Farm.

If you're based in Queenstown you won't need a car, as it's small and pleasantly walkable. However, to explore the surrounding area a car is invaluable. All the major car hire firms have offices at the airport or try one of the local companies such as Jucy rentals (www.jucy.co.nz). Around town the Connectabus (www.connectabus.com) has three colour-coded routes.

There is a taxi rank on Camp Street; local firms include Alpine Taxi (03 442 6666) and Queenstown Taxis (03 442 7788).

Layer North Face and Patagonia to wrangle Queenstown's rollercoaster weather and work a sporty look, but bring smarter threads for bar-hopping.

JRR Tolkein's orc-packed *The Lord of the Rings* trilogy – director Peter Jackson shot parts of the film in Queenstown. *Rita Angus: An Artist's Life*, by Jill Trevelyan, is the first biography of the talented NZ artist, who painted landscapes around Queenstown, Wanaka and Central Otago.

Regional fish, seafood, lamb and steak are all perfect post-bungy jump pick-me-ups, and you won't go wrong with a bottle of much-touted local Central Otago pinot. There are some top restaurants in Queenstown with most countries' cuisine represented.

Winter (June to September) is peak time for ski buffs, with blue skies, white slopes and crisply cool temperatures. The rest of the year, the city and its spectacular natural surrounds warm up for walking, watersports and more extreme thrills and spills.

Queenstown's main dining strips run from Steamer Wharf up Beach Street, splitting into Shotover and Church Streets. During warmer months join the crowds of alfresco diners, and in winter grab a seat in front of a roaring fireplace.

WORTH GETTING OUT OF BED FOR

Queenstown's lakes and alpine mountains are eye-poppingly striking; admire the blockbuster location from atop the Skyline Gondola (www.skyline.co.nz), which sports a café and restaurant.

Although the great outdoors are the big draw here, there are a handful of must-see galleries including Toi o Tahuna, at 11 Church Lane (www.toi.co.nz), which exclusively represents New Zealand art including contemporary Maori talents. Ask owner Mark Moran for the free guide *Galleries & Artist Studios in the Wakatipu* for a more comprehensive cultural crawl.

Queenstown is New Zealand's most famous ski destination, with popular slopes at the Remarkables and Coronet Peak (www.nzski.com), as well as more chilled-out alternatives at Cardrona (www.cardrona.com) and Treble Cone (www.treblecone.com) around smaller lakeside town Wanaka, 100 kilometres north-east. Local buses and return shuttles run to the ski fields. For transport, lift deals and equipment hire head for Snowrental (www.snowrental.co.nz) at 39 Camp Street or Info & Track Centre (www.infotrack.co.nz) at 37 Shotover Street; Alpine Sports (www.alpinesports.co.nz) located at number 39 is also good for sourcing the right gear. For off-piste heli-skiing, try Harris Mountains Heli-Ski (www.heliski.co.nz) or Southern Lakes Heli-Ski (www.southernlakesheliski.co.nz), which both offer private charters. More leisurely pursuits include winery tours and tastings (try www.queenstownwinetrail.co.nz).

It's three and a half hours' drive north-west to spectacular Milford Sound in Fiordland – but New Zealand's top tourist attraction won't disappoint. Sheer rock faces rise dramatically from the water with forests clinging precariously to the craggy cliffs. A cruise out onto the Sound may also conjure up seals and dolphins. Lots of tour operators run day trips out of Queenstown, including Real Journeys (www.realjourneys.co.nz). Milford Sound Scenic Flights (www.milfordflights.co.nz) also offers aerial sweeps across it; return flights from Queenstown take about an hour, or team your trip with a lake cruise for a four-hour adventure.

Daredevil kids over 10 can enjoy vertiginous bungy jumps, care of AJ Hackett, or the Secrets of Bungy Tour lets them sample the madcap bungy scene without leaving terra firma (www.bungy.co.nz). The beachside playground in Queenstown Gardens will please younger children, and all kids should get a kick out of the Underwater Observatory at Main Town Pier (03 442 6142). Large windows reveal the huge trout, long-finned eels and scaup (diving ducks) that call Lake Wakatipu home; throw in a Kawarau Jet jet-boat ride for added aquatic thrills (www.kjet.co.nz).

There are endless scenic walks in the area ranging from one-hour strolls to eight-hour treks; the DOC visitor information centre at 37 Shotover Street (www.doc.govt.nz) has a free guide, Queenstown Walks and Trails. For longer tramping, the three- to four-day 32-kilometre Routeburn Track will make you feel the burn, but its scenic subalpine rainforest location will make up for it (reserve your spot ahead of time).

With its tempting bakery and deli, the Mediterranean Market (www.mediterranean.co.nz) is the place to fill up your gourmet hamper. Pick up a bottle of the region's toasted pinot noir and settle back on a lakeside bench or do battle with seagulls on the shore.

Queenstown is brimming with adventure and sports stores but there are a few sartorial gems too; at 1, The Mall, Angel Divine (03 442 8988) stocks hot NZ designers including Kate Sylvester, and ethical fashion label Untouched World (03 442 4992) creates beautiful Merino wool garments. Kapa, at 29 Rees Street (03 442 4041), has local and Maori artwork and jewellery. On Saturdays between April and December, a small arts and crafts market is held on the lakeside beside Steamer Wharf. The pretty gold-mining town of Arrowtown (www.arrowtown.org.nz), half an hour's drive from Queenstown, is also good for upmarket boutiques and craft shops.

There's a marked Frisbee Golf Course in Queenstown Gardens where all you need is a frisbee and decent hand-eye coordination.

trying at least one heart-stopping activity, as this is the adrenalin capital of the world. Bungy jumping, skydiving, hang gliding, jet-boating, caving, canyoning, white-water rafting, climbing, mountain biking or kayaking are all readily on offer. Horse treks, walking and fishing are less of a white-knuckle ride.

Ever since AJ Hackett (www.bungy.co.nz) introduced to the world that crazy elastic-band-tied-to-ankle sport, way back in 1988, the town has been trying to outdo itself with faster, higher and scarier challenges. The 43-metre-high Kawarau Bridge is the site of the world's first commercial bungy, but you can also try jumping at night from the 47-metre-high Ledge Bungy. If that sounds too tame, try the Nevis option, where you leap from a stomach-churning 134-metre-high pod suspended over the river of that name.

January After bringing in the new year with a bang, Queenstown hosts a festival dedicated to its famous drop during the Central Otago Pinot Noir Celebration, held over two days at the end of January (www.pinot celebration.co.nz). **March** The annual Wakatipu Disc (Frisbee) Golf Tournaments are held in Queenstown Gardens. **April** In nearby Arrowtown, the streets floweth over with festivities for the Autumn Festival (www.arrowtown autumnfestival.org.nz). **June–July** Queenstown's snowtastic Winterfestival is celebrated over 10 fun-filled days from late June to July (www.winterfestival.co.nz).

'Our attention was consumed by the "living wallpaper": Cecil Peak, front and centre, the Remarkables range to the left and Lake Wakatipu below'

Queenstown

Azur Lodge

STYLE Luxe lakeside lodges
SETTING Lush Queenstown hillside

It's a testament to the sublime comforts of Azur Lodge that, in the renowned Adventure Capital of the World, this keen skier was unable to leave her private villa for the better part of 24 hours. Even snow falling heavily outside didn't make me muster the energy. OK, so I managed to meander up the path to the main lodge at 3pm for an afternoon tea of melt-in-the-mouth brownies and still-warm choc-chip cookies whipped up by our host Maria (very handily a pastry chef in her former life). But that was the extent of my outdoor adventures. Like Gollum and his cave, I quickly slunk back to savour the delights of my sumptuous cavern.

On arrival, I confess to some foreboding as our courtesy car turned off the road hugging Lake Wakatipu and instead headed up into the suburban estate of Sunshine Bay. Any fretting was quickly allayed when we swung onto a dirt track and up the driveway of the Azur. Perched on the crest of the hill was the main lodge, with its nine private villas scattered down the hillside. And not a provincial house – or any other distraction for that matter – in sight. Only the breathtaking panorama of snowcapped mountains and the grandeur of New Zealand's longest lake.

At risk of succumbing to scenery fatigue so early in our stay, we relaxed with a latte in the main lodge where we were introduced to the delightful Keiko, resident chef and conjurer of breakfasts and any other daytime food requests. With Mr Smith itching to hit the slopes for a few afternoon runs, we went down to our villa (number 5), where Maria tried in vain to explain the various amenities on offer. In vain only because our attention was consumed by what Mr Smith astutely referred to as the 'living wallpaper' around us: Cecil Peak, front and centre, the Remarkables range to the left and Lake Wakatipu below.

Mr Smith recovered his composure more quickly than I and was soon whisked away in his snow gear by Corey, a big-mountain skier and relatively recent addition to the Azur team. Having eyed the Central Otago sauvignon blanc on ice, I contemplated spending the afternoon in the jaw-dropping bath with a wine glass for company. But instead I put on my hiking boots and headed off along the Sunshine Bay track for the 40-minute lakeside walk into Queenstown. The fragrant wet track in winter evoked a rainforest, which is an appropriate segue into my afternoon appointment, as I'd arranged to meet with local tea expert Michelle Casson to discuss all things leafy and infused. (I'm into tea.) After taste-testing numerous exotic concoctions and purchasing some must-have brewing paraphernalia, I scurried back to the lodge laden but feeling virtuous enough to now indulge in my bath fantasy.

The Azur bath experience would be hard to eclipse. The deep spa-for-two is set against large bi-fold windows that open to create a Japanese onsen-like effect by letting in the sense of the elements – in this case relentless rain – without the accompanying reality. From this stage I watched the drama of the weather unfold, from wild gusting winds that helped a *Titanic*-era steamboat, the TSS *Earnslaw*, on its voyage across the lake, to a misty fog that settled in to blanket nearby Cecil Peak. My emotions watching this natural theatre rode an equally wide range from blissful to exhilarated, especially when a bird attempted a sortie through the open windows.

(The fact that Damien Rice was rotating with David Gray on the iPod might also explain the mood swings.) At any rate, as a psychologist, I can easily recommend this as the ultimate stress antidote.

Each Azur villa has clearly been designed to maximise the drama outside by keeping the interior luxe but subdued – Queenstown's wilderness is the headline act in the decor here. The beechwood palette never competes for attention, and the furnishings, including the super king-size bed, are comfortable but refined. Photographic prints of mountains and water by Christchurch artist Doc Ross are both fitting and stunning. Topping off the comfort are heated tiles throughout and a gas fireplace in the lounge. But lest I give the misleading impression that the Azur is in any way 'homely', all the mod-cons are available, including wireless internet. Plus, there's a deck for outdoor dining and lounging around when the weather better reflects the Sunshine Bay tag.

The thing that distinguishes the Azur from traditional lodges, and which apparently leads to some confusion among guests, is the decision not to cater dinner. Since Queenstown's finest eateries are only five minutes away by car, this struck Mr Smith and I as reasonable. Instead, the Azur offers the best of both worlds. The first night we mingled with other guests and staff over pre-dinner drinks and canapés, where we gleaned local insights from Corey about skiing options and jostled with Elvis, the resident pooch, for prime position at the fireplace. Ready for dinner, we were then driven by Sharon to Wai restaurant in Queenstown where we feasted on seafood, lamb, cheese and more wine. Treating us like indulged teenagers, Sharon duly collected us after we'd called to say we'd finished. On our second night, when I shamefully couldn't bring myself to leave the Azur grounds, we instead ordered in Thai, which Sharon brought to our villa (with complimentary pinot noir) and artfully assembled with candlelight at our own dining table.

We floated out the next day, resolving that it would be remiss of us not to return in the summer. Just to see what those snowcapped peaks look like when it's a little warmer, of course.

REVIEWED BY ROSEMARY PURCELL

NEED TO KNOW

Rooms Nine villas.

Rates NZ$900–$1,300, including airport and town transfers, breakfast, minibar drinks, afternoon tea, apéritifs and canapés. Excludes tax at 12.5 per cent.

Check-out 11am, or a bit later for a fee. Check-in, 2pm.

Facilities Library, Jacuzzi. In rooms: minibar, LCD TV, Denon DVD/CD player, iPod dock, free WiFi, Linden Leaves toiletries, private decks.

Children Baby cots are free. They can split double beds into twins or provide extra beds for NZ$70 plus tax. High chairs, toys, microwaves and patio safety features are also on tap, as is babysitting at NZ$20 an hour.

Also On arrival at Azur you're welcomed with a glass of wine, beer or a soft drink on the house – and a run-through of Queenstown's highlights.

IN THE KNOW

Our favourite rooms All villas come with separate lounging areas, ensuite bathrooms replete with rainforest showers and double spa baths, and huge windows bringing the outside in – but we like number 5 for its privacy.

Hotel bar Although there's no dedicated public bar, there's a sociable drinks scene at Azur. Each evening a buffet bar is set up in the main lodge with a tempting selection of local wines, spirits and beer for guests to quaff before dinner.

Hotel restaurant Azur Lodge doesn't have a restaurant but it does provide breakfast, afternoon tea and evening drinks and canapés. In-room dining can be arranged (eat out on the deck for sublime views) or the concierge can book you into the best local restaurants.

Room service Meals can be ordered in from local restaurants until 10pm, and your table set and cleared by Azur's staff. Burgers, pizza or Thai can also be sourced for a 20 per cent fee.

Dress code A high-performance fleece for that 'mountain climber at rest' look.

Local knowledge The area's mix of wildly beautiful nature and fun, high-octane sports means you can go hiking, skiing and skydiving, or just relax into more leisurely pursuits such as wine tasting.

LOCAL EATING AND DRINKING

The Bathhouse (03 442 5625) at 15–28 Marine Parade, Queenstown Bay, offers fine dining right by the lapping waters of Lake Wakatipu. Showcasing local produce from Central Otago, this is a stylish spot for an organic coffee, glass of white, a casual lunch or more formal dinner with an optional tasting menu (when reservations are essential). **Gantleys Restaurant** (03 442 8999) at Arthurs Point Road is another upmarket affair with an award-winning wine list served up in an appealing historic stone building in landscaped gardens. **Wai Waterfront Restaurant** (03 442 5969), on the lakeside at Steamer Wharf, is known for its strong Central Otago wines, local seafood and freshly shucked melt-in-your-mouth New Zealand oysters, and offers à la carte choices and a seven-course tasting menu. For a friendly local that serves tasty pizza, pasta, salads and good wines, from budget to more rarified options, head for **Vknow** (03 442 5444) in Fernhill. If fine-cut steak and wild, organic food is more your bag, then make a trip to **Botswana Butchery** (03 442 6994) at Archers Cottage, 17 Marine Parade. Set in an old villa, it has cosy nooks inside and a large patio outdoors.

GET A ROOM!

Use our free online booking service: check availability and make reservations through www.mrandmrssmith.com.

 SMITH CARD OFFER A bottle of local bubbly and chocolates in your villa on arrival.

Azur Lodge 23 MacKinnon Terrace, Sunshine Bay, Queenstown 9300 (03 409 0588; www.azur.co.nz)

'Ushered upstairs, we were drawn from the ground floor's Copenhagen cool to Kyoto-style red-and-black enamels'

Queenstown

The Spire

STYLE Urbane five-star suites
SETTING Alpine church-side lane

lake hooded by snowcapped peaks; we learned that in a town with about 11,000 residents and more than a million visitors a year, there's not one traffic light. That's how smoothly time flows here. The Spire is located in the very heart of New Zealand's all-season adventure capital and it is the town's chicest retreat, discreetly hidden in a narrow lane, behind a stacked-stone façade. Delivered to the door, what bags we had were whisked away, and we stepped into the Spire's cosy foyer to be met by Mel, Jan's partner, the hotel's general manager. Mel exuded courtesy and warmth and – that universal sign of all useful people – proffered hard news. She knew where my bag was (before the airline did, I suspect), had made arrangements for it to be on the earliest flight the next day, and had also planned how to keep up morale until it arrived.

Mindful of our needs, Mel ushered us upstairs, and we were drawn from the ground floor's Copenhagen cool to Kyoto-style red-and-black enamels on the three upper levels. Our Double King Suite's decor returned us to calming creams and autumnal tones in stone, timber and fabrics, our room warmed by a minimalist gas fireplace, a rich, brown fur throw on the designer couch and the softest strains of Verdi and Vivaldi. Framed through the floor-to-ceiling balcony window was the apse and steeple of the town's 19th-century stone church. Even a bottle of champagne was on ice and a side plate of chocolates awaited. We were then assured that our peace and privacy would be uninterrupted. (Even mundane but essential matters of keeping rooms refreshed are handled with the utmost discretion; we discovered the next morning that the staff uses a combination of monitoring and two-way radios to sneak in diplomatically when guests are out.)

Soon enough, although bag-less, I was showered and luxuriating in a Spire-provided robe. Mrs Smith was purring in the Eames recliner, soothed by the fragrant, local Evolu products. My towelling get-up though, however comfortable, was not best suited to Queenstown's after-dark scene – even when teamed with ski boots – so the kind people downstairs organised for a fine, earthy Central Otago pinot noir and a pair of juicy burgers to be

Time spent on the best powder runs can be compared to our slalom towards Queenstown and the Spire. Anticipation gives way to calm. Power demurs to grace. And, in our case, after soaking up a few moguls, we settle into a tranquil rhythm. Why the bumpy start? At Queenstown airport, Mrs Smith got her bags and I got my ski boots. And that's all. Just as I was wondering what exactly I'd be wearing to the Champagne Bar at the hotel I'd heard so much about, in stepped Jan, who had driven from the Spire to greet us. The quietly spoken Dane calmly gathered our belongings, brushed off the setbacks and set about lifting our spirits, in a prosaic, Scandinavian kind of way.

Jan's poise as he drove us to our contemporary hideaway helped us pause and delight in Queenstown's pale grey delivered to our room. (Fergburger, a local brand, is incomparable in its genre and witty in its titles: do not leave town without trying its tasty takeaways.)

Food is something at which the Spire excels, as the sensational breakfast the next morning revealed. My rösti and ham arrived like a precious meteorite hurtled to earth: all crusty dark on the outside and buttery, magma-soft potato in the centre. Mrs Smith enjoyed a special herbal tea served with graceful ceremony, and we were both uplifted by the pop-modern colour of the Rosenthal china.

In fact, the whole place was very easy on the eye: iconic furniture by Eames and Starck, as well as one-off artworks by contemporary New Zealand talents, make the Spire stand out from other hotels by miles. There's even a well-appointed boardroom for business meetings – or some Texas hold 'em or cable sports if you'd prefer.

In-house know-how at the Spire was the most thrilling influence on our stay. Before we arrived, there were tips about on-piste and heli-skiing options. Then, during our trip, more advice was given about the area's wine, food, history, geography and art. Exemplifying the adage 'measure a team by its depth', Mel, a former software executive, leads from the front. She harnesses an executive's experienced intuition with well-honed curiosity about the guest and their interests.

This care saw us escorted to the not-to-be-missed restaurant showcase for Amisfield wines in nearby Arrowtown, where we were exhorted to try an idiosyncratic hot chocolate with chilli. Later we were encouraged to sample dark ale and tapas with the locals at Eichardt's Bar on Queenstown's waterfront. And then there were Mrs Smith's squeals that evening at the pillow gifts (a travel kit of Evolu delights). All this they took care of. So, did the Spire arrange the perfect timing of the powder dump at nearby Coronet Peak? Or organise for the panoramic beauty as I crested the ridge below Green Gates in a spray of crystals? I don't know for sure, but given their knack for hospitality, I wouldn't rule it out: that is the dedication to detail at this most heavenly of hotels.

REVIEWED BY JOHN CARRUTHERS

'Mrs Smith was purring in the Eames recliner, soothed by the fragrant, local Evolu products'

NEED TO KNOW

Rooms 10 suites.

Rates NZ$725–$1,085, including à la carte breakfast, champagne and chocolate on arrival, and airport transfers. Excludes tax at 12.5 per cent.

Check-out 11am, but there is flexibility. Check-in, 2pm, unless by prior arrangement.

Facilities DVD/CD library, free WiFi throughout. In rooms: flatscreen TV, iPod dock, DVD/CD players, Bang & Olufsen phone, minibar, pillow menu, Evolu toiletries, balcony.

Children Baby cots are NZ$70 a night plus tax; extra beds, NZ$180. Babysitting can be arranged with qualified nannies from NZ$15 an hour.

Also A masseur or beauty therapist can come to your room – perfect for smoothing ruffled feathers after Queenstown's many outdoor activities. Alternatively, the Spire's two miniature schnauzers, Merlot and Shiraz, are on hand for soothing strokes.

IN THE KNOW

Our favourite rooms We especially love Room 6 for its pretty views of the church spire that gives the hotel its name, but king-size beds, luxe linens, stone-clad fireplaces, design classics and large private balconies feature in all suites.

Hotel bar Laid-back lounge music and soft lighting make the Inspire Champagne & Wine Bar, by the lobby, the ideal champagne-cocktail-sipping spot. Perch at the bar counter or chill out in romantic tabled seating by the fire.

Hotel restaurant Simple and intimate, Inspire Restaurant offers breakfast only (exclusively for guests), but the Spire can advise you on great cafés and restaurants within walking distance for eating out.

Top table By the window, overlooking the garden.

Room service Take breakfast in your room or on your balcony; the hotel can order in take-away food at any time of the day or night, including burgers and pizza.

Dress code This season's luxe lakeside loungewear.

Local knowledge The Spire can arrange almost any activity; this is the adventure capital of the world, so have a go at something extreme. Take your pick from adrenalin-rush heli-skiing, bungy jumping or jet-boating. Gentler pursuits such as golf, hiking and horse riding are also on offer, or unwind at the lake with a picnic hamper or packed lunch, provided with 24 hours' notice.

LOCAL EATING AND DRINKING

Elegant lakeside **Wai Waterfront Restaurant** (03 442 5969) at Steamer Wharf, Beach Street, has one of the best locations and reputations in Queenstown. Known for its seafood, lamb and freshly shucked local oysters, there's even a seven-course tasting menu. For a rustic Italian downtown, head for the daily menu and wood-fired oven at **Bella Cucina** (03 442 6762) at 6 Brecon Street, and get fresh pasta, pizza and breads. Or check out well-respected **Amisfield Winery and Bistro** (03 442 0556), a country-style eatery with a pretty courtyard at 10 Lake Hayes Road, 15 minutes' drive from central Queenstown. Enjoy wine tastings as well as appetising organic and locally sourced produce to complement the tipples. The outdoor terrace with roaring fire at **Barmuda** (03 442 7300) on Searle Lane draws the crowds whatever the weather, and the original cocktail list keeps them here until closing. Vibrant local **Vudu Café** (03 442 5357) at 23 Beach Street serves up generous, tasty breakfasts, lunches and dinners; there's a great play area for kids and online access for anyone with laptop in hand. For burgers with attitude, hotfoot it to **Fergburger** (03 441 1232; www.fergburger.com) at 42 Shotover Street in town, loved by locals for its savvy, satisfying take on fast food.

GET A ROOM!

Use our free online booking service: check availability and make reservations through www.mrandmrssmith.com.

 SMITH CARD OFFER A bottle of Central Otago pinot on arrival.

The Spire 3–5 Church Lane, Queenstown 9300 (03 441 0004; www.thespirehotels.com)

KAIKOURA

COASTLINE Ocean-lapped, snow-capped mountains
COAST LIFE Whale watching and wine quaffing

A name which translates as 'meal of crayfish' gives a taste of the scene in store. Lying midway between Christchurch and Picton on the spectacularly rugged east coast of New Zealand's South Island, the seaside town of Kaikoura is blessed with a soul-stirring surf-and-turf setting. Wildlife lovers, immerse yourselves in dolphin-spotting and more – a catalogue of much-protected marine life is at your flippers, including whales, seals, penguins and albatross. Or mingle with this vibrant fishing community and meet inspiring artists and craftsfolk whose wares make great mementos of this fascinating former whaling station with a rich Maori heritage. By the way, the surf's not half bad either.

GETTING THERE

Planes Sounds Air (www.soundsair.com) links Wellington with tiny Kaikoura Airport, seven kilometres south-west of town, or larger Blenheim Airport (www.blenheim airport.co.nz) to the north. Wellington International Airport (www.wellingtonairport.co.nz) is under an hour's flight from anywhere in the country; Christchurch (www.christchurchairport.co.nz) is another international option. Domestically, try Air New Zealand (www.airnew zealand.com); and Qantas (www.qantas.com.au) or Pacific Blue (www.flypacificblue.com.au) from Australia.

Trains Tranz Scenic's TranzCoastal service runs daily between Picton and Christchurch, stopping off at Kaikoura, departing from Picton at 1pm and Christchurch at 7am. The train journey is an easy-on-the-eye way to enjoy the Kaikoura coastline as it weaves between mountain and sea (www.tranzscenic.co.nz).

Automobiles Allow well over two hours from either Picton or Christchurch; from Blenheim, just under two. Christchurch is an especially scenic route.

LOCAL KNOWLEDGE

Taxis There are no local firms as such, but there are shuttle services that operate sightseeing trips and airport transfers. Try www.kaikourashuttles.co.nz.

Packing tips Outdoor gear is the local uniform; and don't forget your splash-proof camera for marine snaps.
Recommended reads It may be set on the North Island coast, but Witi Ihimaera's 1987 novel *The Whale Rider*, about a young Maori girl's ability to communicate with whales, will make for a perfect read in Kaikoura.
Local specialties As the name indicates, this is a seafood lover's heaven, with crayfish a must on the menu. Other local delights include grouper, cod, mussels and paua, as well as kumera, a kind of sweet potato long cultivated here. There are also organic options, award-winning wineries and sweet treats such as fudge. And it's not just the edibles that make the restaurants worth visiting – the aesthetics are just as tasty thanks to those show-stopping views.
Do go/don't go November until February is usually the warmest and driest time to visit; March is often a rainy month and temperatures drop in winter (June until August). If you're planning some whale watching, summer (December to March) is the best time to spot orcas (killer whales), June to September is prime time for southern right whales, and giant sperm whales can be seen year-round, along with dusky dolphins and fur seals (all sightings are very weather-dependent).

And... Get closer to the jaw-dropping mountains that frame Kaikoura's coastline with some skiing at Mount Lyford Alpine Resort. Slopes are generally open from June to October, depending on snow conditions, and there's transport available from Kaikoura, 60 kilometres away, with various shuttle services (www.mtlyford.co.nz).

WORTH GETTING OUT OF BED FOR

Viewpoint Take advantage of this pristine rendezvous and look up, up, up at night – sights like this are a pipe dream from light-polluted city locations. Stargaze for an hour and a half with Kaikoura Night Sky Tour (www.kaikouranightsky.co.nz; NZ$50 a person). A guide will point out the constellations and let you eyeball Saturn, Jupiter and Mars through a powerful telescope. For a loftier adventure, enjoy a bird's-eye view from the cockpit: Air Kaikoura (www.airkaikoura.co.nz) allows passengers to pilot a plane with a professional instructor for 20-minute flights over the coastal waters.

Arts and culture Trace the area's rich history of Maori culture, European settlers and the whaling industry through the Kaikoura District Museum & Archives at 14 Ludstone Road (03 319 7440). A wing built on whale bones at Fyffe House, the town's oldest building, is an insight into its past (www.fyffehouse.co.nz). A dozen or so craft stores and galleries add allure to the Art Trail – get a guide from the visitor centre on West End (www.kaikoura.co.nz).

Activities Whale watching is a must here, as the area's striking above-ground landscape – mountains plunging into the sea – is repeated underwater, with a deep canyon and unusual currents attracting marine life. Whale Watch (NZ$145 an adult; NZ$60 a child, aged 3–15; www.whalewatch.co.nz) offers daily tours with regular year-round sightings of giant sperm whales, as well as migrating humpback, pilot, blue and southern right whales, depending on the season. Wings Over Whales (NZ$165 an adult; NZ$75 a child, aged 3–14; www.soundsair.com/whales) allows you to spot whales, as well as dolphins, seals and ancient Maori sites, from the air, in a small four- or eight-seater plane. You can also swim with curious seals with Seal Swim Kaikoura (NZ$70–$90 an adult; NZ$60–$70 for children under 14; www.sealswimkaikoura.co.nz), frolic with sea birds care of Albatross Encounter (NZ$125 a person for a four-hour tour;

www.oceanwings.co.nz/albatross) or go fishing (from NZ$55 for a half-hour charter a person; www.fishkaikoura.co.nz). For more of a gourmet outing, tickle your palette with a NZ$5 wine tasting, or NZ$15 tour and tasting, at Kaikoura Winery (www.kaikourawinery.co.nz), which enjoys spectacular coastal views. Catch daily 45-minute tours at 11am, 2pm and 4pm, then head for the café/restaurant for lunch or a vineyard platter afterwards.

Daytripper Get connected with the indigenous culture and hear about customs, spiritual beliefs and ancestral stories with Maori Tours' twice-daily 3.5-hour excursions. Adults, NZ$115; children, NZ$65 (www.maoritours.co.nz).

Best beach For renowned surfing, try Kahutara (19 kilometres south of Kaikoura) and Mangamaunu beaches (15 kilometres north of town), as well as the Meatworks just over the railway line at Hapuku. Contact Board Silly Surf Adventures in Kaikoura for classes or hire (03 319 6464). There's also a safe swimming beach in town opposite the Esplanade.

Children If llamas, wallabies and goats appeal, Kaikoura Farm Park has critters galore for kids to play with (03 319 5033). Saddle up at Fyffe View Ranch, for family-friendly horse treks through bush trails (www.kaikourahorsetrekking.co.nz).

Walks Really gorge on local beauty by tackling the Kaikoura Peninsula Walkway, which loops from the Esplanade in town to Point Kean, and then winds around the cliffs and shoreline to South Bay. The

12-kilometre trail takes about three hours, and you'll pass fishermen, seals, red-billed seagulls and historic Maori *pa* sites along the way (www.doc.govt.nz).

Perfect picnic Roadside caravan Nin's Bin, a 20-minute drive north towards Picton on SH1 (near Rakautara), is a local favourite, serving up crayfish, lobster and green-lipped mussels steamed in white wine, with sumptuous sea views. Eat them while ogling the ocean.

Shopping With arts and crafts one of the headline acts here, unique, local souvenirs are plentiful. Try Southern Paua & Pacific Jewels (2 Beach Road) for pretty things to garnish you and yours. For those with a one-track food-focused mind, local produce is also worth a look-in: head to 33 Beach Road and scoop up some of Hislop Café's organic honey (03 319 6971).

Something for nothing Bring your own snorkelling gear, and check out the marine life along this gorgeous rocky coastline for free. Dolphins, seals, sea birds and even whales may rear their heads, even if you haven't shelled out for a group tour.

Don't go home without taking a dip in Hanmer Springs' warm, mineral thermal pools, just under two hours' drive inland, which have been attracting visitors for 125 years (NZ$14 an adult; NZ$7 a child, aged 3–15; younger kids get free entry). There's a spa too for additional pampering, as well as private pools and sauna and steam rooms, although it'll cost extra to go it alone (www.hanmersprings.co.nz).

COMPLETELY KAIKOURA

Eat crayfish like the locals do at the beachfront Kaikoura Seafood BBQ. Little more than a roadside shack with shaded tables outdoors, the meals served here don't come much fresher. Dishes include whole crayfish, grilled scallops, whitebait fritters and steaming chowder – all served with rice or bread. Hold that thought and try not to salivate, then seek it out at 194 Torquay Street, near the seal colony.

DIARY

June Brave the cold over the Queen's Birthday Weekend in June, when the O'Neill Coldwater Classic surf competition comes to Kaikoura. **October** With such an abundance of good food and wine in the region, it's only right that it's celebrated with a big annual festival. Seafest takes place the first Saturday in October and features the best of food and wine from Kaikoura, Marlborough and North Canterbury, plus entertainment too (www.seafest.co.nz).

'Our room is named after a native
bird, which makes sense
considering it's a bit like a nest:
it's one of five treetop rooms'

Hapuku Lodge & Tree Houses

STYLE Architectural meets arboreal
SETTING Deer-dotted pastures and peaks

Look, I'm not very good at packing lightly; instead of a weekend's worth of clothes I have a month's supply. A fact I instantly regret as Mr Smith and I lug four suitcases up three flights of stairs to our room. Luckily a plate of baked-that-day biscuits is waiting for us as a reward for our work-out. There is no number on the door – our room is called Kotare, after a native bird, which kind of makes sense considering it's a bit like a nest: it's one of the five treetop rooms. There is also a lodge at Hapuku, but surely the only reason you'd stay on ground level is if you're recovering from a hip replacement.

Our room is luxurious, with an inviting king-size bed in the centre, and ridiculously impressive views. Wander to one end and there is a fireplace with two comfy chairs and full vistas of snowcapped mountains; a meander to the far side leads you to the ensuite, which looks out to the sea. There is something very sexy about the bathroom area. Mr Smith is so enamoured of the heated slate floor he lays his clothes on it so they're nice and toasty when he puts them on. The double spa has cushioned headrests, but for the voyeur (not mentioning any names, Mr Smith), the shower is completely encased in glass and looks over a privately owned field to the ocean. 'Only the sheep can see you,' a staff member assures us, 'and they've seen it all before.'

Jaws removed from the floor, Mr Smith and I take off to explore the area. The first thing we see is a colony of seals on the rocks. We decide the collective noun should be a snuggle of seals, as they make the most precarious rock look comfy. Next, we visit Kaikoura Winery. I'm willing to wager there aren't many wineries where you can sip booze while whale watching. Yep, somehow seeing a frolicking pod of blue whales makes the chardonnay taste sweeter.

Happy with our sea-life encounters, we head back to the lodge for dinner. All the guests meet for a pre-supper drink and you can mingle as much or as little as you like. There are only three other residents tonight and, as Mr Smith also goes by the name Captain Have-a-Chat, we're soon all merrily swapping anecdotes.

Now to the food: it is quite simply exceptional. None of that gourmet guff where you're given a massive plate and need a magnifying glass to find the part you eat. The fresh creations are elegantly presented and the portions are man-sized. We choose the eye fillet for two and there is so much left over that the chef offers to make it up as sandwiches with lashings of mustard the next day. Now that's service.

Full of top tenderloin and gallons of New Zealand pinot we stumble back to our room to find someone on staff has lit the fire for us. We change into the supplied dressing gowns. 'It's like walking around wrapped in a flannelette sheet,' says Mr Smith before drawing the burgundy curtains that make the bedroom feel instantly like part of the Queen's Court. Deliciously regal.

After a decent sleep-in and a game of 'I can see the snow, now I can see the ocean' we head over for breakfast. I can formally declare duck hash the breakfast of champions. We grab our sandwiches and venture to Hanmer Springs to enjoy the thermal pools. Now, everything might look close on the map, but trust me: not only do you need a hire car

here, you should also double the time you think it will take to get anywhere. The roads are windy and either hug the coastline or take you over mountain ridges, which can be hairy when massive trucks speed past.

We arrive at Hanmer Springs to find it's not as rustic and natural as we expected. There is, however, something deeply cool about choosing what temperature pool to soak in. Here's a hint: 41 degrees is where it's at. Then Mr Smith spots the waterslides. If anyone had said I'd be in New Zealand in the dead of winter in my bikini racing up icy steps to the top of a waterslide I would have said they were loco, but embracing your inner child is a completely energising experience. The lifeguard joins in and gives us marks out of 10 for our entries into the water.

We're buzzing as we arrive back at our room. Mr Smith decides to light the fire himself and when the flames leap obligingly he dances around the room like Tom Hanks in *Castaway*, exclaiming, 'I made fire.' (I don't want to burst his manly bubble but how hard can it be when you have to hand: propellent, pine cones and perfectly cut wood?)

As we walk to dinner I make a mental packing note: Louboutin heels may look fab, but they aren't really practical on gravel pathways around a lodge. Staff members take drink orders like friends excited to welcome you to their new pad. Rather than imposing, they are so knowledgeable about the local area it feels like they're co-conspirators on your adventure. We are soon telling them tales of conquering the waterslide and, amazingly, they don't look at us like we are immature freaks. Not once.

Dinner again exceeds expectations. We even ask to speak to the chef, and he brags that his rice pudding with poached tamarillo is the best in the world Mr Smith hears the sound of a gauntlet hitting the ground. Minutes later my amateur critic is raising a creamy spoonful to a smirking mouth, an eyebrow arched. A flash of disappointment at not being able to burst the chef's bold claim is swiftly replaced by a look of ecstasy. What else to do after but flop, full of pud, into those fireside chairs but a waddle away? We stare glassy-eyed into the flames and our surroundings feel as comforting as being wrapped up in my dad's favourite old jumper. But thankfully for boutique-hotel lovers, Hapuku Lodge is just that little bit more stylish.

REVIEWED BY SHELLY HORTON

NEED TO KNOW

Rooms 12, including four suites.

Rates NZ$528–$1,050, including breakfast. Tax is extra at 12.5 per cent.

Check-out 11am, but flexible subject to availability. Check-in, 2pm.

Facilities DVD library, free WiFi throughout, guest Mac computer, outdoor heated swimming pool and 25-metre lap pool, hot tub, sauna, gardens. In rooms: flatscreen TV, DVD and CD players, iPod dock, minibar, Evolu, Living Nature and Lavish toiletries.

Children Welcome in the Family Tree Houses and Olive House Apartment; only those over 12 in the main lodge rooms. Baby cots available for NZ$50 a night; extra beds NZ$115, including breakfast.

Also The lodge's knockout 600-hectare grounds, between the towering Kaikoura Seaward Mountains and surf-lashed Mangamaunu Bay, include the family farm's oil-producing olive grove and deer stud.

IN THE KNOW

Our favourite rooms For a cool canopy experience, the modern, wood-clad Tree House Rooms, set in a manuka grove remote from the main lodge, are a must. The five one-bedroom Upper Branch Rooms, perched 10 metres up in the treetops, are the most romantic and private with wraparound windows ensuring neck-swivelling views of mountains, sea and roaming deer from the spa bath, seating nook (complete with wood-burning fire) and deck. Smaller, more affordable Lower Branch Rooms sit below, or book into one of the Family Tree Houses, an interconnected hybrid of the two.

Hotel bar Make yourself a martini or a Manhattan and then relax on comfy couches by a circular stone fireplace in the lodge's spacious lounge and dining area. Open 8am–1am.

Hotel restaurant The lodge's open-plan dining room has a relaxed alpine feel, with simple wood furniture, timber floors and a double-sided fireplace (in summer, eat in the garden). Chef Richard Huber's philosophy is 'farm gate to plate' with contemporary seasonal dishes spanning dry-aged grass-fed rib eye, Hapuku Farm organic greens and oven-roasted Kaikoura crayfish plucked live from the hotel's own tank.

Top table There are a couple of window tables with easy-on-the-eye views of the deer paddock and mountains; or grab a pew at the chefs' work counter beside the open kitchen to watch them whip up your meal.

Room service Available 11am–9.30pm in Lodge Suites only, with a menu mirroring the restaurant's lunch and dinner offerings. You can also pre-order picnics.

Dress code Refined yet relaxed – natural tones will chime in with the surf and turf setting.

Local knowledge It's just a 20-minute walk down to acclaimed surf beach Mangamaunu Bay, or explore the area on one of the hotel's free mountain bikes. The small eco-marine town of Kaikoura is a 15-minute drive away and is the hub for aquatic activities including whale watching (www.whalewatch.co.nz) and dolphin encounters (www.dolphin.co.nz).

LOCAL EATING AND DRINKING

Cliffside boutique **Kaikoura Winery** (03 319 7966) has amazing ocean and mountain views. Two kilometres south of Kaikoura at 140 State Highway 1, it's open daily for tastings of its award-winning wines. At 33 Beach Road in Kaikoura, **Hislop's Café** (03 319 6971), which doubles as an organic wholefoods store, even mills its own flour for its freshly baked goods. Pop in to sample its vibrant local menu and tasty regional wines. The waterfront 1885-built **Pier Hotel** (03 319 5037) at 1 Avoca Street is now a cosy gastropub with an open fire, dishing up robust seafood and pub favourites.

GET A ROOM!

Use our free online booking service: check availability and make reservations through www.mrandmrssmith.com.

 SMITH CARD OFFER A pre-dinner cocktail for two.

Hapuku Lodge & Tree Houses State Highway 1 at Station Road, Kaikoura 7371 (03 319 6559; www.hapukulodge.com)

(offers you can't refuse)

 Look out for the Smith Card offers at the end of each hotel review

As a BlackSmith member, you're automatically entitled to exclusive added extras: we like to ensure your stylish stay is as enjoyable as possible. Activate your free membership now (see pages 4–5) and take advantage of the Smith Card offers listed below when you book any of these properties through us. Each booking also earns you money back into your Vault account, redeemable against future hotel stays – it's our way of saying thank you. For more information, or to make a reservation, visit www.mrandmrssmith.com or talk to our expert Travel Team on 1300 896 627 in Australia; 0800 896 671 in New Zealand; 0845 034 0700 in the UK; 1 866 610 3867 in the US and Canada; or +61 3 8648 8871 in Asia.

AZUR LODGE Queenstown
A bottle of local bubbly and chocolates in your villa on arrival.

BAMURRU PLAINS Top End
A gift-wrapped book on Australian birds.

BELLS AT KILLCARE Central Coast
An exclusive chef's tour of the kitchen gardens, with guidance on seasonal produce.

THE BLOOMFIELD Melbourne
Either afternoon tea, including freshly brewed loose-leaf T2 tea with cakes, or a choice of white or red wine and nibbles.

THE BOATSHED Auckland
A tasting plate of local Waiheke delicacies on arrival.

CAPE LODGE Margaret River
A gift pack of Cape Lodge Estate wine on departure.

CAPELLA LODGE Lord Howe Island
A gourmet picnic or barbecue lunch for two.

EAGLES NEST Bay of Islands
A one-hour massage treatment.

ESTABLISHMENT HOTEL Sydney
Free VIP access to Establishment's lounge bar Hemmesphere and a Hemmesphere CD.

THE FARM AT CAPE KIDNAPPERS Hawke's Bay
NZ$50 spa credit.

GAIA RETREAT & SPA Byron Bay
AU$100 spa treatment voucher.

HAPUKU LODGE & TREE HOUSES Kaikoura
A pre-dinner cocktail for two.

THE HENRY JONES ART HOTEL Hobart
A bottle of Tasmanian wine.

HUKA LODGE Lake Taupo
Lunch for two including a bottle of NZ house wine, either within the Lodge or as a picnic.

THE ISLINGTON HOTEL Hobart
20 per cent off dinner (including drinks).

LIMES HOTEL Brisbane
AU$20 bar tab voucher.

LIZARD ISLAND Great Barrier Reef
A Lizard Island oil burner.

THE LODGE AT KAURI CLIFFS
Bay of Islands
NZ$50 spa voucher on arrival.

THE LOUISE Barossa Valley
A bottle of sparkling wine on arrival.

LYALL HOTEL AND SPA Melbourne
A bottle of Chandon NV (Australian
sparkling wine) on arrival.

MOLLIES Auckland
Home-baked cookies and fruit
on arrival.

NORTH BUNDALEER Clare Valley
A gift box of handmade Haigh's Chocolates,
an iconic South Australian brand founded
in 1915.

PRETTY BEACH HOUSE Central Coast
A signed copy of chef Stefano Manfredi's
cookbook *Cook for All Seasons* or a PBH
backpack and water bottle for coastal
bush walks.

THE PRINCE Melbourne
A bottle of sparkling wine and
free parking.

QUALIA Great Barrier Reef
A bottle of champagne.

QUAMBY ESTATE Launceston
A round of golf.

ROYAL MAIL HOTEL The Grampians
A copy of photographic journal *A Dunkeld
Portfolio* by Richard Crawley.

SAL SALIS NINGALOO REEF
Ningaloo Reef
Complimentary one-way scenic charter flight
from Exmouth Learmonth Airport to Sal Salis
Ningaloo Reef (for a minimum two-night
stay with two people travelling together).

SOUTHERN OCEAN LODGE
Kangaroo Island
AU$50 spa treatment voucher.

THE SPIRE Queenstown
A bottle of Central Otago pinot on arrival.

STONEBARN Southern Forests
A glass of quality Australian sparkling
wine on arrival, a bottle of local wine
and a Stonebarn memento.

VICTORIA'S AT WATEGOS Byron Bay
Tropical fruit platter and a bottle of
Australian sparkling wine on arrival.

WHAREKAUHAU LODGE & COUNTRY
ESTATE Wairarapa
A three-hour guided farm tour.

(useful numbers)

DIALLING CODES
Australia: +61 **New Zealand:** +64
(NB: drop the 0 off the area code if calling from overseas)

AIRLINES (DOMESTIC)
Air2there (NZ: 0800 777 000; INT: +64 4 904 5130; www.air2there.com)
Air New Zealand (AU: 132 476; NZ: 0800 737 000; www.airnewzealand.co.nz)
Jetstar (AU: 131 538; NZ: 0800 800 995; www.jetstar.com)
Qantas (AU: 131 313; NZ: 0800 808 767; UK: 0845 774 7767; US: 1800 227 4500; www.qantas.com)
Rex (AU: 131 713; INT: +61 2 6393 5550; www.rex.com.au)
Skywest (AU: 1300 660 088; www.skywest.com.au)
Tiger Airways (AU: 03 9335 3033; INT: +65 6580 7630; www.tigerairways.com)
Virgin Blue (AU: 136 789; NZ: 0800 670 000; INT: +61 7 3295 2296; www.virginblue.com)
Sounds Air (NZ: 0800 505 005; INT: +64 3 520 3080; www.soundsair.com)

AIRLINES (INTERNATIONAL)
Air New Zealand (AU: 132 476; NZ: 0800 737 000; UK: 0800 028 4149; US: 1800 262 1234; www.airnewzealand.com.nz)
British Airways (AU: 1300 767 177; NZ: 09 966 9777; UK: 0844 493 0787; US: 1800 247 9297; www.britishairways.com)
Cathay Pacific (AU: 131 747; NZ: 0800 800 454; UK: 020 8834 8888; US: 1800 233 2742; www.cathaypacific.com)
Emirates (AU: 1300 303 777; NZ: 0508 364 728; UK: 0844 800 2777; US: 1800 777 3999; www.emirates.com)
Ethihad Airways (AU: 1800 998 995; UK: 0800 731 9384; US: 1888 8 ETIHAD; www.etihadairways.com)
Jetstar (AU: 131 538, NZ: 0800 800 995; US: 1866 397 8170; www.jetstar.com)
Malaysia Airlines (AU: 132 627; NZ: 0800 777 747; UK: 0871 423 9090; US: 1800 552 9264; www.malaysiaairlines.com)
Qantas (AU: 131 313, NZ: 0800 808 767; UK: 0845 774 7767; US: 1800 227 4500; www.qantas.com)
Singapore Airlines (AU: 131 011; NZ: 0800 808 909; UK: 0844 800 2380; US: 1800 742 3333; www.singaporeairlines.com)
Thai Airways (AU: 03 8662 2266; NZ: 09 377 3886; UK: 0870 606 0911; US: 1800 426 5204; www.thaiair.com)

United (AU: 131 777; UK: 0845 844 4777; US: 1800 864 8331; INT: 1800 538 2929; www.united.com)
V Australia (AU: 138 287; NZ: 0800 828 782; US: 1800 444 0260; INT: +61 7 3333 6888; www.vaustralia.com.au)
Virgin Atlantic (AU: 1300 727 340; UK: 0844 874 7747; US: 1800 821 5438; www.virginatlantic.com)

AIRPORTS (AUSTRALIA)
Adelaide Airport (www.aal.com.au)
Ballina/Byron Airport (www.ballina.info/airport)
Brisbane Airport (www.brisbaneairport.com.au)
Cairns Airport (www.cairnsairport.com.au)
Darwin Airport (www.darwinairport.com.au)
Gold Coast Airport (www.goldcoastairport.com.au)
Melbourne Airport (www.melbourneairport.com.au)
Perth Airport (www.perthairport.com)
Sydney Airport (www.sydneyairport.com.au)

AIRPORTS (NEW ZEALAND)
Auckland Airport (www.auckland-airport.co.nz)
Bay of Islands (Kerikeri) Airport (www.bayofislandsairport.co.nz)
Blenheim Airport (www.blenheimairport.co.nz)
Christchurch Airport (www.christchurchairport.co.nz)
Hawke's Bay (Napier-Hastings) Airport (www.hawkesbay-airport.co.nz)
Queenstown Airport (www.queenstownairport.co.nz)
Rotorua Airport (www.rotorua-airport.co.nz)
Taupo Airport (www.taupoairport.co.nz)
Wellington Airport (www.wellington-airport.co.nz)

FERRIES & YACHT CHARTERS
Central Coast Ferries (AU: 02 4363 1311; www.centralcoastferries.com.au). From Woy Woy.
Fantasea (AU: 07 4967 5455; www.fantasea.com.au). From Airlie Beach to the Whitsunday Islands.
Kangaroo Island SeaLink (AU: 131 301; INT: + 61 8 8202 8688; www.sealink.com.au). From SA's Cape Jervis to Penneshaw on KI.
Spirit of Tasmania (AU: 1800 634 906; INT: +61 3 6421 7209; www.spiritoftasmania.com.au). Melbourne to Devonport, north Tasmania.
Sydney Ferries (AU: 131 500; www.sydneyferries.info)
Fullers (www.fullers.co.nz). Ferries from Auckland to the Hauraki Gulf Islands and Devonport, North Shore.
Interislander (NZ: 0800 802 802; www.interislander.co.nz). Ferries between NZ's North and South Islands.

Charterworld (INT: +61 2 8005 0054; www.
charterworld.com). Crewed yachts, Australia and NZ.
Cruise Whitsundays (+61 7 4946 4662; www.
cruisewhitsundays.com). Airlie Beach-based.
Fair Wind Charters (INT: +64 9 402 7821; www.
fairwind.co.nz). Bareboat or skippered yachts, Bay
of Islands, NZ.

MAPS, MOTORING AND MORE
**www.whereis.com; www.street-directory.com.au;
www.street-directory.co.nz**
The Australian Automobile Association
(INT: +61 2 6247 7311; www.aaa.asn.au)
Automobile Assocation (NZ: 0800 500 222; www.
aa.co.nz). NZ's 24-hour emergency breakdown service.
Avis (AU: 02 9353 9000; NZ: 09 526 2847; www.avis.com)
Budget (AU: 1300 362 848; NZ: 0800 283 438; www.
budget.com.au; www.budget.co.nz)
Classic Car Hire World (www.classiccarhireworld.
com). Classic and sports cars, worldwide.
Europcar (AU: 1300 131 390; INT: +61 3 9330 6160;
NZ: 0800 800 115; www.europcar.com.au)
Hertz (AU: 133 039; INT: +61 3 9698 2555; www.
hertz.com)
Scro Australia (AU: 1300 793 682; INT: +61 2 9505
8500; www.scronline.com.au). Oz-wide sports car rental.
Thrifty (AU: 1300 367 227; NZ: 0800 737 070; www.
thrifty.com)

TAXIS AND TRANSFERS
Australia Wide Taxi Network (131 008;
www.131008.com). Dial from anywhere in Oz.
New Zealand Taxi Federation (04 499 0611; www.
taxifederation.org.nz). NZTF-approved cabs nationwide.

TRAINS
Rail Australia (www.railaustralia.com.au) lists websites
and contact numbers for each state-run rail company.
Tranz Scenic (NZ: 0800 872 467; INT: +64 4 495
0775; www.tranzscenic.co.nz) operates NZ routes.

UP, UP AND AWAY
Aviation Tourism (AU: 02 9317 3402 & 07 4946 8249;
www.avta.com.au). Tours from Sydney and Whitsundays.
Heli Experiences (AU: 0413 961 918; www.heli
experiences.com.au). Melbourne and VIC tours/charters.

Glacier Southern Lakes Helicopters (NZ: 0800 801
616; INT: +64 3 442 3016; www.glaciersouthernlakes.
co.nz). Queenstown and Milford Sound NZ tours.
Heletranz (+64 9415 3550; www.heletranz.co.nz).
Auckland and NZ tours, including Bay of Islands.
Helipro (www.helipro.co.nz). NZ helitours and charters.
Air Australia International (AU: 08 9332 5011;
www.airaustralia.net). South-west WA charters.
Air South (AU: 08 8234 3244; www.airsouth.com.au).
Adelaide and SA regional airline and charters.
Altitude Aviation (AU: 1800 747 300, INT: +61 2 4945
4522; www.altitudeaviation.com.au). Oz-wide charters.
Hinterland Aviation (INT: +61 7 4035 9323; www.
hinterlandaviation.com.au). Cairns-based charter flights.

TOURIST BOARDS
Tourism Australia (AU: 02 9360 1111; NZ: 09 915
2826; UK: 020 7438 4601; US: 1 310 695 3200;
www.tourism.australia.com).
Tourism New Zealand (AU: 02 8299 4800; NZ 04 4628
000 & 09 9144 780; UK: 020 7930 1662; US: 1 310 395
7480; www.newzealand.com).

CITY & GOURMET GUIDES
Daily Addict (www.dailyaddict.com.au). Finger on the
pulse of stylish Sydney.
Gourmet Traveller (www.gourmettraveller.com.au).
Restaurant and bar reviews in Australia and New Zealand.
TimeOut Sydney (www.timeoutsydney.com.au). The
online face of the city listings magazine.
TwoThousand (www.twothousand.com.au);
ThreeThousand (www.threethousand.com.au);
FourThousand (www.fourthousand.com.au);
FiveThousand (www.fivethousand.com.au);
SixThousand (www.sixthousand.com.au): snapshots of
subculture and events in Sydney, Melbourne, Brisbane,
Adelaide and Perth, respectively.

SAVVY TRAVEL WEBSITES
Ecotourism Australia (AU: 07 3252 1530; www.
ecotourism.org.au). Eco Certified Oz tourism operators.
JiWire (www.jiwire.com). Find WiFi hotspots in Oz/NZ.
SeatGuru (www.seatguru.com). Find the best plane seat.
Timeanddate (www.timeanddate.com). International
dialling codes and time zones for stopwatching your calls.

(who are Mr & Mrs Smith?)

Our reviewers are hand-picked people we admire and respect, from top chefs to designers and journalists, all of whom have impeccable taste, of course, and can be trusted to report back to us on Smith hotels with total honesty. The only thing we ask of them is that they visit each hotel anonymously with a partner and, on their return, give us the kind of insider lowdown you'd expect from a close friend.

REVIEWERS WHO'S WHO

Helen Bodycomb MASTER MOSAICIST

Her work has taken Helen everywhere, from the north of Italy to central Malaysia, as both a teacher and student of the delicate art of mosaics. Often found concentrating on a small area of a design, this artist is clearly a believer in the old adage 'the devil's in the detail', something that should make hotel owners quake with fear. When not travelling the globe, Helen can be found practising her craft in a studio in Central Victoria.

John Carruthers NEW VENTURER

With fretful investors and clamouring customers, it's a brave high-tech CEO who heedlessly books the designer getaway. But disappear (however briefly) we all must to rejuvenate mind and body – or ultimately pay the price, says John. With a well-honed bias towards colder climes, he rations his travel escapes to occasional tented wilderness, a powder-hound's quest for the ultimate ski experience and northern hemisphere cities (while Mrs Smith patiently pines for sun-drenched beaches). All of which calls for both nerve and a critical eye for beauty: just what you'd expect from a former photojournalist.

Andrew Chiodo MENSWEAR DESIGNER

Considered one of Australia's top designers, Andrew can usually be found keeping a watchful eye on his eponymous retail operation in Melbourne. An attention to detail finely tuned after two decades in the fashion business, combined with the fact that he is normally too immersed in work for regular holidays, makes him a discerning traveller. His belief? Whether it's the stitching on a shirt or gift left on a hotel bedroom pillow, it is the little things that really matter.

Carrie Choo ON-THE-PULSE BLOGGER

Life hasn't been the same for Carrie since she founded her website *Daily Addict*, a style-savvy guide to what's hot in Sydney, at the start of 2008. Inspired by her constant quest for entertainment and enlightenment, she has put her love of writing, 10 years in corporate marketing and a fascination with people to good use, lifting the lid on the best the city has to offer. She travels extensively and is addicted to caffeine, fashion, French films, Adriano Zumbo cakes, playing poker and exploring the worldwide web.

Kirstie Clements EDITOR-IN-CHIEF

Having worked at *Vogue Australia* for more than 20 years, editor-in-chief Kirstie has had the opportunity to stay in some of the world's most magnificent locations. However, as befitting one who helps define enduring style, she's not a fan of the superficially trendy, the supercool or the €65 breakfast. She is at her happiest when about to take off somewhere new, finds airport lounges strangely thrilling, and has finally, after two decades, learned how to pack light.

Amy Cooper SEEN-IT-DONE-IT SCRIBE

Amy's fascination with hotel minutiae comes as no surprise to her parents, who recall a child curiously obsessed with ice machines, shoe polishers and the housekeeper's cupboard during family holidays. UK tabloid journalism and its long hours spent lurking in hotels in pursuit of celebrities suited her well, but after editing women's magazines, writing dating columns in Australia and co-authoring a book about bad movies, Amy found her true calling writing about bars, parties and travel for *The Sun-Herald*. She remains at heart a frustrated hotelier. To this end, she recently mastered the art of towel sculpture and is particularly good at elephants and lobsters. Mr Smith is a tolerant man.

Angus Fontaine HOTEL-LOVING HACK

At one stage simultaneously a crime reporter, fishing columnist, beer judge and editor of Australia's highest circulating men's mag, Angus gave it all away to kick in high-society doors as the writer/host of Discovery Channel's behind-the-scenes travel show *Five Star Insider*. Today, he's editor-in-chief of *Time Out Sydney*, a father of three and a household name (at his place, anyway).

David Grant EVENTS GURU

The invisible hand behind eight Olympic Games and some of the sexiest parties from Sydney to New York, David has spent the past 25 years creating magical, celebratory environments for the world's most discerning and luxurious brands (and yet he still finds time to cue rock stars and mow red carpets). Because he enjoys the vicarious pleasure of delighting others with his sense of theatre, style and service, David loves nothing better than having that returned to him, and so has an eclectic, high-maintenance travel bent that drives Mrs Smith mad (although she rarely complains as she rolls over in bed at 38,000 feet somewhere above Afghanistan).

Stuart Gregor PR AND WINE WIZARD

Stuart takes the taste out of tastemaker. He is a slightly overweight, balding man who has a wardrobe full of brown shoes, jeans and golf shirts. He does, however, have a monumental wine cellar that makes him popular at parties. He runs a luxury and lifestyle PR firm called Liquid Ideas working with many of the smartest brands in the market. Before he ran out of adjectives, Stuart used to write about wine, penning six books and Australia's most-read wine column for five years. He eats, he drinks, he shoots, he scores. He lives with Mrs Smith, his two children and a dog in Sydney.

Shelly Horton STAR REPORTER

As celebrity writer for *The Sun-Herald* in Sydney, Shelly is one of the busiest gals in the business. When she's not interviewing famous faces (such as Tom Cruise, Paris Hilton and even the Dalai Lama), Shelly splits her time between weekly appearances on Channel Seven's *The Morning Show* and a guest spot on Richard Glover's drive programme for ABC Radio. And just in case that doesn't impress, she can say the alphabet really fast... backwards.

Deborah Hutton MEDIA LUMINARY

A former model, magazine editor and now spokesperson and ambassador for brands such as Qantas, Deborah has spent most of her life on the road, in the air and between the four walls of more than her fair share of hotel rooms – usually, however, for work. These days, she's more than happy to spend a few days on a luxury break just for her own indulgence, and has developed a passion for golf. Deborah has lost count of how many times fellow travellers have asked her: 'Don't I know you from somewhere?'

Christine Manfield GLOBETROTTING GOURMET

Most of us don't need any excuse to traverse the globe but Christine says she has one anyway. As a chef, author and restaurateur (Chris is the force behind Sydney eatery Universal), she's always on the lookout for inspiration, indulgence and adventure. Luckily, she is also a gypsy at heart, having spent time in London where she opened a restaurant (East@West) and regularly guiding gastronomic luxury travel trips to places like Morocco, India and Spain. Her motto in life? Leave no stone unturned.

Andrew McConnell CHEF AND CULTURE VULTURE

Tasmania might become Andrew's favourite holiday destination; having just returned from Hobart for Mr & Mrs Smith he was named Chef of the Year by *The Age Good Food Guide*. He's certainly left his culinary mark on his hometown Melbourne, where he now owns and runs restaurants Cumulus Inc and Cutler & Co with his partner Pascale Gomes-McNabb (having forged an enviable reputation at Three, One, Two and Circa, the Prince). While discovering new tastes is obviously high on his list of travel priorities, Andrew is also an art lover and avid gallery goer.

Paul McNally EPICUREAN EDITOR

Sydneysider Paul's first review, a write-up on a Hobart restaurant, appeared in the final issue of *Black + White* magazine before it folded – so he's hopeful his latest contribution won't have a similar jinxing effect on *Mr & Mrs Smith*. He's written for various food, bridal and jewellery mags – although he thinks you shouldn't hold the last two against him – as well as contributing quirky ice-cream recipes to a cookbook. Paul spends all his spare cash on good food, red wine and plane trips.

Rosemary Purcell FORENSIC PSYCHOLOGIST

As an active researcher, Rosie has a vast résumé of international travel, courtesy of the many conferences that constitute the only perk of academic life. Sadly most of these travels involve destinations whose main claim to fame are major convention centres. Thankfully her passion for skiing and high-altitude mountaineering has taken her to far more exotic and far-flung places that should, hopefully, bolster her cred with *Mr & Mrs Smith* readers.

Charles Rawlings-Way TRAVEL AUTHOR

Having trained as an architect and worked as a barman in London (he was a master at putting the little shamrock atop a Guinness), cinema cleaner, croissant chef and deckhand on a fishing trawler, Charles gave up all that glamour to draw maps for *Lonely Planet*. Thankfully that lead him to travel writing and he's since contributed to 15 of the company's best-selling tomes. In his bottom drawer at home in Adelaide you'll find a 320,000-word epic entitled *The Great Unpublished American Road Novel*. And, yes, it is still unpublished.

Liane Rossler DESIGNER

For more than two decades, Liane has been one of the co-owners and designers of Sydney jewellery and homewares company Dinosaur Designs. Although you can find her designs in just about any corner of the world, you're much more likely to find her close to home. As a Climate Project Ambassador – trained as such by none other than nobel laureate Al Gore – she's more concerned with her environmental footprint than finding the latest hotspot in Helsinki or hip bar in Bahrain. When she does find herself holed up in a hotel, Liane places personal service over gold-plated taps.

Margie Seale PAGE-TURNING PUBLISHER

There is a reason Margie can often be spotted at the international airport pleading the case for her overweight luggage: as the managing director of Random House Australia & New Zealand, her suitcase is always laden with manuscripts. She thinks the cornerstone of a good holiday is to give in to at least a couple of days of pure luxury, especially after a gruelling walking trip (of which she's racked up quite a few). When not working, Margie can usually be found on a couch with an ocean view. Reading a book, of course.

Sarah Thomas ROVING REPORTER

After leaving Wales behind, Sarah found herself in London working for a travel publishing company. It gave her the opportunity to blag her way into some of the world's most amazing hotels – the Dorchester and Le Meurice, for example – and a taste for the high life and all things nomadic. With nothing more than a backpack, Sarah arrived in Sydney four years ago as a freelance journalist and hasn't been able to tear herself away. She writes for *The Sydney Morning Herald*, *Travel + Leisure* and *GQ*.

Simon Thomsen FOOD CRITIC

An award-winning food and travel writer, Simon has spent the past four years expanding his waistline as restaurant critic for *The Sydney Morning Herald*. He was also co-editor of the SMH *Good Food Guide* for six years and has been known to drive for five hours just to go to lunch. His work appears regularly in *Travel + Leisure*. He is currently developing an online restaurant guide, which he would like to imagine will be a sort of foodie version of *Mr & Mrs Smith* by Mr T.

Sigrid Thornton ACTOR

Having performed on stage and screen since she was a teenager, it's not surprising that Sigrid is one of the most recognisable faces in Australian performing arts. One of her first television roles, back in the mid-Seventies, was in the long-running cop show *Homicide*, and since then she's starred in iconic Australian productions including *The Getting of Wisdom*, *SeaChange* and even *Prisoner: Cell Block H*. Travel for her is about satisfying all the senses and to that end she always packs a special brass pepper grinder, just in case.

MR & MRS SMITH TEAM

Mr & Mrs Smith Directors

Managing director James Lohan is one half of the couple behind Mr & Mrs Smith. James' first company, Atomic, was behind some of London's most popular club nights. (His millennium New Year's Eve party was voted 'number-one place to be in the world' by *FHM Magazine*). He built on this success by designing and producing events for clients such as Finlandia vodka and Wonderbra. He then went on to co-found the White House bar, restaurant and members' club. Since Mr & Mrs Smith's first book, James has visited almost 1,000 hotels and, now a dad, he's become a keen advocate of our child-friendly hotel collection *Smith & Kids*.

Online and marketing director Tamara Heber-Percy, co-founder of Mr & Mrs Smith, graduated from Oxford with a degree in languages, then left the UK for Brazil, where she launched a new energy drink. Since then, she has worked at one of the UK's top marketing agencies as a consultant for international brands such as Ericsson and Honda and in business development for Europe, the Middle East and Africa. She left the corporate world in 2002 to head up her own company, the County Register – an exclusive introductions agency – and to launch Mr & Mrs Smith.

Asia Pacific co-founder and managing director Simon Westcott grew up in London, but has made Melbourne home for more than 10 years. A graduate of Oxford and Indiana universities, he is a former global publisher and director of *Lonely Planet*, and a current contributing editor for *Travel + Leisure*. He has travelled extensively in Australia, NZ, Asia, Europe and North America, always and only with a single soft leather holdall from Gurkha.

Financial director Edward Orr has worked in investment banking and managed companies in their early stages for more than a decade. As a result, he's stayed in hotels on every continent on the globe – and, generally, he doesn't like them. This makes him qualified not only to look after the finances of Mr & Mrs Smith, but also to have penned the odd review. He can confirm that Smith hotels really are special enough to be a treat, even for the most jaded corporate traveller.

Publishing director Andrew Grahame launched the UK's first corporate-fashion magazine in 1990. After moving into fashion shows, exhibitions and conferences, he transferred his talents from clothing to finance, launching Small Company Investor. He started a promotions company in 1993 and, after a spell as a restaurant/bar owner in Chelsea, turned his hand to tourism in 1997, creating the award-winning London Pass and New York Pass, which give visitors access to the cities' attractions. Andrew co-produced our TV series *The Smiths' Hotels for 2* for the Discovery network.

Mr & Mrs Smith in Melbourne

Associate director Rodrigo Calvo grew up in Bolivia, but hit the road days after his 18th birthday to study marketing (and country music) in Austin, work as an ad man in Boston, and enjoy island seclusion in Elba, before heading back to South America to launch a marketing consultancy and tinker with vintage cars. The consultancy took off; the cars are another story. Rodrigo crossed paths with Mr & Mrs Smith while reading for his MBA in London, and immediately set to work expanding the brand in the US. Luckily for Smith, his next attack of wanderlust coincided with the opening of our Melbourne office, and he hotfooted it over to Australia to be part of the Asia Pacific launch team.

VP of hotel relations Debra McKenzie has lived and breathed hospitality throughout her working life, with time spent in front-of-house and managerial roles at the RitzCarlton and Hayman Island Resort. After honing her palate in the Sydney restaurant world, Debra went on to globetrot for Kiwi Collection from Australia to Europe – perfect training for her role as head hotel-hunter in Mr & Mrs Smith's Asia Pacific office. She also flexes her muscles as a photographer and stylist, working in Vancouver and Sydney with blue-chip clients.

Editorial manager Sophie Davies grew up in Turkey, Indonesia and Iran, exiting stage left during the revolution. After studying at Oxford, she lived out her foreign-correspondent fantasy as a news researcher for Japanese TV, before swapping bento for boy bands with a features gig at *Just Seventeen*. Having freelanced for *Time Out* and *The Telegraph*, her love of design led to a six-year affair with UK *Elle Decoration*, where as assistant editor Sophie learned how to spot a good table at 20 paces and honed her hotel-appreciation skills. When Smith's Melbourne office beckoned, it was time to leave London (and her beloved Arsenal football team) for pastures new.

Mr & Mrs Smith in London

Associate director Laura Mizon spent her younger years in Spain and, after graduating from Manchester University, returned to her childhood home to work for four years at an independent record label in Madrid, promoting the emerging Spanish hip-hop movement. When she joined Mr & Mrs Smith as a freelancer in 2004, it soon became clear that Laura was to play a key role. She is now responsible for building relationships with like-minded brands and all things operational.

Editor-in-chief Juliet Kinsman helped create Mr & Mrs Smith's distinctive voice and she has sampled many a lovely hotel and rental cottage in the process. As well as tasting the high life for work and obsessing over apostrophes, she shares insider secrets with *The Times* through to *Forbes* and co-presented our show *The Smiths' Hotels for 2* for the Discovery Channel. Born in Canada with stints in Africa, America, Greece and India, Juliet has recently been tackling the challenge of globetrotting with a toddler in tow. Who says you can't enjoy a little luxury travel *en famille*?

Managing editor Anthony Leyton joined Smith in 2007 to provide short-term help launching a handful of hotels in Asia. He sometimes wonders why no one's noticed he hasn't left yet. Before being embraced by the Smith family, he worked for *The Independent* and *Push*

Guides and penned pieces for publications both top-drawer (*The Telegraph*) and top-shelf (*Fiesta*). He has had a love of travel ever since he found bullet holes in the walls of a hotel room in New Orleans.

Head of hotel collections Katy McCann grew up in the south of Spain and later became editor of *In Madrid*, the largest English-language publication in the city. She was tracked down by Mr & Mrs Smith in 2004 to develop and expand our hotel collections, which fitted in perfectly with her love of travel and her multilingual prowess. Having seen more than 2,000 hotels over the last six years, Katy is probably the world's most qualified person to ensure each property is the perfect addition to the Smith collection.

Head of hotel relations Peggy Picano-Nacci was born in Indonesia and grew up in France. The past 15 years have seen her earn an unrivalled understanding of what makes a great boutique hotel tick. A former sales manager at the Dorchester and an alumnus of *Small Luxury Hotels of the World*, where she was responsible for the French, Spanish and Portuguese territories, she has also made use of an alarming array of languages while working closely with our member hotels.

Head of PR and marketing Aline Keuroghlian has worked in travel for 15 years. Stints at Armani and London's quirky Sir John Soane's Museum helped cultivate her love of stylish things. After university came several years of guiding professionals across Italy for niche tour operator ATG Oxford, which made use of her maternal heritage. Nowadays, she puts both her sense and sensibility to work by dealing with some of the most beautiful hotels in the world, as featured in Mr & Mrs Smith's collections.

Head of relationship marketing Amber Spencer-Holmes may be a Londoner, but she has cosmo credentials, having lived in Sydney and Paris before reading French and English at King's College London. Prior to joining Mr & Mrs Smith, Amber made waves in the music industry running a number of well-respected record labels. She is married to our TuneSmith columnist Rob Wood.

(where in the world)

ASIA

Bhutan Paro, Thimphu
China Beijing, Hong Kong, Nanjing, Shanghai, Yangshuo
India Karnataka, Kerala
Indian Ocean Maldives, Mauritius, Seychelles
Indonesia Bali, Jakarta, Lombok, Sumba, Yogyakarta
Japan Kyoto, Yamagata
Malaysia Kuala Lumpur, Langkawi
Singapore Singapore
Thailand Bangkok, Chiang Mai, Hua Hin, Khao Lak, Koh Phi Phi, Koh Samui, Krabi, Phuket

AUSTRALASIA

Australia Adelaide, Barossa Valley, Blue Mountains, Brisbane, Byron Bay, Central Coast, Central Highlands, Clare Valley, Far North Queensland, the Grampians, Great Barrier Reef, Great Ocean Road, Hobart, Hunter Valley, Kangaroo Island, the Kimberleys, Launceston, Lord Howe Island, Margaret River, Melbourne, Ningaloo Reef, Northern Beaches, Red Centre, Southern Forests, Sydney, Top End
New Zealand Auckland, Bay of Islands, Hawke's Bay, Kaikoura, Lake Taupo, Queenstown, Wairarapa, Wellington

EUROPE

Austria Vienna, Zell am See
Belgium Antwerp, Brussels
Cyprus Limassol
Czech Republic Prague, Tábor
Denmark Copenhagen
Estonia Tallinn
France Ardennes, Beaujolais, Bordeaux, Brittany, Burgundy, Côte d'Azur, Dordogne, Languedoc-Roussillon, Lorraine, Normandy, Paris, Pays Basque, Pays de la Loire, Poitou-Charentes, Provence, St Tropez, Tarn, Vaucluse
Germany Berlin, Munich
Greece Athens, Mykonos, Santorini
Iceland Reykjavík
Ireland County Meath, Dublin
Italy Aeolian Islands, Amalfi Coast, Capri, Florence, Milan, Piedmont, Puglia, Rome, Sardinia, Sicily, Sorrento, South Tyrol, Tuscany, Venice
Monaco Monte Carlo
Netherlands Amsterdam
Portugal Alentejo, Cascais, Douro Valley, Lisbon
Spain Barcelona, Basque Country, Cadiz Province, Córdoba, Costa de la Luz, Empordà, Extremadura, Granada, Ibiza, Madrid, Mallorca, Marbella, Ronda, San Sebastián, Seville Province, Tarifa, Valencia
Sweden Stockholm
Switzerland Adelboden
Turkey Istanbul
United Kingdom Bath, Belfast, Berkshire, Birmingham, Brecon Beacons, Brighton, Cardigan Bay, Carmarthen Bay, the Chilterns, Cornwall, the Cotswolds, County Durham, Devon, Dorset, East Sussex, Edinburgh, Gloucestershire, Hampshire, Harrogate, Kent, Lake District, Liverpool, London, Manchester, Norfolk, Northamptonshire, North Yorkshire, Oxfordshire, Peak District, Pembrokeshire, Powys, Snowdonia, Northeast Somerset, Suffolk, Trossachs, Vale of Glamorgan, Wester Ross, West Sussex, Wiltshire, Worcestershire

THE REST OF THE WORLD

Belize Ambergris Caye, Cayo, Placencia
Brazil Bahia, Rio de Janeiro
Canada Montreal, Toronto
Caribbean Antigua & Barbuda, Barbados, Grenada, Mustique, St Barths, St Lucia, Turks & Caicos
Guatemala Flores
Mexico Colima, Jalisco, Mexico City, Puebla, Riviera Maya, Yucatan
Morocco Atlas Mountains, Essaouira, Marrakech, Ouarzazate
South Africa Cape Town, Garden Route & Winelands, Hermanus, Johannesburg, Kruger, Madikwe, Western Limpopo
United Arab Emirates Dubai
United States Austin, the Berkshires, Boston, the Hamptons, Las Vegas, Litchfield Hills, Los Angeles, Miami, Napa Valley, New York, Palm Springs, Portland, San Diego, San Francisco, Smoky Mountains, Sonoma County, Washington DC
Zambia Lower Zambezi

www.mrandmrssmith.com

Smith

Welcome to the wonderful world of Mr & Mrs Smith, where you'll find everything you need to mastermind your next unforgettable trip away. Our brilliant boutique-hotel bibles are full of inspiring places to stay in Australia and New Zealand, the UK, Europe and the US, with top tips for making the most of your destination on arrival. Or get the inside track online at www.mrandmrssmith.com, where you can book a room or just plan your dream getaway. Whether you're after a romantic weekend away or a fabulous family holiday, the fun starts here...

JOIN THE CLUB

If you've just got your hands on this book, then congratulations: you're now a complimentary BlackSmith member for a year, meaning you get free gifts at every Smith hotel you stay in (goodies on arrival range from a bottle of bubbly to spa treatments). You can also enjoy exclusive hotel offers, money back from the Vault (our loyalty scheme) to put towards future trips, access to our expert Travel Team and brilliant benefits with chic partner brands. Just remember to activate your card first (see pages 4–5).

And if you want to treat yourself further, then why not upgrade? As a SilverSmith member, you'll double your earning power with the Vault (getting four per cent of every hotel stay back again). Plus you'll get great Half-Price Hotel offers, amazing room deals from our Last-Minute Club (LMC) and travel discounts to speed you on your way.

Our top membership tier, GoldSmith, confers even more privileges: all Black and SilverSmith benefits, plus our full concierge service. We'll happily handle your hotel and flight bookings, theatre and restaurant reservations and even organise someone to feed your pets while you're away. You can also take advantage of automatic room upgrades at hotels when available, free airport lounge access, exclusive Eurostar fares, eligibility for Hertz's President Circle (their top car hire loyalty scheme), and the chance to bank five per cent of every hotel stay towards your next booking with the Vault.

INSPIRATIONAL ESCAPES

Our Australia/New Zealand guide is the latest in a series of coolly collectable books from the Smith stable, cherry-picking the best hotels from around the world with original ideas for stylish destinations to visit. Whether you're headed to the UK, Europe or globetrotting further afield, we've got it covered, with around 600 hot hotels spanning cosy inns, blissful beach retreats, hip urban hang-outs and sensual spas. Add in entertaining reviews and savvy suggestions, and you've got a capsule kit for an effortless getaway. What's more, each one comes with an exclusive BlackSmith membership card, entitling you to gifts and discounts galore. Order our indispensable guides at www.mrandmrssmith.com/shop and get packing...

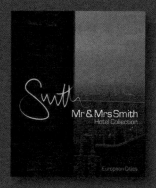
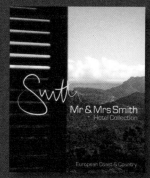
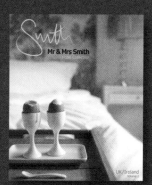

GET A ROOM!

For a one-off gift, treat someone to a weekend away at any of our fantastic 600-plus hotels worldwide, with a Mr & Mrs Smith's Get a Room! gift card. Sexily packaged in a slim black box, they're perfect for surprising partners, family or friends (maybe try and get invited along too). For details, or to order online, see www.mrandmrssmith.com/hotel-gift-voucher.

[applause]

thank you

Earl Carter and his assistant Fraser Marsden for fabulous photography and an heroic high-speed odyssey around the Antipodes, and Wanda Tucker for helping make it happen; wordsmiths extraordinaire Sophie Davies, Juliet Kinsman and Carrie Hutchinson for their many labours of love, and Samantha Anderson and Nikki Haynes for pitching in; designer Lauren Camilleri and project manager Paul McNally for their creativity, patience and professionalism, and to everyone at Bloom for their original brand genius and design savvy; picture editor Lisa Steer for her deft research and fine eye; Warren Smith at Splitting Image and Lena Frew at C and C Printing for repro and printing; Sandy Grant, Keiran Rogers and Astrid Browne at Hardie Grant for many favours and forgivenesses and for bringing this to a bookstore near you; Stuart Gregor, Sally Lewis, Rowena Fitzgerald and Gillian Martin from Liquid Ideas for pumping up the volume; all our tastemaker reviewers and their significant others for sharing inspirational stories of their stays. And, last but not least, to the rest of the two Smith teams on either sides of the world that gave exquisite and elongated birth to the original brand, the current book and our new bits of warehouse and web real estate down under: James Lohan, Tamara Heber-Percy, Edward Orr, Laura Mizon, Anthony Leyton, Lucy Fennings, Kate Pettifer and Jasmine Darby in London; and Debra McKenzie, Rodrigo Calvo, Tamara Ryan and Sabrina Corelli in Melbourne. To a Smith, they are all talented, hard-working, sassy and smart.

Smith

Mr & Mrs Smith

(index)

(the small print)

Published in 2009 by Mr & Mrs Smith (Asia Pacific) Pty Ltd
© Mr & Mrs Smith (Asia Pacific) Pty Ltd 2009

Mr & Mrs Smith (Asia Pacific)
1-C, 205–207 Johnston Street,
Fitzroy, Melbourne, VIC 3065, Australia
Telephone: +61 (0)3 9419 6671
Fax: +61 (0)3 9419 6673
Email: info@smithhotels.com.au

Mr & Mrs Smith
2nd floor, 334 Chiswick High Road
London W4 5TA, United Kingdom
Telephone: +44 (0)20 8987 6970
Fax: +44 (0)20 8987 4300
Email: info@mrandmrssmith.com

Editorial Sophie Davies, Juliet Kinsman, Carrie Hutchinson
Design Lauren Camilleri
Project management Paul McNally
Photography Earl Carter, except as indicated below
Cover Sal Salis Ningaloo Reef, shot by Earl Carter
Wallpaper Spring Floral by Florence Broadhurst,
courtesy of Signature Prints
Printed and bound in China by C and C Printing. This book
is printed on paper from a sustainable source.
ISBN 978-0-646514-505 (CIP data is available from the NLA)

Photography credits
Getty Images: 14–15, 25, 54, 56, 66, 68–69, 130, 132, 162, 172, 206, 216–217, 219, 238, 268, 271, 280, 302; *Lonely Planet Images:* 13, 22–24, 38, 40, 67, 88, 90, 103–105, 118–120, 131, 133, 140, 142–143, 150–153, 163–164, 174–175, 184, 195–196, 207–209, 237, 252–255, 269–270, 281, 288–291, 293, 300–301, 303, 319, 326–327; *Robert Harding Picture Library:* 236, 239; iStock: 39, 41, 89, 141, 165, 218, 278; *Vivid Sydney:* 12. *Courtesy of the hotel:* Gaia Retreat & Spa: 28; Pretty Beach House: 52; Capella Lodge: 55, 57–62; Royal Mail Hotel: 91; Quamby Estate: 121; The Louise: 135; Southern Ocean Lodge: 154–158; Sal Salis Ningaloo Reef: 173; Stonebarn: 183; Bamurru Plains: 197; Limes Hotel: 210–214; Lizard Island: 220–224; Qualia: 226–230; Eagles Nest: 259; Huka Lodge: 282, 284–286; Wharekauhau Lodge & Country Estate: 292, 294–296; Hapuku Lodge & Tree Houses: 317–318. NB: The painting featured in the photograph on page 110 is *The Gift*, by Skye Targett, 2008.

Warranties
Although Mr & Mrs Smith has taken all reasonable care in preparing this guide, we make no warranty about the accuracy or completeness of its content and, to the maximum extent permitted, disclaim all liability arising from its use. If hotel details change or accidental errors appear in print, the publishers will apply the corrections in the following edition of this publication. Opinions expressed here are those of the individual reviewers and do not necessarily represent the opinions of the publishers. The publishers shall not be liable for any deficiencies in service, quality or health and safety at any particular hotel. All and any complaints or claims for redress must be made directly to the hotel concerned.

Hotels
The hotels featured in the Mr & Mrs Smith collection have paid a fee towards the costs of research and booking administration. Inclusion is by invitation only; hotels cannot buy their way into the collection. Mr & Mrs Smith is funded by private investment and is independent of all hotels.

Membership terms and conditions
Hotel offers for Mr & Mrs Smith cardholders are subject to availability and are valid once only per booking made. The card is non-transferable and members recognise and accept that they visit any hotel voluntarily and entirely at their own risk. The publishers cannot accept any responsibility for hotels failing to honour cardholder offers, or for change of ownership causing discontinuation of offers. The publisher is not liable for any loss, damage, expense, disappointment or inconvenience suffered by any cardholder or user of this guide. For full terms and conditions, go to www.mrandmrssmith.com/legal.